Rebels and Robbers
Violence in Post-Colonial Angola

Assis Malaquias

NORDISKA AFRIKAINSTITUTET, UPPSALA 2007

Indexing terms:

Violence
Social structure
Obstacles to development
Political aspects
Political power
Civil war
Peace
Nation building
National security
Post-conflict reconstruction
Angola

Language checking: Elaine Almén

Index: Margaret Binns

Cover photo: Angola War. Military training for members of Movement for the Liberation of Angola in Kinknzu, Zaire. August 27, 1973. © Tramonto

ISBN 978-91-7106-580-3

© The author and Nordiska Afrikainstitutet 2007

Printed in Sweden by Elanders Gotab AB, Stockholm 2007

Dedication

*To my mother Amélia Ussova Malaquias
and to the memory of my father Mimoso Nelson Malaquias,
for their inspiration*

*To my daughters
Chyara Malaquias and Nafela Malaquias,
for their love*

Contents

Acknowledgements

I owe an immense debt of gratitude to many people who, over the years, have encouraged me to write this book. Many of them were fellow African(ist) graduate students at Dalhousie University who were attracted to Halifax by our dynamic and devoted mentor, Professor Tim Shaw. Under Tim's guidance, this group – including David Black, John Inegbedion, Abilah Omari, Sandra McLean, the late Joshua Mungenyi, and Larry Swatuk – became an informal think tank where impromptu, lengthy, and intense discussions about Africa regularly took place. I learned much from those discussions, often held at the Grad House. I am most thankful to this group of friends and colleagues for the camaraderie and all the help and encouragement they gave me.

I am also indebted to my colleagues in the Department of Government at St. Lawrence University. For the past decade, this extraordinary group of individuals – Patti Ashlaw, Alan Draper, Gus diZerega, Fed Exoo, Sandy Hinchman, Grace Huang, Joe Kling, Val Lehr, Laura O'Shaughnessey, Ansil Ramsey, Karl Schonberg, and Bob Wells – have provided me with the perfect environment to write this book. Their encouragement and support played a critical role in my ability to conclude this project while fulfilling my various other responsibilities as a member of the department and within the wider St. Lawrence community.

This book received its final touches while I was on sabbatical at the University of the Western Cape in South Africa in the fall of 2004. I am very thankful to the head of the Department of Political Studies, my friend and colleague Keith Gottschalk, for ensuring that I had an office and a computer to finish my manuscript. In addition to providing me with the material conditions to finish the book, he regularly dropped in to offer a cup of coffee and his brilliant insights about the complexities of the regional context of which Angola is an important part.

Sonja Johansson of the Nordic Africa Institute quickly recognized the project's potential and played a critical role in guiding it through the final stages. I thank her and the anonymous reviewers who carefully read the manuscript and offered constructive comments on both form and substance.

Above all, I am most thankful to the many Angolans who generously shared with me their insights about the conflict analyzed in this book.

Preface

After more than four decades, violent conflict has been absent from Angola for four years. The key challenge for this richly endowed country in the decades ahead is to undertake the arduous transition from negative to positive peace. Given the legacies of colonial and post-colonial violence, the achievement of positive peace is by no means guaranteed – at least not in the foreseeable future. This book highlights this challenge by analyzing some of the critical historical and contemporary factors hindering the attainment of positive peace in Angola.

The book had a long gestation period. It is the culmination of years of research and writing about the political economy of Angola's turbulent transitions: first toward independence and statehood and, later, toward peace. Over the years, the focus of my research has expanded from the relatively narrow relationship between oil and conflict to the political and economic dynamics of transition away from a system dominated by a single political party overseeing a command economy toward a system based on multiparty politics and free-market economics. I had not, initially, set out to write a book. But the number of requests I regularly received to write and speak about the conflict in Angola suggested that there was sufficient interest among scholars, students, and the general public to justify writing a book on the subject.

The book's long gestation also reflects its ambitious scope. When analyzing Angola's conflict, it is not difficult to fall into the temptation of reducing the conflict to a single major analytical variable: whether ethnicity, ideology, resources, personality, and so on. Such variables can, admittedly, be useful as lenses through which Angola's recent challenges can be viewed. Undoubtedly, ethnicity played an important role in creating the conditions for the long civil war. Likewise, the ideological rivalries that developed in the context of the wider global conflict between East and West during the Cold War contributed to the length, intractability, and lethality of Angola's conflict. But ideology alone cannot explain why this particular conflict lasted for several decades. Even when, ideology was no longer a major factor fueling global instability, Angola did not follow international trends deemphasizing ideological differences as a way to resolve conflicts. Instead, Angola's conflict only came to an end after the death of one its key personalities. This would appear to confirm the centrality of the personal level of analysis in understanding the dynamics of the conflict. But a focus on the personalities is not sufficient to fully explain the causes, dynamics, and length of the conflict. Peace, even of the negative kind, was delayed because war was too profitable for too many key domestic players. In other words, the availability of economic resources played a key role as well.

The book recognizes that multiple factors must be taken into account to gain a clear view of the big picture. Such factors are all pieces of a complex puzzle. The process of putting all the pieces together was both challenging and enjoyable. Admittedly, this is not a static puzzle because it is shaped by changing challenges facing Angola.

Canton, N.Y., October 2006

Assis Malaquias

Introduction

Violent conflict has been the dominant feature in the last four decades of Angola's history, making it one of Africa's worst post-colonial tragedies. Once justifiably regarded as a potential sub-regional leader in southern Africa, due to its considerable natural resources, it flirted instead with the possibility of becoming a 'collapsed state' for much of the first quarter century of its existence as an independent state.

What started out in 1961 as a national liberation war to destroy an oppressive colonial system gave way, during the decolonization process in 1975, to a protracted civil war that over nearly three decades, mutated through various, increasingly violent, stages. These changes were primarily a consequence of the domestic participants' changing strategies for achieving power. These changing strategies were, in turn, pragmatic responses to various regional and international developments such as foreign military interventions, the superpowers' Cold War calculations, the end of the Cold War and the collapse of the former Soviet Union in 1991, and the end of apartheid in 1994. But beyond the strategic calculations, there were also real "greed and grievance" factors motivating the participants and sustaining the conflict. In many respects, both grievance and greed have motivated the participants in the Angolan conflict. Thus, if the anti-colonial phase of the conflict was driven mainly by the struggle over political and civil rights as well as economic opportunities denied by the colonial system to indigenous populations, the post-colonial phase was a consequence of the inability of three nationalist groups – divided by ideology, ethnicity, region, social class, and race – to find a workable agreement on how best to share power and wealth after independence. Two major consequences arose from this failure to share power and wealth: first, the new state was regarded as less than legitimate by a significant portion of the population that had no political voice within a highly restrictive political system and consequently did not receive tangible benefits from it. Second, it legitimized violence as a means to destroy what was perceived by those excluded from the system as an artificial, unfair, and undemocratic political construct. Jonas Savimbi, the main rebel leader, was able to capitalize on these two factors in his overall strategy to challenge the post-colonial state.

The peculiarities of the rebellion led to a quick termination of hostilities after Savimbi's death in 2002. But this military outcome resulted in a process for ending the civil war – cease-fire, demobilization of rebel forces and their integration into state structures – that excluded a broader political context for addressing the fundamental issues that ignited and sustained it. Significantly, at the political level, the governing party still retains a near-monopoly while, at the economic level, the interests that emerged during the civil war to control national natural resource rents maintain their privileged position. This book explores how this lack of resolution over grievance and greed issues affects prospects for sustainable peace in post-conflict Angola. Specifically, how will these unresolved issues affect political reform, social reconciliation, and economic reconstruction aimed at restoring to health a society that has been so thoroughly ravaged and traumatized by violent conflict?

Admittedly, the prospects for sustainable peace in post-colonial Angola have never been better. Savimbi's death represented the symbolical end of the civil war that was confirmed by a rapid sequence of other equally momentous events including the capture and surrender of the remaining rebel leadership – leading to cessation of hostilities – and, consequently, the implosion and demilitarization of UNITA,[1] the rebel group Savimbi had founded and led since 1966. Savimbi's violent departure from the national scene thus granted Angola an opportunity to permanently break the post-colonial cycle of violence and begin a new era of peace and development. This optimistic scenario, however, must be tempered by the fact that Savimbi was only one, albeit important, element of a complex conflict that gripped a violent society. Even before Savimbi's death, the civil war in Angola had already evolved into a major criminal enterprise. Once regarded primarily as an ethnic conflict exacerbated by Cold War ideological rivalries, Angola's protracted conflict became a convenient cover under which the warring elites enriched themselves. Thus, although Angola's long post-colonial agony has come to an end, this is true mainly as far as the civil

---

1. União Nacional para Independência Total de Angola.

war is concerned. The end of UNITA's rebellion simply provides Angola with the best opportunity yet to finally create the conditions for sustainable peace and development. But, UNITA rebels were not solely responsible for Angola's misery. Since coming to power in 1975, but especially since the death of Angola's first president Agostinho Neto in 1979, the governing MPLA[2] has produced an increasingly corrupt and kleptocratic regime that systematically and illicitly appropriated a significant portion of revenues accrued from the sale of oil.

Paradoxically, the violence – both physical and structural – inflicted upon the country by its rebels and robbers has helped to create important political and economic bases for state-building and indigenous-driven development that were absent at the time of independence. Post-colonial violence in Angola, however devastating it was, served two critical conditions for a viable state. First, the civil war helped to develop a sense of national identity and common purpose as well as the acceptance of the legitimacy of the state as constituted and its structures of governance. Second, it facilitated indigenous large-scale capital accumulation.

At the time of independence, the nationalist movements held three distinct and mutually exclusive visions for post-colonial Angola. The visions put forth by FNLA[3] and UNITA were heavily tinged by the ethnocentric, regional, rural-based, and often racist views of their respective leaders. Such views were antithetical to those held by MPLA. MPLA's victory in the civil war can, therefore, also be interpreted as a victory of a more inclusive notion of nation and citizenship. But at a more basic level, the destructive dynamics of the war fused a nation together. Undeniably, the effects of the long civil war on Angola's human fabric are pervasive, impacting directly or indirectly upon every citizen. For example, prolonged physical violence resulted in between 750,000 to 1 million war-related deaths. In addition, 440,000 Angolans sought refuge beyond national borders. But more than four million Angolans were trapped inside the country as internal refugees. Most of these internally displaced people were forced out of the countryside and into relatively more secure urban areas. For the duration of the war, these individuals learned new modes of interacting with people from different regions and, in the process, forged a new sense of national identity that few other less violent processes could achieve. The indiscriminately destructive nature of the war had many other consequences as well whose

---

2. Movimento Popular de Libertação de Angola.

3. Frente Nacional de Libertação de Angola.

visible effects include the large number of destitute war amputees and street children. Less visible but equally important, the war also caused widespread social trauma as a consequence of war-related deaths of family members and the state of permanent personal insecurity. It is this collective trauma and insecurity – a direct consequence of the long violent conflict – that united most Angolans in their desire to end the immediate suffering and the more long-term goals of regaining control over their lives as a first step to rebuilding families and communities in the post-colonial state. Thus, ultimately, the war also established the legitimacy of the post-colonial state and the structures of governance that had evolved since independence. Whereas at the end of colonialism the three nationalist movements with competing ideologies could stand as equals with different blueprints for the post-colonial project, the civil war helped to determine who would be the main architect of this project.

The civil war also helped to define the structures and dynamics of post-colonial wealth accumulation. The massive exodus of the colonial economic elite was one of the consequences of the haphazard decolonization process. Thus, the new Angolan state had to quickly devise ways to undertake its own processes of wealth accumulation. Initially, inspired by its commitment to Marxism, the governing MPLA entrusted this key responsibility upon the state itself. However, as in most countries that attempted similar approaches elsewhere, the Angolan state failed to deliver in the area of wealth accumulation. Thus, beginning in the 1980s, the state began to devolve this responsibility to trusted individuals within the ruling elite. These individuals were given opportunities to – both licitly and illicitly – accumulate enormous fortunes. In addition, the dynamics of the civil war provided a most convenient cover for the government and the rebels to plunder the country's vast resources without regard for accountability, let alone the development needs of the people they purported to govern and/or liberate. Thus, an estimated USD $1 billion/year in government receipts from oil production simply disappeared in the so-called "Bermuda triangle", i.e. between the state oil company (SONANGOL), the central bank, and the Futungo de Belas presidential palace. Similarly, UNITA rebels earned about USD $500 million/year in diamond revenues from the mines they controlled after the early 1990s. Thus far, most of these fortunes remain in offshore bank accounts. Until recently, the relatively small portions of the monies repatriated to Angola were used in grotesque forms of conspicuous luxury consumption. However, increasingly, there are noticeable signs that the wealth accumulated during the war is being used along more developmental lines – in construction, light industries, services, and commercial farms.

Although the end of the civil war has finally given Angola an opportunity to fulfil its potential, important challenges remain. The country must overcome the twin cultures of violence and corruption that grew unchecked during the civil war. For Angola, escaping post-colonial corruption promises to be just as difficult as escaping post-colonial violence due to a combination of important factors. The onset of the civil war during the decolonization period prevented the citizens from moving beyond interrogating and challenging an intrinsically oppressive and corrupt colonial society in need of thorough dismantling. Instead, the war robbed society of alternatives for self-reinvention. Even worse, it created conditions for the new self-appointed societal caretakers which were ideal for corruption. With the post-colonial state under domestic and international threat, the governing elites increasingly saw self-preservation as the dominant objective. The grand and revolutionary projects for societal transformations that inspired the anti-colonial war were postponed by the civil war. But the civil war may have done lasting social damage as far as corruption is concerned. The civil war period coincided with a large boom in oil and diamond production. However, due to the general lack of transparency and accountability partly caused by, and resulting from, the civil war, the monies accrued from the sale of oil and diamonds were captured by government and rebel elites respectively. Alarmingly, though expectedly, the habit of corruption that was first embraced by the elites now dominates all levels of society with potentially serious negative consequences for social stability as well as political and economic development. From petty corruption – the demanding and/or acceptance of small bribes as a normal occurrence – to grand corruption whereby high officials appropriate large sums of public funds for private ends, Angola faces a potentially more resilient and destructive foe than the rebels it battled for more than a quarter century. How society rids itself of this evil will determine the extent to which it can achieve sustainable positive peace and, possibly, the viability of the post-colonial state.

Purpose and themes

This book reviews some key aspects of Angola's movement away from the political economy of conflict and kleptocracy toward sustainable peace. It suggests that the next critical step for Angola after overcoming the violence imposed by the civil war involves the equally difficult process of changing

the nature of the state with the objective of eliminating the structural violence that oppresses and impoverishes the average citizen. Thus, one of this
book's key premises is that, to be sustainable, peace for Angola must mean
much more than the absence of war. It must also involve "the establishment
of positive, life-affirming, and life-enhancing values and social structures"
(Barash and Webel, 2002:3). In other words, Angola must seek to achieve
positive peace.

Negative and positive peace

Peace is commonly viewed from either a negative or positive perspective.
From a negative perspective peace can be defined simply as the absence of
war, "a condition in which no active, organized military violence is taking
place" (Barash and Webel, 2002:6). But peace can also be defined more
positively not simply as absence of war but, additionally and critically, in
terms of a positively defined condition of social justice (Galtung, 1969:183).
Positive peace, then, results in good management, orderly resolution of societal conflicts, and harmony associated with mature relationships (Boulding 1978:3). In other words, the elimination of physical violence – whereby
"human beings are hurt somatically, to the point of killing" (Galtung,
1969:169) – is an insufficient condition for peace. Peace also involves the
elimination of psychological violence – i.e. "violence that works on the
soul", such as "lies, brainwashing, indoctrination of various kinds, threats,
etc." – as well as structural violence defined as *social injustice* (Galtung,
1969:171). For Galtung, focusing on structural factors that prevent human
beings from realizing their full potential – the "violence that works on the
soul" – is just as important as focusing on the "violence that works on the
body" (Galtung, 1969:169). During wars, for example, there are identifiable
actors that actually perpetrate the physical violence which is measured in
numbers of dead and injured – making it personal and direct. But structural violence can also kill, mutilate, hit or hurt (Galtung, 1969:170), albeit
more "slowly, and undramatically" (Galtung and Hoivik, 1971:73). There is
no denying that "misery in general and hunger in particular, erode and finally kill human beings" (Galtung, 1985:145). Often, the numbers involved
are similar to those produced by war. Galtung's elaboration of structural
violence is worth quoting at some length:

> The violence is built into the structure and shows up as unequal power and
> consequently as unequal life chances. *Resources* are unevenly distributed, as
> when income distributions are heavily skewed, literacy/education unevenly

distributed, medical services existent in some districts and for some groups only, and so on. Above all the *power to decide over the distribution of resources is* unevenly distributed. The situation is aggravated further if the persons low on income are also low in education, low on health, and low on power – as is frequently the case because these rank dimensions tend to be heavily correlated due to the way they are tied together in the social structure (Galtung, 1969:170).

Galtung is clear in arguing that this type of violence may not necessarily be intentional: "individuals may do enormous amounts of harm to other human beings without ever intending to do so, just performing their regular duties as a job defined in the structure" (Galtung, 1985:145). As Hoivik puts it more forcefully in other words, "the cause of structural violence lies in the structure of society itself" (Hoivik, 1997:60). Therefore, from this perspective, an agenda for building a more peaceful society would require a proactive and determined societal effort on the part of both state and citizens to eliminate the domestic causes of structural violence.

This notion of positive peace, more so than negative realist views, provides an appropriate conceptual framework for understanding important processes in countries like Angola that must not only create conditions able to resist a relapse into war as the means for settling disputes but also harmoniously work toward realizing the goal of achieving sustainable positive peace. Specifically, for Angola, this approach would suggest that the major post-civil war challenge is to build sustainable peace by dismantling the structural violence that has permeated society through much of the colonial and post-colonial periods of this country's history. In many respects, this challenge is not dissimilar to previous struggles for liberation – first, against colonialism, and then, after independence, against UNITA's insurgency. Much like colonialism and the post-colonial rebellion, the post-colonial state must now be thoroughly deprived of its ability to inflict structural violence upon its citizens. To put it positively, all citizens must have the freedom and the means to realize their full potential in life; they must all have the ability to control their destinies.

For Angola, this new process of liberation requires, minimally, meeting and overcoming several important and concurrent challenges. A crucial first step involves UNITA's thorough transformation, even reinvention, into a viable political party while creating the socio-economic and political conditions that permanently prevent a relapse into conflict. The immediate first step in this direction has already been concluded and involved both disarming the rebel group and reintroducing former combatants into civilian life. To the Angolan government's credit, these twin processes of disarmament and reintegration were conducted magnanimously so as to enable UNITA members to peacefully fulfil their political, economic, and cultural aspirations within civil society with dignity. But preventing a relapse into conflict will also necessitate a longer-term process of addressing the fundamental structural causes of the violence in Angolan society, with particular attention given to how wealth, power, and opportunities are distributed. Sustainable peace will require that all citizens – not simply the elites – have equal access to wealth and economic opportunities within an open, inclusive, and transparent political system. As currently structured, the Angolan state mainly serves the ruling elite's political and economic interests while the majority of the population survives in conditions of poverty. In other words, now that UNITA's rebellion has come to an end, Angolans are faced with the gigantic task of transforming a state that has acquired too many criminal traits. Alas, simply ending UNITA's criminal insurgency and pruning the state of its criminal tentacles will not guarantee sustainable peace unless both processes are accompanied by a concerted effort to bridge the many schisms that currently separate Angolans.

The main theme of the book is sustainable peace after protracted civil war. Sustainable peace requires more than war termination. War termination involves creating political, economic, social, and symbolic incentives for would-be combatants to opt out of war as a means to promote their political and economic interests. Sustainable peace, the most important challenge for Angola in the coming decades, involves more than war termination through cease-fires, peace accords, pact-making, and elections. It requires the building of social and political structures and frameworks that prevent a return to conflict. Sustainable peace for Angola will require a commitment from the key national actors to permanently play by the rules rather than defecting when those same rules appear not to favour them or when conditions are created to by-pass the rules through non-political means. Indeed, it requires that the losers have guarantees that they will not be marginalized or otherwise punished. Sustainable peace also requires de-emphasizing politics as the easiest way for personal enrichment. Alternative occupations and outlets must be found. In sum, sustainable peace requires the creation of conditions that, over time, nurture reconciliation while discouraging conflict.

Structure of the book

This book is divided into nine chapters. *Chapter 1* provides reviews on how three important legacies – human diversity, natural resource wealth, and colonialism – helped to shape Angola's political economy.

Chapter 2 analyzes the dynamics of physical violence and focuses on its main perpetrators – colonialism, and the nationalist movements. Colonial violence took various forms including slavery, forced labour, and anti-nationalist counter-insurgency warfare. The nationalist movement, given its fractured nature, added important dimensions and layers of physical violence into society that survived the end of colonialism and transformed themselves into new forms during the post-colonial era. Divided by profound schisms – including ideology, ethnicity, class, and race – the liberation movements were unable to create a united front against Portuguese rule. Consequently, they spent as much effort fighting among themselves as they did fighting the colonial presence. More terribly, they brought their unresolved disputes into the post-colonial arena, thus setting the stage for a civil war that would last for 27 years after the departure of the colonial administration.

Chapter 3 focuses on the external dimension of the physical violence that has consumed Angola, especially in the post-colonial period. The haphazard process of decolonization was not only defined by Portugal's precipitous departure but also by the direct involvement of both the United States and the former Soviet Union as they attempted to install their respective surrogates in power with the help of willing client states. The United States provided support to both FNLA and UNITA through Zaire (now the Democratic Republic of Congo) and tacitly approved South Africa's backing of UNITA. Similarly, the former Soviet Union supported MPLA through Cuba.

Chapter 4 discusses the main agent of physical violence in post-colonial Angola: UNITA. It suggests that Angola's post-colonial conflict involved, primarily, a transformation of violence – both in terms of character and its target. From political violence to remove colonial occupation, Angola now faced a criminal violence aimed at imposing a new form of oppression upon the same peoples in whose name the first war had been fought. Although UNITA's poorly articulated justification for its long guerrilla campaign pointed to the governing elite's monopoly on power and wealth, its original ideals for a more open and inclusive political system were soon overshadowed by the rebels' own transformation into a criminal enterprise. Under Savimbi's erratic yet charismatic leadership, UNITA underwent a long and agonizing period of political and military self-destruction. Periodic and exhaustive purges robbed the group of its best and brightest political and military leaders. Thus, UNITA's own political and military blunders had predictable and inevitable implications for its long-term survival prospects. For example, at the political level, UNITA's unwillingness to clearly distinguish soft and hard targets during the civil war resulted in considerable erosion of support even among the Ovimbundu, the ethnic group the rebels claimed to represent. At the military level, the option to prematurely adopt a conventional posture against the government in the early 1990s, after its own defeat at the polls – even more so than its original option to participate in the civil war in 1975 – will be regarded as the rebels' single most costly strategic failure, leading to their ultimate demise. This chapter also focuses on the political economy of violence to explain how UNITA underwent its various adaptations and incarnations. It argues that, especially after independence, UNITA was primarily a guerrilla army occasionally masquerading as a political party. This group's military character ultimately hindered its ability to play a more constructive role in post-colonial politics. Post-Savimbi UNITA had an excellent chance to reinvent itself as the champion of Angola's poor and marginalized. But, alas, it commited yet another characteristic blunder by failing to understand that it could not reinvent itself with the leftovers of an old leadership committed to the goals and spirit, if not the methods, of UNITA's late leader. Reinventing UNITA means, first and foremost, transforming this group into an inclusive and democratic political party led by individuals capable of defining and articulating forward-looking national goals like, for example, how to reshape the state to serve the interests of all citizens, not mainly those of the elites. In other words, only radical change will ensure UNITA's continuing relevance.

Chapter 5 focuses on the main source of structural violence in Angola: the MPLA regime. It sheds light on the forces that caused the MPLA regime's own changes and how it transformed the character of the state – from the revolutionary zeal that characterized the immediate post-independence period to its current problematic condition. MPLA has abandoned its commitment to people-centred ideals in favour of a more elitist and, ultimately, kleptocratic system of governance. Now, both political power and the country's vast oil wealth are concentrated in the hands of the President and his small entourage of close friends and relatives. This group and its immediate clients adeptly used the civil war both as a source of direct financial gains – through the appropriation of public funds for private uses and via the sizeable commissions involved in arms transactions – and as a convenient shield against demands for accountable and/or transparent governance. Sustainable peace in Angola will require the loosening of this elite's stranglehold on power and wealth. With the civil war over, Angola requires new leadership to win the major development struggles that lie ahead. As the last party congress demonstrated, MPLA is not ready to embrace new, capable and/or accountable leadership. Moreover, despite rhetorical pronouncements, MPLA is unprepared to reverse its drift away from its original people-centred ideals. Although a return to Marxism-Leninism is neither practical nor desirable, MPLA's earlier focus on distributive justice must be recaptured to facilitate the attainment of economic development, social harmony, and political stability. This will remain MPLA's key challenge and its best option to sustain popular support in post-civil war Angola.

Chapter 6 reviews Angola's attempts to achieve peace after independence. The main political forces in Angola have consistently attempted to reconcile their differences through pact-making. But they have all failed! Peace was finally achieved on the battlefield, not at the negotiating table. What led to the failure of various peace agreements was not simply UNITA's recalcitrance. Those peace agreements dealt almost exclusively with the basic arithmetic of political power-sharing defined in terms of how government posts would be shared. This was the easy part because, for the main protagonists in the civil war, defeat was not measured simply in political and military terms. It also meant the real possibility of relegation to the margins of the political system, or worse, due to lack of independent sources of funding. In other words, the loser would depend on the generosity, not simply magnanimity, of the victor. Therefore, since, in its last stages, the war had become a contest for valuable resources, lack of access to revenues through legal channels created important incentives for renewed violence. In other words, control of Angola's vast oil and diamond revenues was also very much at stake, but this issue was not given adequate attention. This peculiarity systematically operated to sabotage the peace processes.

Chapter 7 focuses on the challenges of post-conflict governance in a divided society and suggests that how Angola deals with the issue of ethnic identity, a perennial backburner with tremendous explosive potential, will significantly impact upon the prospects of post-conflict peace. Like most African countries, Angola is also fractured along ethnonational lines. Colonialism forcibly included within Angola several would-be nations with distinct histories and aspirations. It is unrealistic to expect that these communities will fizzle out any time soon especially when the state – given its problematic patterns of distributing both wealth, power, and opportunities – is not particularly friendly to the average citizen. It is not inconceivable, therefore, that a state like Angola, brittle by birth and further enfeebled by nearly three decades of civil war, may succumb to the centrifugal forces of ethnonationalism. Chapter 7 looks at possible ways of reconciling Angola's many pre-colonial ethnic communities with the modern post-colonial project of nation-state building.

Ultimately, the success of the post-colonial nation-state building project that has now been given another chance in Angola will greatly depend on how the citizens perceive this undertaking. The perception that this process will result in the erection of a citizen-friendly state will go a long way in ensuring a successful outcome. Otherwise, as has occurred in several other African countries, discontent will fan residual violence into acquiring new shapes and forms. The post-colonial state must, therefore, constantly build avenues that facilitate a necessary organic connection with citizens – to seek both their input and endorsement of the policies that, at the end of the day, must be designed for their benefit. In other words, the state must seek to actively promote and protect wide social sites and spaces commonly know as civil society. This discussion is the focus of *Chapter 8.*

While domestic civil society can act as a critical stabilizing factor that prevents future eruptions of physical violence, long-term sustainability will continue to depend largely on international involvement from all key global actors as Angola overcomes the devastating effects of civil war. Therefore, *Chapter 9* returns to a discussion of the external dimensions of sustainable peace. Specifically, it suggests that to achieve broad national reconciliation and sustainable peace at the domestic level, Angola must re-calibrate its foreign policy towards an open engagement with major international powers like the United States as well as other key global players, especially the International Financial Institutions (IFIs).

In closing, the book reiterates that sustainable peace must be just. The ultimate challenge for Angola is the building of a just society.

Background

Legacies of diversity, wealth, and colonialism

Angola is a resource-rich country of 14 million people that occupies approximately 1,246,700 square kilometres on the Atlantic coast of southwestern Africa. Even by post-colonial African standards, Angola's recent history is distinctive. Prospects for post-colonial development have been conditioned by the hopes inspired by its rich human and natural endowments and constrained by the country's complex legacies.

Endowments

The people

Angola comprises several large ethnic communities, including the Ovimbundu, Mbundu, and Bakongo – representing three-fourths of population – and several smaller communities like the Lunda-Chokwe, Nganguela, Nyaneka-Humbe, Ovambo, and the Khoisan – the original non-Bantu inhabitants of the region from which Portugal carved out present-day Angola.

Portuguese explorers first arrived at the mouth of the Congo River in 1483, in their search for a maritime route to Asia. By the time of first contact with the Portuguese, the peoples of this region of Africa had developed several important kingdoms, including the Kongo Kingdom, encompassing parts of three current African states: Angola, the Democratic Republic of Congo, and the Republic of Congo. In the late 15th century, the Kongo kingdom was at the height of its power – dominating the west coast of central Africa. Ruled by a monarch, Kongo was divided into six provinces, five of which had their own subordinate rulers. The central province of Mpemba was governed by the king personally and contained the royal city of Mbanza Kongo. This city lay on a well-cultivated territory surrounded by many small villages. Its population was once estimated to be as many as 100,000 people. The surrounding provinces were Nsundi to the north, Mpangu to the northeast, Mbata to the southeast, Mbamba in the southwest, and Sonyo on the coast west of the capital (Birmingham, 1966:2). This kingdom's origins can be traced back to the late fourteenth century when members of the Bakongo people crossed the Congo River south into northern Angola and established their capital at Mbanza Kongo. From there, the Bakongo quickly increased their power by expanding geographically while granting a high degree of autonomy to the peoples they conquered, resulting in the creation of a powerful decentralized political entity with the Kongo kingdom at its core.

Immediately south of the Kongo kingdom existed the Ndongo kingdom of the Mbundu people whose ruler, the Ngola a Kiluanje, was a tributary of the Kongo's Manikongo. Portuguese interest, and subsequent exploitation of this area and its people, peaked toward the latter part of the sixteenth century when Paulo Dias de Novais established a colonial settlement in Luanda in 1575. Soon, the Portuguese began to refer to the entire region under their control – both real and imaginary – as Angola, a slight deformation of the Ndongo king's title.

South of Ndongo, the Ovimbundu people had created several important kingdoms. Known as "the most important African traders below the equator" (Duffy, 1959:193), their trading caravans "traveled as far as the Congo River in the north, the Kalahari Desert in the south, and the great lakes of east Africa, seeking slaves, ivory, beeswax, corn, and palm oil to exchange at the ports of Benguela and Catumbela for cloth, guns, and rum of European manufacture" (Samuels and Bailey, 1969:115). The Ovimbundu achieved great economic prosperity between 1874 and 1911 when they dominated the rubber trade that had replaced the slave trade as a key sector in the regional economy. This prosperity, however, could not be sustained as it took place within a context of increasingly aggressive Portuguese attempts to dominate the Ovimbundu, especially after 1890 – in the aftermath of the Berlin Conference of 1884–5 that finalized the European partition of Africa – when Portuguese began to settle in Bié (Vie) and Bailundo (Mbailundu) in large numbers. In 1902, the Mbailundu king – Mutu-ya-Kevela – led the last major effort against the Portuguese who, by then, were expropriating Ovimbundu land while subjugating them into forced labour. Mutu-ya-Kevela's campaign delayed Portugal's ability to exercise full control over much of the central highlands for a decade. The Portuguese eventually prevailed and were able to establish effective control beginning in 1912. But full control over the Kwanhama kingdoms, further south, did not occur until 1915. The Lunda-Chokwe kingdoms, to the east of the Ovimbundu, were also not conquered until the early 1920s.

Currently, the Bacongo represent about 15 percent of Angola's population and reside mainly in the northern provinces of Cabinda, Zaire and Uige. The Mbundu, representing about 25 percent of the population, occupy the areas around the capital city, Luanda, and east as far as the Cassanje area of Malanje province. The Ovimbundu are, by far, the largest ethnic group. They represent 35 to 40 percent of Angola's population and dominate the areas with the highest population density in the country—the central plateau provinces of Huambo, Bie and Benguela. This ethnic diversity has dominated politics and society in Angola since the first contact with Europeans. Unfortunately, it has consistently been a source of weakness, not strength. For example, the ethnically diffused nature of resistance against Portuguese encroachment and dominance facilitated the imposition of colonial rule. Although sporadic anti-colonial resistance took place during Portugal's presence in Angola, the various kingdoms and chiefdoms threatened by colonial domination were not able to create a united front. From this perspective, the disunity that characterized the anti-colonial movement after WWII and the inability to establish an inclusive political system after independence has long historical antecedents. Equally important, by forcibly including within their colonial possessions different ethnic groups with different histories and aspirations, colonialism set the stage for a very problematic process of state building in Angola and elsewhere in Africa after independence. Regrettably, the main nationalist movements in Angola (FNLA, MPLA, and UNITA) drew a significant portion of their following from distinct ethnic groups in the country – Bacongo, Mbundu and Ovimbundu – that once constituted distinct kingdoms: Kongo, Ndongo and Bailundo respectively.

Natural resources

Endowed with rich agricultural land, abundant water resources, and immense mineral resources, Angola is potentially one of the richest countries in Africa. As Campbell (2000:159) puts it, "the wealth of the country is now legendary". Scientific surveys have established that Angola can be subdivided into five main regional geological units, each containing a distinct combination of valuable mineral deposits. The first geological unit, where Pleistocene to Cretaceous marine sediments are deposited in a series of coastal basins, is located on the western margin of Angola. These rocks hold the country's oil reserves. The second region – containing Quaternary to Tertiary sedimentary cover rocks, comprising sand, quartzitic sandstones, gravels and clay – extends over nearly half of Angola, including the entire eastern part. Most of Angola's diamond production comes from these rocks. Third, Mesozoic to Palaezoic sediments are found mainly in the Cassanje Graben, a north-central to north-western geological depression. Diverse sub-volcanic and volcanic bodies occur, including kimberlites and carbonatites along a major south-west to north-east trend line across Angola. Fourth, Upper Proterozoic fold belts occur along the margins of Angola's Precambrian shield, the most important being the West-Congo, Damara and Maiombe-Macongo. They are characterized by the occurrence of base metal mineralisation and a variety of industrial minerals. Fifth, Lower Proterozoic to Archean rocks form the Angolan, Maiombe, Cassai and Bangweulu shields and the Kwanza horst. Granitic-gneissic terrains, meta-volcano-sedimentary and meta-sedimentary (greenstone) belts can be differentiated. Complex Lower Proterozoic greenstone belts are present in south-central Angola (Riddler, 1997:16). In sum, Angola has vast resources in gold, platinum, nickel, chrome, iron, copper, manganese, kaolin, gypsum, quartz and zinc. The most important of the country's natural resources, however, are oil and diamonds.

To fully grasp the significance of Angola's oil deposits, one should first take a broader continental overview. The continental margin of West Africa comprises seven major oil producing areas or basins. They include: (1) Abidjan, straddling Côte d'Ivoire and the Tano and meta sub-basins in Ghana; (2) Offshore Benin, structurally defined by the Romanche Fracture Zone in the west and the Okitipupa High (in Nigeria) in the east with the western flank extending to Togo; (3) Niger Delta, located between Okitipupa High in the west and Cameroon in the east and including the Rio-Del-Ray-Cameroon-Fernando Po Basin; (4) Gabon Coastal, extending from the southern part of Cameroon, through Equatorial Guinea to Gabon, where it is bounded to the south by the Gabon Fracture Zone; (5) Lower Congo, extending from Congo to Angola, bounded to the north by the Gabon Fracture Zone; and, (6) Kwanza Basin, stretching along the entire western coast of Angola (Akinosho, 1999:34). Geologically, Angola is situated along two of the most productive basins in Africa: Lower Congo and Kwanza. Belgium's Petrofina made the first commercial oil discovery in 1955 at Benfica in the Kwanza basin. Since then, twelve billion barrels of oil have been discovered. Major discoveries and aggressive exploration have made Angola the second largest oil producer in sub-Saharan Africa after Nigeria.

Angola's diamond resources are possibly the largest in Africa (Premoll, 1992:32) and the country is ranked among the top ones in the world in terms of quality and its reserves, considered "virtually limitless and evaluation of their true potential will take years of prospection" (Helmore, 1984:530). Diamonds were first discovered in Angola in 1912. Since then, about 700 kimberlites have been identified throughout the country, most of them aligned along a southwest-northeast trend across Angola into the Democratic Republic of Congo. More kimberlites are expected to be discovered by a combination of satellite image interpretation and ground geochemical exploration, modern techniques being used successfully in other major diamond producing countries. The erosion of kimberlite pipes, especially in Lunda Norte province, has produced significant quantities of alluvial diamonds that can be mined with relatively unsophisticated, even rudimentary, tools. The end of the war will enable the government to impose its rule in these diamond-rich areas and allow foreign investment to finally begin to flow again to explore Angola's large number of kimberlite pipes.

In important respects, Angola's wealth in terms of human resources initially enticed Portuguese explorers to conquer the land while, later, the discovery of vast natural resources vindicated the early explorers' decisions while also justifying continued colonial presence.

Dynamics of occupation and resistance

Early colonial penetration

The rulers of Kongo treated the Portuguese who first landed on the shores of their kingdom not so much as explorers or conquerors but as citizens of a distant but equal power. Indeed, soon after Diogo Cão's arrival, Kongo and Portugal exchanged diplomatic representatives. This initial diplomatic exchange quickly developed into a mutually beneficial relationship between the two sovereign entities. For example, Kongo exported ivory and other goods to Portugal in exchange for technical assistance. The relationship between the two countries grew even closer after the death of Kongo's king Nzinga Nkuwu in 1506. His successor – who adopted the Portuguese name Afonso – asked for Portuguese support in various areas, particularly in education and religion.

Alas, the mutually beneficial relationship between Kongo and Portugal soon changed as the explorers directed their attention towards exploiting Kongo's vast human and natural resources. The ensuing slave trade that soon came to dominate Portuguese-Kongo relations was a direct result of a fundamental shift – fuelled by commercial interests – in Portugal's imperial calculus. Slaves from Kongo, not diplomatic relations, would enrich the empire and thus help sustain its international relevance. For Kongo, the slave trade marked the beginning of a painful descent, especially after the death of Afonso in the 1540s. With their kingdom profoundly debilitated socially and weakened politically, the rule of Kongo kings after Afonso was characterized by instability and upheaval due to external invasions and internal wars of succession. A couple of other events sealed the fate of this kingdom. The first occurred in 1565 when Portugal made explorer Paulo Dias de Novais a *donatário* (proprietary landlord) of Angola (Duffy, 1962:50). From then on, as far as Portugal was concerned, the Kongo kingdom was no longer a sovereign entity. Kongo's military response to Portugal's manoeuvers was ineffective due to the kingdom's unstable internal situation. In 1665, the Portuguese put a final end to this resistance with a decisive victory at the Battle of Mbwila, an event that marked the end of the Kongo kingdom as a unified territorial and political entity.

As in the kingdom to the north, Portugal's newfound interests in Ndongo profoundly disrupted the kingdom's social, political, and economic bases. Equally important, it also altered the relationships between Ndongo and Kongo by influencing how the two kingdoms perceived each other. Thus, the *Manikongo*'s military incursion into Ndongo in 1556 can be interpreted as an attempt to reestablish Kongo's uncontested domination that existed prior to the Portuguese arrival. But the *Manikongo* misperception of his kingdom's relative power ultimately led to the defeat of his army by a thitherto compliant satellite. After Ndongo's victory, it sought full independence and was able to achieve it with Portuguese help. However, as with the Kongo before, Portugal's good relations with Ndongo were short-lived. The explorers soon initiated attempts to militarily conquer Ndongo and, as in the north, explore the kingdom's human and mineral resources. Again, military resistance proved futile as the Portuguese in 1671 captured the Ndongo capital of Pungu-a-Ndongo.

In the sixteenth century, as the Portuguese were finalizing the conquest of Ndongo, they were also coming into contact with the Ovimbundu – a third major population group that inhabited the lands south of Ndongo. For much of the sixteenth century, the Portuguese launched inland exploratory expeditions from their coastal base in Benguela which, by 1617, had evolved into a permanent colonial settlement. These missions culminated with the establishment of an inland stronghold in Caconda in 1580 and Porto Amboim in 1584. From these outposts, Portuguese explorers began a systematic penetration of the Ovimbundu kingdoms in the late seventeenth century. Although, initially, Portuguese explorers were motivated by the lure of mineral wealth, they soon turned to slavery.

Like the kingdoms to the north, the Ovimbundu were initially able to resist Portuguese encroachment and domination. As early as 1660, Kapango I, the king of Tchiyaka, forced a Portuguese expeditionary force to retreat before it could reach the central highlands. Later, in 1718, the Tchiyaka led a "coalition of kingdoms" to drive out the Portuguese from their fortress in Caconda and from much of the region (Chilcote, 1967:72). Although the Portuguese successfully invaded the kingdoms of Tchiyaka, Ndulu, and Mbailundu in the wars of 1774–1776, they did not succeed in fully dominating these kingdoms until the first decade of the twentieth century. Indeed, some of these kingdoms prospered economically while keeping the Portuguese at bay. The Ovimbundu kingdoms, for example, parlayed their strategic location in Angola's central highlands as well as their military prowess and "aggressive entrepreneurial activity" into an important base for capturing significant opportunities to engage in trade of both humans and natural resources (Newitt, 1981:96). Colonialism effectively put these entities on a different and extraordinarily complex path of development.

Colonialism

After 1575, when Portugal established a trading post in Luanda, it attempted to penetrate the hinterland through various campaigns that often involved protracted military clashes with the local populations. The "final phase of conquest" whereby Portugal was able to finally achieve military supremacy did not take place until between 1891 and 1918 (Abshire, 1969:76). Portugal's effective administrative control over the entire colony was only achieved after World War II due partly to a large influx of settlers. Several colonial policies – in the areas of immigration, land expropriation, taxation, forced labour, cash crop production – ensured the settler community's control of the main sources of wealth and power (Birmingham, 1982:344; de Andrade, 1982:80, Heywood, 1987:358; Pitcher, 1991:43). This structure of exploitation also served as a base for the reordering of colonial social structures to permanently enrich the settler community while impoverishing and marginalizing local populations.

The marginalization of Angola's indigenous populations amounted to what has been described as Portuguese apartheid (Cabral, 1982a:8–9). As in neighbouring South Africa, settler colonialism in Angola established highly unequal structures that placed the minority white settler community at the top of the social structure while *indigenas* (indigenous) Angolan peoples were relegated to the very bottom with mulattos and *assimilados* occupying the middle levels. The colonial system robbed the *indigenas* of the ability to realize their potential by severely curtailing political, economic, and social rights. For example, although they constituted by far the majority of the population, *indigenas* had no right to vote. Furthermore, they were segregated into *muceques* (shantytowns), had to carry identity cards at all times, and were forced to pay a head tax, and were "subject to the obligation, moral and legal" to provide their "free" labour to the colonial authorities (Bailey, 1969:167). Indeed, a master-servant relationship constituted the socio-economic foundation of the colonial system in Angola. Even the *assimilados* could only aspire to go so far since the colonial legal framework clearly stipulated the highest levels a non-white could reach. Assimilation, therefore, became a constant reminder of the intrinsic violence of colonial society.

Assimilation was a form of psychological violence against Angolans in the sense that it involved an experience akin to "a process of cultural decomposition that aimed at producing a *colonial subject*" (Kabwegyere, 1972:303). Assimilation separated Angolans from their pre-colonial identities, values, and languages while teasing them with socio-economic and cultural conditions they could never fully reach. Within a fundamentally oppressive colonial society, Angolans could only achieve the purported goals of assimilation – i.e. to be certified as "civilized" and thus become a Portuguese citizen – by rejecting their past and embracing alien identities, values, and languages in what MPLA (1982:139) referred to as "cultural genocide".

To become *assimilado*, an Angolan had to comply with several stringent requirements:

> The applicant had to be eighteen years of age and prove his ability to speak Portuguese. He had to demonstrate that he earned sufficient income for himself and his family. He had to be of good character and possess those qualities necessary for the exercise of the public and private rights of the Portuguese citizen. He had to submit a birth certificate, a certificate of residence, a certificate of good health, a declaration of loyalty, and two testimonies of his good character. In addition he had to be able to pay various fees and petty taxes which amounted to from ten to twenty pounds. The wife and children of the *assimilado* could also acquire citizenship if they spoke Portuguese and could demonstrate their good character (Duffy 1962:165).

From a pragmatic perspective, the *assimilado* status was appealing for many Angolans because it could represent a small degree of freedom from within the wider violence of colonialism even if it might concurrently heighten their suffering. Thus, with assimilated status, a person could "travel without permission; he did not have to pay the head tax; he was exempt from contract labour; he could, theoretically, receive the same pay as a European in the same government position; he could vote" (Duffy, 1962:165). But such a person would have to make a conscious decision to turn his or her back on those tangible and intangible factors that up until then defined him or her as a person – i.e. language, culture, community, etc. In the end, after five centuries, the colonial order was able to assimilate less than 1 per cent of Angolans partly due to the many systemic restrictions and impracticalities but also due to the unwillingness of many Angolans to reject their identities. In practice, however, this policy further divided Angola society. Now, to the various existing socio-economic, regional, and ethnic divisions, another – assimilated vs. non-assimilated – was added. But even *assimilados* did not constitute a homogenous group; they were further divided into the "assimilated-object", and the "assimilated group" (Da Cruz 1982:76).

The "assimilated-objects" included civil servants and employees in commerce and industry. They were heavily represented by *mulattos* who could trace their lineage to families that had accumulated wealth in the early stages of the colonial economy, including in the slave trade. Since the Portuguese constituted less than 1 percent of Angola's population until 1940, the mulatto population had enjoyed a certain advantage in the colonial racial pecking order. Specifically, since the colonial authorities depended on both their skills and loyalty, they occupied a variety of low-level management positions in both government and the private sector. However, around 1950, the mulatto usefulness for the colonial administration began to diminish as the proportion of the settler population slowly rose to about 2 percent, surpassing the number of mulattos. A lowering of their social status followed this decline in colonial usefulness. Since the main preoccupation of the colonial regime was to look after the interests of the settlers both at the political and economic levels, Portugal had no qualms about restricting the realm of activities open to mulattos. In the zero-sum calculus of colonialism, this would lead to more opportunities for white settlers. Thus, two highly restrictive regulations were introduced into colonial labour policies in Angola. First, a higher educational competency level was required to hold administrative and managerial positions. Second, and even more restrictively, the 1921 colonial administration divided the civil service into two branches – European and African – and assigned mulattos and African *assimilados* to the latter, with little hope of ever advancing beyond the level of clerk first-class. This successfully protected virtually all well-remunerated government jobs for the settlers. For the mulattos who tended to identify themselves with the settlers for various social and economic reasons this racial demotion was both devastatingly humiliating and frighteningly disempowering. Understandably, this group of Angolans – once beneficiaries of the colonial system – became radicalized and emerged as important leaders in the anti-colonial struggle. They would also be consistently at odds with the second group of *assimilados* da Cruz identified.

The second group of *assimilados* included people who, "were destined in the colonial context to attain social and economic success" (Da Cruz 1982:76) because they had access to education, including specialized training, both at home and abroad. After the Second World War, the colonial regime increased the numbers of African students allowed into the education system. Also, since the late 1800s, there had been several foreign missionary schools in Angola. These missionary schools, in particular, were instrumental in educating thousands of Angolans as teachers, nurses, clerks. Many of them were then able to compete for government and private sector jobs. Although most did not succeed, some found jobs working for railways, ports, road construction companies, hospitals, and so on. By the 1950s, there was a critical mass of urban Africans who aspired to achieve their full potential within various spheres of colonial society and demanded the space to do so. More important, given settlers' resistance to these demands, many individuals were willing to use various means to achieve greater accommodation within colonial society, not necessarily its overthrow. This explains Da Cruz' lament that the majority of the members of the second group "display behaviour similar to that of the petty bourgeoisie" due to their social condition, education, psychology and "the social functions to which they aspire" (Da Cruz 1982:76). Beyond his lament, however, Da Cruz made an even more important point by indicating that these two groups' respective interests and social conditions gave them different perspectives on colonialism. Consequently, they also approached the solutions to the colonial question differently. While the majority of the assimilated-object group "rejected colonialism in their innermost behaviour", members of the second group simply "opposed colonialism on the basis of patriotism, self-interest, or even solidarity" (Da Cruz 1982:76). This critical distinction had major implications for both the inter- and intra-nationalist group violence that plagued the anti-colonial movements and which carried over, with much lethality, into the post-colonial period.

The leaderships of the main liberation movements were drawn from the two sub-sets of *assimilados*. The MPLA leadership was dominated by the first group. The second group of run-of-the-mill *assimilados*, on the other hand, dominated the leaderships of FNLA and UNITA. Thus, social extraction – in addition to ideology, race, ethnicity, and region of origin – is an important dimension for understanding the violence among the main nationalist movements in Angola and their inability to build a united front against the repressive and violent colonial system.

Nationalism

The colonial regime was jolted in May 1926 by a right-wing military coup that led to the establishment of a one-party regime, known as *Estado Novo* (New State), that survived under several leaders until it was finally overthrown by another military coup – this time led by middle-ranking left-wing officers – in April 1974. The *Estado Novo*, especially through its Colonial Act of 1930, changed the relationship between Portugal and its "overseas possessions". Those territories became "provinces", and were regarded as integral units of both the Portuguese nation and the colonial state. For Portugal – a decaying, resource-poor empire – this constituted a convenient way to continue exploiting conquered territories. It was also an attempt to imbue settler colonialism with a legalistic aura that could justify the repression of any challenge against "national integrity". However, ultimately, increasing repression only served to heighten the determination of Angolans to seek freedom from the oppressive and humiliating colonial stranglehold.

During the 1930s and 1940s, several social, cultural, and sports groups emerged in colonial Angola, particularly in urban areas, with the purported aim of coordinating various emerging forms of anti-colonial resistance. These associations, including LNA and ANANGOLA, became important sites for aggregating and articulating revolutionary ideas arising from continuing and intensifying colonial exploitation, violence, and humiliation, especially the tensions arising from the large influx of settlers after the end of WWII. In the 1950s, these associations increasingly acquired a political character due to the internal effects of colonialism as well as external factors, especially the wave of European colonial disengagement in Africa that started in Ghana in 1957. In many important respects, associations like LNA and ANANGOLA were the embryos of the nationalist movements that led the armed anti-colonial struggle which started in 1961. As discussed below, serious cleavages prevented these groups from creating a united anti-colonial front, with important implications both for the conduct of the liberation war and the post-colonial nation-building project.

The anti-colonial war came to an end not on the battlefield but as a result of the 1974 military coup in Portugal mentioned above. Tired and dispirited by the long colonial wars – not only in Angola but also the better organized and more deadly nationalist wars led by PAIGC in Guinea-Bissau and FRELIMO in Mozambique – a group of mostly middle-ranking left-wing officers deposed the regime that had ascended to power via the 1926 right-wing military coup and installed a left-leaning regime committed to a rapid decolonization process. The new regime quickly, albeit haphazardly, undertook the difficult decolonization process whose success hinged not so much on colonial disengagement as cooperation among the nationalist groups within a transition government that would pave the way to elections – then regarded as the first step to post-colonial peace, stable governance, and development. Regrettably, given the complex societal fissures inherited from colonialism – including deep divisions among the nationalist movements and their propensity for violence against each other – the decolonization process soon degenerated into a killing frenzy before stabilizing into a long and equally deadly civil war. One of the nationalist groups, MPLA, eventually emerged victorious in the narrow sense that it held on to the capital city and was able to inaugurate the new state. But the legacies of the long colonial period effectively hampered this new state's ability to fulfil the aspirations of its newly emancipated citizens.

The colonial legacy

The length and nature of the Portuguese colonial presence in Angola left a legacy which has constrained Angola's development. For over 500 years, the Portuguese colonial system was based on the exploitation of Angola's human and natural resources. The longevity of the colonial presence is, to no small extent, a testament to Portugal's ability to adapt to the opportunities of the colonial enterprise. For Portugal in Angola, these opportunities revolved around the slave trade, coffee, and oil. The exploitation of these resources not only greatly helps to define the nature of colonialism, it also goes a long way to explaining its endurance.

As discussed in the next chapter, the slave trade, mostly to Brazil, defined the first period in Angola's existence as a Portuguese colony, and lasted until 1870. The abolition of slavery marked the beginning of the second period which also coincided with the push to consolidate territorial occupation and establish effective colonial administration throughout Angola. These processes gained considerable speed after World War II when Portugal increasingly relied on both settler immigration and indigenous forced labour – "*contrato*" – as the cornerstone of its colonial "development policy" for Angola. Hundreds of thousands of settlers were encouraged to migrate to Angola where they seized the colony's best agricultural land and helped to expand the booming agricultural sector dominated by coffee production. The resulting coffee boom in turn led to further settler migration to Angola. Favorable prospects for external trade, combined with new colonial policies for industrial regulation, agricultural incentives, labour laws, and monetary policy, led to a dramatic increase in the settler population after World War II: from 44,000 in 1940 to approximately 325,000 by 1974 (World Bank 1991:176). But given Portugal's own condition of economic under-development, this colonial migration was problematic inasmuch as "over half of the 325,000 white settlers had never gone to school and the vast majority of the rest had less than four years of education result[ing] in the Portuguese occupying almost every position in the modern economic sector from engineers and doctors to taxi drivers" (World Bank, 1990:175). Therefore, indigenous Angolans had few employment opportunities within the formal sector of the colonial economy. Fewer still were able to acquire professional training.

A third period began as a result of Portugal's response to the anti-colonial armed struggle and coincided with a liberalization of the colonial economy allowing rapid oil-driven industrialization to take place in conjunction with the coffee economy. The uprisings of 1961 in Angola forced Portugal to reconsider its long-term presence in the territory. Not willing to follow the example of other colonial powers, however, Portugal began to take serious steps towards further integrating Angola's economy into that of the metropolis through increased investment in agriculture, mining, manufacturing, and transportation. Problematically for Angola's long-term development prospects, however, this integration involved an expansion of the settler community's power and wealth while continuing to relegate the indigenous populations to the margins of the economy and society.

The last phase of Portuguese colonialism in Angola – from the start of the armed struggle in 1961 until the disintegration of the Portuguese empire in 1974 – coincided with a period of economic boom in the colonial economy. Angola's fertile lands and vast network of rivers provided great incentives for the development of commercial agriculture, especially coffee production. Increased investments during the 1960s, as well as highly favourable world prices for this commodity, created a boom in coffee production and consolidated Angola's position as the second largest African producer of coffee. In 1973, the last full year of Portuguese administration, Angola exported 218,660 metric tons of coffee. Other important cash crops included sisal, cotton, sugar, cassava, bananas, coconuts, beans, tobacco, wheat, rice, millet, sorghum, fruits, cocoa, and peanuts. Livestock production experienced a sharp increase after the introduction of disease-resistant breeds. Angola had approximately 4–5 million head of cattle in 1973. Timber production was also making an important contribution to economic growth in the pre-independence period. Most of the timber resources are concentrated in the tropical rain forests of the Cabinda enclave, where mahogany and other valuable species are found. By 1973, production of logs had reached 555,149 cubic metres.

The industrial sector in Angola was also developing very rapidly during the last years of Portuguese domination. The extractive industries ranked immediately behind agriculture in terms of importance to the economy. Portugal relied on foreign capital to undertake large-scale mining operations. These large foreign companies holding concessions with exclusive prospecting and exploitation rights over vast portions of the country were instrumental in the production and development of some of Angola's most important mineral resources: oil and diamonds. At the time of independence, Angola had a respectable manufacturing industry geared almost exclusively to the production of goods for the domestic market. The processing of local agricultural products such as food crops, sisal, cotton, and tobacco, was the principal form of manufacturing activity, comprising 36 per cent of the gross production value of the industrial sector in 1973 (Herrick et al., 1967:298).

The Portuguese colonial authorities also made significant investments in the transportation sector. By 1973 there were 72,300 kilometres of roads in existence. Of these, 8,500 kilometres were paved and 27,300 kilometres had an improved gravel or dirt surface, thus allowing for year-round usage. The remaining 36,500 kilometres were made up of dirt roads. Earlier in the 20th century, Portugal laid the foundations in Angola for one of the best railway infrastructures in Africa. The first railway – the Luanda Railway – was initially only 275 kilometres long, running from Luanda to Ambaca. By the end of the colonial period it had doubled in length. Construction of a second railway, the Moçamedes Railway, began in 1905. This railway was designed as an instrument to establish Portuguese control over the southern portion of the territory and facilitate the exploration of important mineral resources in the area, mainly iron ore. The Benguela Railway – the crown jewel of the country's transportation system – is the main railway in Angola. Construction of this railway started in 1912. This 1,340 kilometre railway stretched from the port-city of Lobito on the Atlantic coast to the border with Zambia where it connected with the railway systems of neighbouring countries. Angola's transportation infrastructure also included four important commercial ports and dozens of airports. By the time of independence, then, Angola had what appeared to be a strong economic base. However, given the dynamics of colonial exploitation – i.e. the centrality of the settler community and the marginalization of indigenous communities – this economic base was unsound. The exodus of the Portuguese settlers during decolonization precipitated an economic collapse whose consequences are still felt after almost three decades.

Portuguese exodus and economic decline

The exodus of the Portuguese settler population from Angola represented a serious setback for the new Angolan state. The Portuguese and their descendants constituted a community of about 340,000 out of a total population of approximately 6 million at the time of independence. By early 1976, 300,000 of these settlers had left Angola (Bhagavan, 1986:7). This exodus was caused primarily by the heightened anxiety resulting from the violence and uncertainties that characterized Angola's transition to independence. To understand the impact of this exodus it is important to consider that the settlers controlled literally all political and economic life in the colony. The majority of the African population was segregated and relegated into a state of permanent dependency within the colonial political economy. On the eve of independence, then, Angola was left without the people – business-people, commercial farmers, senior and mid-level civil servants, engineers, doctors, teachers, shopkeepers, and many other skilled personnel – who had organized and controlled most political and economic activities in the country. Making matters worse, the departing settlers took with them "every asset that could be transported" (World Bank 1991:6).

The departure of the Portuguese settlers led to drastic reductions in productive activities. The exodus of the settler population had its most immediate and dramatic effect in the agricultural sector. Their commercial farms, as previously noted, constituted the principal suppliers of agricultural products both for domestic consumption as well as for export. Another important role of the settlers was that of intermediaries between the subsistence farmers and the urban and export markets, i.e., they bought agricultural products from the subsistence farmers and transported them to the major commercial centres where the products were shipped to the rest of the country and overseas markets. The removal of this crucial link in the chain of agricultural production and distribution caused major short-ages in the supply of agricultural goods throughout the country. Predict-ably, the mass departure of the Portuguese settlers precipitated the onset of a major economic downturn: between 1974 and 1976 "every sector of the economy experienced sharp output declines" ranging up to 100 per cent (World Bank 1991:6). The post-colonial state was mostly unprepared to meet this challenge, especially since its attempts were hampered by the onset of a protracted civil war.

Civil war

The major political, military, economic, and social problems that conspired against the post-colonial state were glaringly visible at the time of independ-ence from Portugal on 11 November 1975. The political crisis surrounding the granting of independence to Angola arose from the three main nation-alist groups' inability to form a united front during the fourteen-year strug-gle against Portuguese colonialism. This was compounded by their failure to agree on a power-sharing formula for a post-colonial political system.

When a group of disgruntled young officers of the Portuguese Armed Forces overthrew the regime of Marcelo Caetano in Lisbon on 25 April 1974, the nationalist movement in Angola was in disarray. Unlike in Mozam-bique and Guinea-Bissau – the other Portuguese colonies in Africa where the colonial power was on the defensive due to the greater cohesiveness and organizational skills of FRELIMO[1] and PAIGC[2] respectively – the libera-tion movement in Angola was not on the verge of defeating the Portuguese army. Although the anti-colonial armed struggle against Portugal started in Angola in 1961, endemic disagreements fueled by personal jealousies, ethnic/racial differences reflecting the various social bases of the nationalist groups, and ideological antagonisms reflecting their external help within the Cold War context – i.e., MPLA, FNLA and UNITA were supported by the former USSR, the USA, and China respectively –seriously hindered

---

1. Frente de Libertação de Moçambique (Front for the Liberation of Mozambique).

2. Partido Africano para a Independência da Guiné e Cabo Verde (African Party for the Independence of Guinea and Cape Verde).

the nationalist movement's ability to pose a real military threat to Portugal's colonial rule. Divisions between the nationalist groups were further exacerbated by deep internal schisms: by the early 1970s, MPLA had split into three factions and FNLA had spawned UNITA.

Given the highly fractured nature of the nationalist movement in Angola and consequent inability to take advantage of the momentous changes brought about by the collapse of the colonial regime, many of the unresolved problems that marred the liberation struggle were brought unchecked into the realm of post-colonial politics with calamitous consequences. The three liberation groups rejected post-colonial peaceful coexistence and power-sharing and each attempted to usurp the political power left up for grabs by inviting in foreign armies to crush the opposition. Thus, MPLA, FNLA, and UNITA welcomed Cuban, Zairian (and western mercenaries), and South African armies respectively into Angola in the months leading up to independence.

At independence Angola had essentially three governments: MPLA backed by Cuban troops controlled Luanda, the capital, and little else; UNITA controlled Huambo, the second largest city and several southern provinces with South African help while FNLA, supported by Zairian troops, held the northern provinces.

In the early stages of this internationalized civil war Cuban troops prevailed over the South African and Zairian armies. Demoralized and humiliated for failing to install their respective allies in power, both the South African and the Zairian armies retreated within months of independence. However, independence and the defeat of UNITA/SADF and FNLA/Zairian armies in 1976 constituted a short pause in the civil war. The new Angolan state was forced to survive under constant external military threat. This threat to the new Angolan state was closely linked with the South African apartheid regime's policies in southern Africa after the collapse of the Portuguese settler regime and the instrumentalization of UNITA by external powers – especially South Africa but also the United States – as a proxy in their regional destabilization strategies.

At the end of the initial phase of the civil war (1975–1976) UNITA was virtually destroyed and MPLA was ready to consolidate its power. The coming to power of P.W. Botha in South Africa, however, thwarted this aspiration. Until becoming prime minister in September 1978, Botha had been South Africa's defence minister. As such he supervised South Africa's disastrous 1975–76 intervention in Angola's civil war. As prime minister, Botha's regional policy was based on the white regime's "total strategy" designed to prevent a perceived "total onslaught" by communist forces in the region. The implementation of the "total strategy" relied heavily on Special Forces, covert operations and proxy armies like UNITA.

Broadly, "total strategy" was a comprehensive set of policies designed by the apartheid regime to ensure its survival, through a combination of reform and repression, in the face of several developments that confronted South Africa in the 1970s. First, domestically, apartheid was confronted with the re-emergence of new forms of organized, large-scale black opposition to the racist regime. The 1976 Soweto uprising heralded both a new phase in the liberation struggle and its bloody repression demonstrated the regime's determination to use any means to preserve the status quo. Second, also at the domestic level, restrictions on the mobility and training of black labour threatened to aggravate an increasingly untenable economic situation. Third, regionally, the collapse of Portuguese colonialism and the independence of Angola and Mozambique under socialist governments showed that apartheid South Africa's position in the region was increasingly imperilled. Finally, at the international level, the growing condemnation of South Africa and its isolation from its major allies indicated the need for dramatic changes.

The "total strategy" ultimately failed because it was inherently problematic at various levels. It was particularly problematic inasmuch as it attempted to internationalize the problems confronting the apartheid state. The main proponents of this strategy argued that the source of instability and conflict, both inside South Africa and across the region, was neither apartheid nor colonialism but external intervention. Therefore, from this perspective, it was necessary to ensure that neighbouring states refrained from actively supporting the armed liberation struggle for South Africa and Namibia and that no "communist" power gained a political or military foothold in the region. Angola became a prime target in South Africa's total strategy primarily because its Marxist regime allowed both the ANC and SWAPO to set up bases and carry out military operations from bases in it. Just as troubling for South Africa was the presence of thousands of Cuban troops and Soviet military advisers in Angola.

Beginning in 1980 – partly as a response to regional changes including Zimbabwe's independence under Robert Mugabe's ZANU – the SADF moved away from mere small-scale assistance to UNITA to large military operations inside Angola. Thus, in June 1980, the SADF launched *Operation Skeptic* in response to an alleged increase in SWAPO attacks in northern Namibia from its bases in southern Angola. This operation marked the beginning of continuous large-scale SADF operations in Angola. An important side-effect of such operations was to revitalize UNITA. Advancing behind SADF, UNITA occupied territory and kept most weapons captured by the South African army. Several towns in the Cuando-Cubango province – including Mavinga, Cuangar, and Luenge – were thus "liberated" by UNITA in 1980. In August 1981, SADF launched *Operation Protea* which was followed in November by *Operation Daisy*. These invasions provided the smoke-screen for UNITA to consolidate its base in Cuando-Cubango, make significant advances in Moxico province, and begin intensive guerrilla operations in the populous and agricultural rich central plateau. This enabled UNITA to intensify guerrilla activity across the country and caused the MPLA government to become increasingly dependent on Cuban military assistance to remain in power.

Major SADF interventions in Angola escalated into the late 1980s. In 1987, for example, SADF staged a massive intervention in response to a combined Angolan-Cuban-Soviet offensive that threatened the rebel base at Jamba. By 1988 the civil war had reached a high point with massive SADF intervention to save UNITA from the advancing MPLA and crack Cuban units at the battle of Cuito-Cuanavale. This small military base witnessed what has been described as "the fiercest conventional battle on African soil since Erwin Rommel was defeated at El Amein" (Campbell 1989:1). A South African invasion force of approximately 8,000 troops equipped with heavy artillery, armoured cars and surface-to-air missiles had laid siege to Cuito-Cuanavale after SADF's long-range artillery staved off an Angolan army assault on the town of Mavinga. Had Mavinga been captured, the Angolan army would have removed the biggest obstacle en route to UNITA's headquarters at Jamba. To defend Cuito-Cuanavale, the Angolan army deployed 10,000 troops supported by the 50th division of the Cuban army and more than 400 tanks. The battle ended with a "crushing humiliation" for the SADF who had become "trapped by the rainy season, bogged down by the terrain, and encircled" by Angolan and Cuban troops (Campbell 1989:1).

The battle of Cuito-Cuanavale had a major impact in terms of re-invigorating a stalled negotiation process. The intense military confrontation demonstrated to Cuba and South Africa – both small, sub-imperial interventionist forces – that unbearable loss of lives would be involved in protracted military engagements. Consequently, both countries accepted the American proposals for a "comprehensive settlement" in the region, involving both the withdrawal of Cuban troops from Angola and the implementation of UNSCR 435/78 regarding Namibia's independence. Unfortunately, the settlement of the Namibian problem did not halt the escalating war in Angola. South Africa and increasingly the United States did not give up the idea of installing UNITA in power through military means if necessary.

American involvement in the Angolan civil war heightened in the 1980s and was based on two policy initiatives – "Constructive Engagement" and the "Reagan Doctrine". Constructive engagement was the policy devised by the Reagan administration to "help foster a regional climate conducive to compromise and accommodation in both Southern and South Africa" (Crocker, 1992:75). This policy emerged from the Reagan administration's view that southern Africa's problems were fundamentally intertwined and solutions to those same problems could only be found if that basic interdependence was recognized. Those charged with implementing Reagan's policies in Africa argued that the task of constructive engagement was "to demolish the myths and fantasies of violence which for decades had transfixed black and white South Africans – the government's 'total strategy' against the 'total Marxist onslaught,' otherwise known as the ANC's 'armed struggle' campaign waged from neighbouring lands vulnerable to the SADF's 'destabilization wars'" (Crocker, 1992:78).

Constructive engagement was intended to move beyond a simple concentration on the ultimate goals of the process of change taking place in the region – i.e. the establishment of non-racial post-settler political orders – to focus on the process itself by addressing the steps and sequences that might lead to it. In concrete terms, this policy committed the United States to "take seriously its responsibility to create a regional climate conducive to negotiated solutions and political change" (Crocker, 1992:77). This, for the United States, also involved forcing an end to "Soviet-Cuban adventurism" in the region (Crocker, 1992:77).

If constructive engagement had a primarily politico-diplomatic tone, the parallel "Reagan Doctrine" had a manifest strategic and military rationale. It was conceived as "a full-blown, global campaign" for providing overt American support for anti-communist guerrilla movements around the world to exploit Soviet "imperial vulnerabilities" at low cost (Crocker, 1992:292). The Reagan Doctrine had an almost immediate impact on the Angolan civil war, as it did in other parts of the world like Afghanistan and Central America. Buoyed up by both the overt as well as covert American help, UNITA significantly escalated its operations after 1985 until signing a peace accord with the government in 1991.

In retrospect, the civil war in Angola shows that the post-colonial state was not in a position to successfully carry out a counter-insurgency war. At the end of the anti-colonial war in 1974, MPLA had approximately 3,000 guerrillas who formed the core of the post-colonial army. Transforming poorly trained guerrillas into a well-trained professional army would have been a difficult task even in optimal circumstances, i.e. no external invasions and civil war. Cuban and Soviet advisers hastily attempted to form a well-trained professional army after independence. However, this army was simply not prepared to cope with the scale of the conflict in the 1980s partly because UNITA had grown into a well organized military structure including conventional regular army and guerrilla units with significant external support including secure sanctuaries as well as generous logistic and back-up support from South Africa and the United States. Later, from the late 1980s, UNITA acquired considerable wealth by mining Angola's vast diamond deposits and used it to procure the military means to take over the state. Although the rebel group ultimately failed to overthrow the MPLA government, it largely succeeded in severely curtailing the Angolan state's administrative space and effectively destroyed the infrastructures inherited from colonialism.

In sum, at the end of the 1980s, a combination of domestic and international factors was threatening the viability of the new and fragile Angolan state. Internally, Angola faced a multidimensional crisis that hindered the state's ability to carry out its basic functions. In this sense, the Angolan state was on the verge of collapse: the civil war had paralyzed the state, rendering it inoperative inasmuch as its reach and authority outside the capital and a handful of major cities were decreasing rapidly and resulting in its incapacity to provide security, let alone law and order, to citizens; the state's authority was being challenged by a rebel group that ruled over a large portion of the country with its population and had a working political-military apparatus together with an organized economy, albeit primitive; the legislative process became irrelevant since laws could not be implemented due to lack of state authority as well as the absence of discipline and control in the state bureaucracy; and the economy outside the oil sector was in a shambles due to a combination of historical factors and post-colonial policies. These domestic pressures were compounded by interrelated changes at the regional and global levels. The magnitude of the government's domestic problems had reached such alarming proportions that their resolution could no longer be attempted through decrees from the capital. A more profound approach, involving fundamental transformations at all levels, was needed to overcome this multi-faceted crisis. This eventually led to political as well as economic liberalization and, ultimately, the end of the civil war.

CHAPTER 2

Violence and Fractured Nationalism

Violence – both physical and structural – has dominated Angola's post-colonial history. This situation was not entirely unexpected because the major immediate forces that conditioned the new state's character – especially the colonial order and, paradoxically, the national liberation movements who fought to overthrow it – were both violent. This violence increased in intensity, especially after the mid-1970s as the liberation war metamorphosed into a civil war which, over nearly three decades, mutated through various escalating stages. These mutations were primarily a consequence of the domestic participants' changing strategies for achieving power which, in turn, represented pragmatic responses to various regional and international developments such as the military coup that deposed the colonial regime in Portugal in April 1974, the superpowers' Cold War calculations, the end of the Cold War in 1991, and the end of apartheid in 1994.

In addition to war, the post-colonial society has confronted an equally debilitating and resilient foe – structural violence – which may ultimately determine its long-term stability. Escaping post-colonial structural violence will be just as difficult as escaping its colonial antecedents and the physical violence associated with the civil war due to a combination of internal and external factors. The onset of the civil war during the decolonization period robbed post-colonial society of opportunities for self-reinvention after the collapse of an oppressive and corrupt colonial society. Even worse, the civil war presented the new post-colonial elites with ideal conditions for corruption and other forms of structural violence due mainly to two interrelated factors. First, with the post-colonial state under domestic and international threat, the governing elites increasingly saw self-preservation as the dominant objective, leading to the postponement of the grand and revolutionary projects for societal transformations that inspired the anti-colonial war. Second, the civil war era coincided with a large boom in oil and diamond exploration that brought increasingly large revenues into state coffers. Problematically, due to the general lack of transparency and accountability partly caused by the dynamics of the civil war, the monies accrued from the sale of oil and diamonds were captured by the new elites. These elites adeptly used such revenues to further their particular interests – i.e. personal enrichment – for as long as the war lasted. This chapter provides a succinct overview of the main sources of the violence that has dominated Angolan society and politics. It suggests that colonialism and the liberation movements have been important generators of these malignancies.

Colonial violence

Admittedly, it would be inaccurate to suggest that Africa was a peaceful Eden before the advent of colonialism. Indeed, since pre-colonial Africa was as heterogeneous at the political, economic, and social levels as other parts of the world, the relations among African societies involved both cooperation and conflict. Significantly, however, for the vast majority of these societies which came under European domination, colonialism represented "the most cruel and disruptive period in African history" (Gordon and Gordon, 1996:2). European colonialists fundamentally changed Africa through violent means such as the slave trade, the creation of new and arbitrary territorial boundaries, the integration of the new colonies into the global political economy based on unequal and exploitative relationships, and cultural trashing via the imposition of foreign lingua francas, religions, as well as "superior" European values and symbols of identity. As Cabral (1982a:8) succinctly put it, colonialism manifested itself as "total control of the collective and individual life of Africans, either by persuasion or violence". Africa is yet to recover from the traumatic effects of the "permanent violence" that European colonialism inflicted upon the continent (Cabral 1982b:63). In some respects, Angola and the other former Portuguese colonies represent particular cases in European colonization – not simply in terms of the length and depth of the colonial presence but as it pertains to the consequences of "the most retrograde kind of colonial system" imposed by what had been "an impoverished and backward European nation" (Rodney, 1981:138). Portuguese colonialism was so uniquely violent as to stand out as a "reign of evil" (Cabral 1982a:10). During almost five centuries of presence in Angola, the Portuguese used a variety of violent means – physical, psychological, and structural – to exercise and retain control over the colony: slavery, forced labour, and military campaigns used in an ultimately failed effort to crush anti-colonial liberation movements.

The slave trade

Portuguese explorers were some of the pioneers in establishing European-African relations. These relations were not, however, mutually beneficial for much longer than the intial contacts for two main reasons. First, the Portuguese regarded themselves as a superior people with a duty to uplift inferior African peoples (Abshire, 1969:91). Second, they were primarily interested in exploiting Africa's human and natural resources. Since Africans could be captured relatively easily and traded for a very high rate of return in world markets, the Portuguese quickly became very active in the slave trade along the west coast of Africa. Slaves quickly became "the most common merchandise in the Portuguese-dominated opening period of the seaborne trade between Europe and Africa" (Duffy, 1959:8; Elbl, 1997:31).

After the establishment of the Portuguese colony at Luanda in 1575, Angola became the "Black Mother", the major supplier of African slaves (Duffy, 1959:50) to the "new world". Moreover, unlike other colonial authorities elsewhere in Africa, Portuguese authorities did not simply facilitate the slave trade; they were at the apex of this complex and lucrative trade system. As Duffy points out, "the principal dealer was usually the governor, whose interest in the trade was not necessarily his own capital, but the power and facilities of his office plus whatever privileges were contained in his *regimento*" (Duffy, 1959:60). Thus facilitated by colonial authorities, Portuguese slave trade expeditions in Angola "might be gone for weeks, months, or years, often bringing or sending back 400, 500, or 600 slaves" (Abshire, 1969:99). An estimated 4 million of these slaves eventually survived the hellish sea journey to the "new world". If one slave died for each one that survived the ordeal of capture, long walk to the coast, caging, and the boat ride to the Americas, Angola was emptied of about 8 million people (Curtin, 1969:31). Even then, it is important to take into account Elbl's caveat that any estimate about the number of slaves exported from Africa based on surviving numerical data is "necessarily minimalist". Still, even a minimalist perspective provides the horrific scope and impact of slavery for Angola – eight million people is more than Angola's total population at the time of independence!

Although the major participants in the Atlantic slave trade agreed to officially abolish it in 1836, this practice survived throughout the Portuguese territories until 1875. But the official abolition of slavery did not mean that, thenceforth, Angolans would be free. No longer able to export slaves from Angola, Portuguese colonial authorities shifted instead to a system of forced labour in the colony to continue exploiting Angola's human resources.

Forced labour

For hundreds of years, Portugal exploited its colonies' human and natural resources while subjecting Africans to "a sub-human standard – little or no better than serfs in their own country" (Cabral 1982a:8). Under the 1878 *Regulamento para os contratos de serviçais e colonos nas províncias de África* (Regulation for contracts of servants and colonists in the African provinces) Portugal replaced slavery with a slightly less heinous system of forced labour whereby former slaves became contract labourers or *serviçais*. In practice and predictably, slave masters simply kept their slaves. The difference resided mainly in the new label for the Africans kept in servitude – from exportable slaves to domestically exploited contract labourers. Significantly, such changes had little impact on how slave traders in the interior went about their business; instead of buying slaves, they now "contracted" for them (Duffy, 1962:131). Furthermore, the *Regulamento* had a "vagrancy clause" that turned all those Angolans not fully employed into contractable vagrants who colonists could "legally" force into five-year contracts (Duffy, 1962:131). Thus, under "conditions equivalent to slavery" (Rodney, 1981:167), Portuguese owners used this forced labour throughout the colonial empire and beyond – from Angola's own coffee plantations, to Mozambique's sugar plantations, to Sao Tome & Principe's cocoa plantations, and to South Africa's mines.

Colonial military violence

Military conquest and repression played a critical role in the colonial enterprise. In fact, the colonial administration in Angola was, in substance, clearly military in structure and consequently, "rarely did a year pass during the four centuries since 1575 when there was not a colonial campaign somewhere in Angola" (Wheeler, 1969:428). These military missions of conquest, generally referred to by the Portuguese as "pacification campaigns", were instrumental in expanding the colonial writ into the hinterland and in subduing the local populations. An eyewitness described such campaigns as "going out with troops and smoking out the terrorists" (Martelli, 1962:304). The military played an even more repressive role after nationalist groups in Angola initiated the anti-colonial war of liberation.

On 4 February 1961, hundreds of Angolans stormed Luanda's central jail in an attempt to free several hundred nationalist leaders who had been detained by the colonial authorities during the previous two years. Seven Portuguese policemen were killed in the resulting melee. The predictable violent response from the colonists resulted in the killing, wounding and arresting of several hundred Angolans. In addition, for the rest of the month, "the African slums were repeatedly raided by marauding white groups, who indiscriminately murdered and pillaged. Political prisoners in the Luanda gaol were executed and buried in mass graves. White hoodlums roamed Luanda's streets at night, beating, often fatally, any Africans they encountered" (Duffy, 1962:215). Extreme political repression was led by detachments of the *Polícia Internacional e de Defesa do Estado* (PIDE) – the notoriously brutal secret police – that had been sent to the Portuguese overseas possessions in an attempt which ultimately failed to insulate Portugal from the winds of change sweeping away colonialism in Africa. Although PIDE eventually brought the Luanda uprising under control, Portugal could not control the much larger part of the iceberg underneath the surface. An even bigger, more violent nationalist explosion took place on 15 March 1961 when UPA guerrillas attacked the main coffee production centres in northern Angola.

The following situation confronted the colonial authorities in Angola in April 1961:

> ... over 100 administrative posts and towns, in three districts of northern Angola from the Congo border to within 30 miles of Luanda, the capital, had been either wiped out, taken, or paralysed by African nationalist groups; over 1,000 Europeans were dead, and an unknown number of Africans; the economy of north Angola was crippled; communications were largely cut or damaged; and thousands of Portuguese refugees were camped in Luanda, or on their way back to Portugal (Wheeler, 1969:431).

Colonial responses to the 1961 events involved the massive deployment of troop reinforcements and war materiel in the colony. By 1968, Portugal had increased its troop presence to about 50,000, representing a sixteen-fold increase over 1961 (Wheeler, 1969:431), and maintained such levels until 1974. With such military might colonial authorities were able to inflict considerable damage upon the nationalist groups fighting for liberation. Ultimately, however, they failed to prevail mainly because colonial authorities did not have a monopoly on violence. The national liberation movements quickly developed their own violent capabilities. Peculiarly, however, these groups did not simply target colonialism, its manifestations and symbols. They were equally violent toward each other.

Fractured Nationalism

National liberation movements "do no emerge on a fine day out of the mind of some superman or at the instigation of some foreign power. They are born out of popular discontent. They emerge over long periods to combat oppressive conditions and express aspirations for a different kind of society. They are, in short, the agents of class and national struggle" (Bragança and Wallerstein, 1982:iii). Angola produced three main agents of struggle – MPLA, FNLA, and UNITA – that deserve particular attention.

MPLA

MPLA emerged in 1956 as an umbrella organization for various nationalist groups agitating for the end of Portuguese colonialism in Angola. Some of the major groups that integrated MPLA included PCA and PLUA. Its major base of support emanated from the Mbundu, representing about twenty-five percent of the population, who lived in the areas around the capital city, Luanda, and east as far as the Cassange area of Malanje province. MPLA also drew support from the embryonic African intellectual elite in the Luanda area, including influential *mulattos* and a small number of liberal whites.

During the 1950s, much of the struggle took the form of cultural activities to showcase African culture, the publishing of minor anti-colonial and anti-racist material – mostly political stories and poems – and the distribution of political leaflets. As mentioned above, in 1957, Portugal deployed its feared secret police to Angola in an attempt to help control the growing nationalist tide. However, by 1959, as these nationalist activities increased in intensity and began to assume the character of a more overt threat to the colonial administration, the latter responded by undertaking mass detentions of prominent nationalist voices in the country, especially in and around Luanda where most of the MPLA leadership resided.

The 1960s, therefore, began gloomily with the colonial administration attempting to suppress the impeding nationalist storm. In 1960, the colonial administration imprisoned Agostinho Neto – the young Angolan medical doctor and president of the MPLA Steering Committee – who later became post-colonial Angola's first president. The imprisonment of Agostinho Neto led to a mass demonstration by the villagers of his native village of Icolo e Bengo. The Portuguese authorities' military response resulted in thirty villagers dead and two hundred wounded (Chilcote, 1972:181). This was followed in January 1961 by the Baixa de Kassanje massacre. There, as elsewhere in the region – including neighbouring Icolo e Bengo – the local populations were forced to grow cotton as a cash crop. In early 1961, local cotton growers organized a strike to protest against low prices and, more generally, as a political act of defiance against the settler authorities. Unsurprisingly, this action was met by military force. MPLA would later claim that "the colonists repressed the strike with aerial bombardment, using American napalm bombs, which destroyed more than seventeen towns and killed more than 20,000 Africans" (Chilcote, 1972:181). It is in this context of violence that, on 4 February 1961, a group of Angolans attacked the central Luanda prison where many nationalist leaders were held, thus marking the beginning of a fourteen-year armed struggle to liberate Angola from colonialism.

The onset of the armed nationalist resistance against Portuguese colonialism brought serious challenges for MPLA. In fact, MPLA was in disarray within a year of the start of the liberation war. The inability to achieve a leading role in the incipient armed anti-colonial struggle and the failure to achieve a united front with the more powerful UPA had brought MPLA to a leadership crisis. In May 1962, this crisis spilled into the open as MPLA's steering committee meeting in Leopoldville (now Kinshasa) removed Viriato da Cruz from his position of secretary-general, a post he had held since helping to found MPLA in 1956. With his own party facing a profound crisis, Neto pursued his long-standing goal of uniting all nationalist groups, to no avail. Indeed, MPLA was left out of GRAE when it was formed on 3 April 1962. Thus, MPLA's denouncing of GRAE as "anti-unitarian, discriminatory, and arbitrary" (MPLA, 1972:239) can be best interpreted as an attempt to disguise its own increasing marginalization. Yet, undeterred by this growing marginalization, on 5 August 1962, Neto led an MPLA delegation to negotiate with FNLA on the possibilities of bringing about the elusive united front. Neto proposed three possible avenues for cooperation: total fusion between the two parties that constituted FNLA (i.e. UPA and PDA) and MPLA, simple collaboration between FNLA and MPLA, or a military alliance between the three parties individually or between FNLA and MPLA (Chilcote, 1972:267–8). But the FNLA delegation was more interested in getting Neto to retract damaging allegations by some of his party's leaders against the rival movement and officially recognize it. Neto replied, ambiguously, that "FNLA is not *representative*, since it groups only A plus B. This does not mean that its existence is not real. It is only *representativeness* that the Front is lacking, and that we would like to give it by encompassing A plus B plus C" (Chilcote, 1972:268). This was simply too much for FNLA to accept at the time because it would have elevated MPLA to an equal status with UPA and PDA within a broad coalition – effectively eliminating FNLA and replacing it with this proposed new entity. After hearing Neto's daring proposal, the FNLA delegation abruptly ended the unity talks. In addition to its natural desire for self-preservation, some other underlying reasons for FNLA's refusal to enter into a common front with MPLA became clearer with a GRAE document issued on 11 December 1962 entitled "Glimpses of the Angolan Nationalist Organizations". The document describes FNLA, GRAE's key partner, as "supported essentially by the black peasants, who have been subjected to forced labour, defrauded of their land, and classed as 'noncivilized' by Salazar's racist government. These peasants constitute ninety-three percent of the total population of Angola" (Chilcote, 1972:150). The document then proceeded to castigate MPLA – which GRAE regarded as a group comprising "leftist Europeans", members of the Angolan communist party and Marxists – for failing to understand that the anti-colonial war was both "peasant and northern" in origin. Moreover, GRAE suggested in the same document, peasants were rightly suspicious of this group of half-castes and *assimilados* because, after independence, it would form the basis for "a class of *compradores*" if they were "allowed to monopolize the leadership of the revolution in the name of their cultural superiority" (Chilcote, 1972:151). From this standpoint, a common front with MPLA would be tantamount to political and cultural suicide because it would defeat the very objectives FNLA/GRAE were fighting for, i.e. political, economic and cultural empowerment for the vast majority of disenfranchised, exploited, and humiliated peasants. Regrettably, this fundamental difference – later described in detail by Da Cruz – would stay unresolved for the remainder of the anti-colonial war and beyond. In the meantime, however, MPLA continued to seek political relevance.

In December 1962, MPLA held its First National Conference in Leopoldville where it elected a new party executive led by Agostinho Neto (Marcum, 1978:30). But, within six months, this new leadership faced an open revolt. On 5 July 1963, several key MPLA members, headed by former secretary-general Viriato da Cruz, "dismissed" the movement's new leadership. To remain politically alive, on 10 July 1963 Agostinho Neto led his faction in creating the FDLA. This involved forming an alliance with three minor groups – MDIA, MNA, NGWIZAKO – and UNTA. While announcing the creation of FDLA, Agostinho Neto declared that the integration of FDLA's representatives in GRAE was "necessary" (Neto, 1972:218). However, with little leverage, Neto was still unable to convince Holden Roberto to make space within GRAE for himself and/or his followers.

Viriato da Cruz attributed MPLA's turmoil to four main factors: internal conflict resulting from the heterogeneous composition of the movement's social strata, internal leadership struggle, inter-movement rivalry, and "the use of myths" (Da Cruz 1972:208–212). First, MPLA brought together Angolans from various socio-economic backgrounds – from *assimilados* to the downtrodden masses – without a common political outlook on the struggle ahead, including the post-colonial project. Consequently, they formed blocs within MPLA on the basis of their respective interests, origins, socio-political situations, and social aspirations. More problematically, "each bloc offered its own solutions to problems of organization and ideology, to problems of united front tactics, of external alliances, of the socio-economic structures of Angola after independence, etc" (Da Cruz, 1972:209). Second, intellectuals and *assimilados* believed that their presence in the leadership of the liberation movement was "indispensable" to "avoid the excesses of the peasants and guarantee the progressive result of the revolution" (Da Cruz 1972:209). Da Cruz attributes this peculiar view of the MPLA leadership to their own collective fear that "a result of the popular revolution would be a drastic change in the conditions under which they had acquired privileges and advantages" (Da Cruz 1972:209). Third, MPLA was in a weaker position vis-à-vis FNLA, its rival in the armed struggle. FNLA was stronger militarily due to the support it enjoyed from the newly independent Congo (Kinshasa). Therefore, as discussed earlier, FNLA did not show interest in creating a united front with MPLA that would allow the latter to undertake military actions in northern Angola, i.e. within FNLA's own main areas of operation. FNLA was more interested in a more outright absorption of MPLA. Frustrated, MPLA leaders sought "new tactics" for seizing power in Angola. These new tactics "consisted of stressing the importance of the military exploits of the MPLA through propaganda in an effort to obtain strong support in the West for the MPLA and to put an end to the aid given the FNLA" (Da Cruz, 1972:210). Finally, MPLA fell victim of the "myths" surrounding the figure of Agostinho Neto, the organization's imprisoned symbolic leader. After his flight from Portugal in May 1962 to join the armed struggle, Neto not only maintained the myths that had been cultivated through "exaggerated propaganda", he sided himself with intellectuals and *assimilados* who dominated MPLA thus accentuating the fractures within the organization.

Relevance for MPLA in the anti-colonial struggle necessarily involved stepping up its military activities inside Angola, especially in the north-central areas of the country where its popular support base resided. This, however, was very difficult because its main rival, FNLA, hindered MPLA attempts to use territory in recently independent neighbouring Congo and, for that matter, much of northern Angola as staging areas for guerrilla activity. Specifically under their leader's orders to "intercept and annihilate MPLA columns that were trying to infiltrate into Angola" (Marcum, 1969:214), FNLA troops did just that – regularly ambushing, detaining, torturing and killing MPLA leaders and their troops attempting to enter northern Angola from Congo (Marcum, 1969:211). FNLA ignored MPLA's insistent and convincing argument that such "anti-patriotic" acts would "reduce the effectiveness of the Angolan resistance movements by introducing a fratricidal conflict onto the Angolan battlefield" (Marcum, 1969:213). Ironically, MPLA did not abstain from intra- and inter-organizational killings. For example, in November 1965, MPLA detained, tried and executed two former members of its leadership structure – Matias Migueis and Jose Miguel – who, with Viriato da Cruz, had broken away from MPLA and joined FNLA/GRAE.

In addition to its internal turmoil, MPLA also faced a very skeptical external environment. For example, by 1963, the OAU asserted that the "continued separate existence of another minor front such as the MPLA" was unhelpful to the rapid achievement of independence by the Angolan peoples (Marcum, 1978:307) and Congo expelled the movement from its territory. It reestablished itself across the river in Congo (Brazzaville) where a coup had brought to power a left-wing government sympathetic to MPLA. From this new base, MPLA successfully penetrated Angola's Cabinda enclave. However, even this success was problematic in the sense that the separatist FLEC was already active in Cabinda by the time MPLA's guerrillas began to set up bases there. Divergent goals – national liberation vs. separation of the Cabinda enclave – prevented cooperation between them.

Problematic penetration through northern borders due to hostility from competing liberation movements, forced MPLA to change its military strategy in the mid-1960s in favour of military operations along the long eastern border with Zambia, a country that gained independence in October 1964. Although MPLA was undergoing a "striking recovery" at the time (Marcum, 1978:169), the eastern front would not prove unproblematic because UNITA, the movement created in 1966 by Jonas Savimbi after his resignation from GRAE in 1964, had also established itself – albeit in embryonic form – in eastern Angola.

True to form, instead of cooperating to face a common enemy, MPLA and UNITA spent much of their precious resources fighting each other. As Minter (1988:13) points out, "as early as 1967–1968 UNITA clashes with the MPLA were at least as common as its confrontations with Portuguese troops". Unfortunately, as Minter (1988:14) also shows, UNITA had developed an "explicit alliance with the Portuguese military" – the first of several costly strategic blunders that UNITA would commit in the following three decades.

For MPLA in eastern Angola in the late 1960s and early 1970s, the consequences of both Portuguese operations – particularly "Operation Attila" (Bridgland, 1987:96; Henderson, 1979:226) – and UNITA activities against them were militarily devastating. Thus, by the end of 1972, MPLA was "finished" as a viable fighting force in eastern Angola. The political consequences emanating from this inability to establish itself in eastern Angola were equally serious. The military pressure by the Portuguese army and UNITA forces triggered another round of MPLA's then perennial internal and often deadly squabbles followed by predictable purges that served to further debilitate it. According to its former vice-president, Daniel Chipenda, starting in 1967, MPLA routinely relied on "executions without trial" to eliminate dissent within MPLA (Marcum, 1978:203). Ironically, Chipenda supporters allegedly planned to assassinate Neto in1972 and 1973 (Marcum, 1978:201–03). The movement's internal divisions appeared so intractable that the Soviet Union withdrew its support during 1972–1973 (Marcum 1978:201). Thus weakened internally and externally while hounded relentlessly by the Portuguese army, MPLA accepted a marriage of convenience with FNLA, its archenemy, to create CSLA on 13 December 1972. However, the gulf separating the two organizations – a result of major personal, ethnic, racial, and ideological divisions – had made such unity unsustainable. Equally important, this attempted unity between liberation movements generated heightened friction leading to deeper fissures within MPLA as commanders on the eastern front, led by Chipenda, upset by their leader's unwillingness to consult them prior to the merger broke away from the leadership and set up their own autonomous organization – MPLA's Eastern Revolt. This was followed, in February1974, by yet another major fracture in MPLA as former leader Mario de Andrade also broke away from the main fold to create MPLA's Active Revolt.

At the time of the Portuguese coup of 25 April 1974, Portuguese intelligence claimed that MPLA had only a few dozen guerrillas inside Angola (Marcum, 1976:413). Adding to its tribulations, MPLA spent the initial post-coup months engaged in "internal squabbling, torture and murder" (Bridgland, 1987:108), hopelessly divided among three factions: Neto's mainstream MPLA, Daniel Chipenda's Eastern Revolt and Mario Pinto de Andrade's Active Revolt. The August 1974 MPLA Congress was called to help resolve the leadership issue. Instead, it further divided the organization as both Neto and Andrade, along with their respective delegates, walked out of the Congress. Chipenda, the only major leadership contestant not to walk out was promptly elected "President" by his supporters (Marcum, 1978:250). Neighbouring heads of state – Marian Ngouabi of Congo, Mobutu Sesse Seko of Zaire, Kenneth Kaunda of Zambia, and Julius Nyerere of Tanzania – attempted to reconcile the three factional leaders, to no avail. Chipenda finally relinquished his "leadership" under intense pressure from neighbouring African heads of state and eventually merged with FNLA in early 1975 during the initial phase of the civil war. Andrade faded into obscurity. In the end, Neto's faction prevailed. By retaining a strong nucleus of mestiços and assimilados mostly from the Kimbundu region around Luanda, Neto ensured victory over all his adversaries. This momentum would serve Neto well as his MPLA now had to successfully face an assortment of powerful internal and external adversaries.

An important key to MPLA's eventual success was its reengagement with the former Soviet Union. Within the Cold War context and the equally significant Sino-Soviet rivalry, the Soviet Union accepted the rekindling of the ties that had been severed two years earlier due to MPLA's military ineffectiveness and its perennial internal squabbles. The Sino-Soviet rivalry is important in this context inasmuch as China was providing MPLA's archenemy, FNLA, with considerable resources including war materiel and military trainers (Marcum, 1978:246; Gunn, 1992:41; Katsikas, 1982:66). For the Soviet Union, an MPLA victory in post-colonial Angola would constitute a significant ideological and geo-strategic coup. It would mean that the envisaged triumph of socialist movements around the world was proceeding at a good pace. Even more important, Angola could provide the front line bases for an eventual liberation of the entire southern African sub-continent under pro-Soviet regimes. The availability of immense natural resources in the region provided an added incentive for Soviet involvement. The opportunity to inflict important setbacks on its main global adversaries – the United States and China – proved irresistible for the former

Soviet Union. Thus, in August 1974, the former Soviet Union delivered $6 million to its Angolan beneficiaries through the Tanzanian port of Dar-es-Salaam (Gunn, 1992:41), marking the resumption of Soviet engagement in the Angolan conflict.

But MPLA could not rely solely on Soviet help to prevail over its enemies. With no army to speak of, it sought assistance from additional foreign sources. First, it secured the support of the former Katangan gendarmes and, later, more decisive help from Cuban troops. Initially, MPLA relied on the "Katanga Tigers" – Katangan soldiers under the leadership of Moise Tshombe who had been part of an attempted secession of the Zairian province of Katanga in 1960. After their defeat by UN forces in 1962, Tshombe and his troops fled to Angola where the Portuguese colonial authorities employed them to combat the anti-colonial national liberation movements. Ironically, after the collapse of the colonial regime, these Katangan troops were used by one of these Angolan movements – MPLA – to achieve a critical military advantage over its domestic rivals in the first stages of the civil war. FNLA, in particular, was decisively defeated even with the help of Mobutu's Zaire.

FNLA

FNLA was founded on 27 March 1962 through the merging of UPA and PDA (Chilcote, 1972:102). However, FNLA claims a much longer historical pedigree as the natural descendant of the *Grande Revolta* (Great Revolt), the insurgency actions led by Chief Tulante Alvaro Buta against colonial occupation in northern Angola from 1913 to 1915. In fact, both UPA and PDA were primarily regional political formations representing the Bakongo community of northern Angola. Their main objective was the restoration of the ancient Kongo kingdom that had disintegrated as a result of the colonial presence.

The regional character of these organizations reflected the long struggle by the peoples of northern Angola to recapture their pre-colonial identities remembered in the context of the once great Kongo kingdom. When Portuguese explorer Diogo Cao first arrived at this kingdom in the early fifteenth century he found a highly sophisticated society. Ruled by a monarch, the kingdom was divided into six provinces, five of which had their own subordinate rulers. The central province of Mpemba was personally governed by the king and contained the royal city of Mbanza Kongo whose population was once estimated to be as much as 100,000 people. The surrounding provinces were Nsundi to the North, Mpangu to the Northeast, Mbata to the Southeast, Mbamba in the Southwest, and Sonyo on the coast west of the capital (Birmingham, 1966:2).

On the eve of the colonial contact, Kongo was "a quietly prosperous farming community" whose central power was "based on a modified type of trade conducted through a system of tribute and reward" (Birmingham, 1977:544–5). This changed dramatically with the colonial presence. Thus, by the middle of the seventeenth century, constant Portuguese interference in the kingdom's internal affairs had reduced Kongo into "increasingly small and fragmented chiefdoms" consumed by civil war (Birmingham, 1975:341). The kingdom never recovered its power and prestige. Indeed, the "scramble for Africa" of the late nineteenth century finalized the kingdom's dismemberment splitting it into what became three African states: Angola, the Democratic Republic of Congo, and the Republic of Congo. The Bakongo community of the former Kongo kingdom constitutes about fifteen percent of Angola's population and they reside mainly in the northern provinces of Cabinda, Zaire, and Uige. Many have traditionally regarded Kinshasa, not Luanda, as their cultural, economic, and political centre.

During the first half of the 20th century, demands by the Bakongo community for redress of the colonial wrongs were ignored by the Portuguese authorities. Exasperated by the colonial authorities' unwillingness to consider their legitimate aspirations, on 14 July 1954, Holden Roberto became leader of a group of exiled Bakongos in the former Belgian Congo – including Eduardo Pinnock, Borralho Lulendo, and Barros Nekaka – and created UPNA to fight for the emancipation, if not liberation, of the Bakongo community of northern Angola. After that, the Bakongo community and, for that matter, most other Angolans, regarded UPNA and its subsequent incarnations as an organization whose main objective was the restoration of the ancient Kongo kingdom in northern Angola. Consequently, its main constituency and, later, FNLA's, remained almost exclusively restricted to the Bakongo community. UPNA failed to expand its constituency, but not for lack of trying.

From its inception, UPNA quickly evolved as an important political force inside Angola, especially in the north, and its leaders emerged as important spokesmen for the anti-colonial liberation struggle on the international stage. This evolution was reflected in the important name change – from UPNA to UPA – that occurred on 9 November 1958. towards the end of the 1950s, the young Holden Roberto had emerged as a key figure in the Angolan anti-colonial struggle.

In many respects, the name change represented a more ambitious re-design and expansion of Roberto's original and very community-oriented anti-colonial project. Now, the anti-colonial struggle would be expanded and fought in the name of the nation – broadly defined to include all the colony's communities – not simply the Bakongo community. Roberto perceptively realized that – within the revolutionary climate prevailing in Africa in the 1950s where the political discourse regarded community-specific projects as "tribalist" – liberation for the Bakongo community had to be framed within a much broader national struggle. In this respect, therefore, it was a national liberation struggle that UPA initiated on 15 March 1961 with a series of devastating attacks in northern Angola. However, from the beginning, UPA actions demonstrated that its national claims hardly went beyond the rhetorical sphere. For example, the attacks that marked its entry into the anti-colonial liberation war targeted both whites and Africans from other communities (Martelli 304), particularly members of the Ovimbundu community that – due to colonial forced labour practices – worked in northern coffee plantations. The memory of this intercommunitarian violence would become yet another divisive factor that prevented the formation of a united anti-colonial front and fed into retaliatory actions that elevated this type of violence to higher levels during the civil war.

Notwithstanding the indiscriminate violence, the immediate effects of the 15 March 1961 events were to elevate Roberto and his organization to a commanding position within the anti-colonial struggle in Angola. Consequently, Roberto was able to bring the other major political formation in northern Angola, PDA, into his organization. PDA had also been formed in the former Belgian Congo by a group of exiles from northern Angola. However, unlike UPNA and UPA, PDA's origins were not primarily in northern Angola's politics of rebellion as political resistance. Instead, this party's lineage can be traced back to *Nkutu a Nsimbani*, the religious revival and solidarity movement that swept northern Angola in the 1940s, led by the charismatic cult figure of Simao Toko. Subsequently, it evolved into mutual help groups – ASSOMIZO and ALIAZO – before acquiring a more political posture as PDA.

For Roberto, the absorption of PDA was a good, albeit insufficient, first step in a more ambitious effort to unite the anti-colonial liberation struggle under his leadership. Thus, for much of the 1960s, Holden Roberto attempted to expand his group's constituency, especially after the momentous political events unleashed by the 4 February 1961 events in Luanda that symbolically marked the start of the anti-colonial war. But FNLA was not necessarily interested in creating a broad united front in partnership with other nationalist groups like MPLA. Instead, FNLA leaders were more interested in absorbing other organizations as had been done with PDA. Marcum (1969:263) argues that "regional, ethnic, ideological, and personal differences did not dissolve into desired consensus because of strategic and moral imperatives". Specifically, the inability to create a united front reflected "fears on the part of a peasant-based movement, led by either little-educated or self-educated men, often restrictively ethnic in origin, that merger with an organization led by an elite, better educated and ideologically more sophisticated or disciplined, would prove suicidal. They suspected that the common front would only prove to be a vehicle by which university-educated mulattoes and African Marxists might pluck power from their less experienced hands" (Marcum, 1969:263). Ironically, Roberto's worse fears materialized more than a decade later as the MPLA, in fact led by "university-educated mulattoes and African Marxists", succeeded in installing itself in power and has governed post-colonial Angola since independence.

To prevent this scenario, FNLA used a three level strategy. First, it would attempt to continue playing the key role in the liberation struggle at the military level through intensified combat action from secure bases in Congo (Kinshasa). In addition it used elimination and cooptation to retain supremacy in the liberation struggle. Thus, FNLA consistently seized every opportunity to physically eliminate MPLA leaders and their guerrillas (Marcum 1978:198). Finally, Roberto attempted to co-opt nationalist leaders into integrating with either his "national front" or his short-lived GRAE, both created in early 1962. Through GRAE, in particular, Roberto sought to transcend, if not necessarily unite, the various nationalist political formations emerging in Angola while keeping himself as the dominant figure in what promised to be the final phase of the anti-colonial struggle. Thus, he offered top places in his "government" to political figures from other communities. For example, Jonas Savimbi, an Ovimbundu, was given the foreign affairs portfolio. Some important figures in one of MPLA's factions – including Viriato da Cruz, Matias Migueis and Jose Miguel – also joined FNLA/GRAE. However, Roberto's attempt to transcend the anti-colonial nationalist groups via a government in exile proved ineffective and ultimately failed. Unrealistically, Roberto expected that, in the face of strong international condemnation and sustained pressure to disengage, Portuguese colonialism in Angola would collapse. Roberto envisaged his GRAE as playing the key role in generating and sustaining that international pressure. Unfortunately, Roberto underestimated the settlers' ability to resist both national as well as international pressures for change. Settler colonialism in Angola was too entrenched to fall without a sustained military struggle. Thus, GRAE reflected Roberto's own political miscalculations, not the reality of the anti-colonial struggle. Besides, given the numerous and interlocking complexities of Angola's colonial condition and in light of the different motivations driving nationalist groups, it was too simplistic to expect that the entire anti-colonial project could be managed by Roberto's UPA/FNLA/GRAE. In addition, GRAE was very weak in the area of the anticolonial struggle that, ultimately, mattered most – the military sphere. Plagued by insubordination and desertions, GRAE's military wing was hopelessly ineffective – permanently needing thorough bottom-up rebuilding. Regrettably, the political will to accomplish such a profound overhaul was also permanently absent. Instability in the host country where GRAE's bases were located and the stepping-up of Portuguese counterinsurgency operations in northern Angola, along the Congo border, further reduced GRAE's military weight to near insignificance.

Unsurprisingly, Jonas Savimbi left GRAE on 16 July 1964 after accusing it of "ineffectiveness" (Chilcote, 1972:154). Savimbi later elaborated on his reasons for resigning from GRAE and pointed to several key issues. First, he was concerned that no progress in the anti-colonial struggle was possible with individuals who, like Roberto, "have surrendered to American interests". Second, Savimbi pointed to the lack of unity among the nationalist movement. Third, GRAE leadership included mainly family members and people originating from Roberto's region. Fourth, Savimbi bemoaned "the dismantlement of the revolutionary army and the end of military activities in the interior of Angola" (Chilcote, 1972:156–165).

Savimbi left at a time when FNLA/GRAE was entering a long period of decay, from which it would never recover. Through the late 1960s, FNLA/GRAE's political and military activities in the liberation struggle were inconsequential. The hasty collapse of Portuguese colonial rule that Roberto optimistically expected to occur soon after the start of the anti-colonial war did not materialize. In fact, unlike other colonial powers in Africa, Portugal responded to the challenge against its rule in the same way other settler governments in southern Africa did: it readied itself for a fight to the bitter end.

Unprepared politically and militarily for this Portuguese doggedness, FNLA/GRAE's resolve sputtered. This lack of resolve had serious negative consequences both for internal cohesion and, equally consequential, for the vigour of the anti-colonial struggle. As a result, by 1972, FNLA/ GRAE was plunged into disarray when some of its top military command- ers at the main military base of Kinkuzu led a mutiny to replace Roberto who was saved only by the intervention of Zairian troops. In the inevitable purge that followed 13 top commanders were executed (Marcum, 1978:188; Bridgland, 1987:96). Persistent internal squabbles, including several more mutinies, and the consequent failure to turn GRAE into a legitimate and effective government in exile led to this organization's demise. Weakened by internal disarray and an equally serious crisis of legitimacy, FNLA ac- cepted OAU's prodding and attempted to create a common front with rival MPLA. However, the joint CSLA created on 13 December 1972 (Bridgland, 1987:95), soon collapsed due to Roberto's insistence on leading this new body.

By 1973, GRAE was all but dead. But Roberto still had FNLA even though this organization was also seriously moribund, mostly as a result of its military ineffectiveness as a liberation movement even in the Bakongo region of northern Angola. At the political level, FNLA's lethargy was a result of Roberto's autocratic style and his propensity to concentrate all decision making powers in his own hands, his systematic elimination of potential rivals from leadership roles (Marcum, 1978:185), and the almost complete reliance on the generosity of the host country.

Thus, by the time the April 1974 revolution took place in Portugal, FNLA was in a political and military quandary. At the political level, it was now haunted by the inability to transform itself into a truly national libera- tion movement: its power base remained both regional and ethnolinguistic – it could count on little popular support in the populous rural areas of the central plateau or in urban areas like Luanda, Benguela, Lobito, and Huila. Militarily, FNLA was also very weak, not having yet recuperated from the 1971–72 purges. Consequently, as he readied FNLA for the very last stage of this anti-colonial struggle – the decolonization process involving formal power transfer from the colonial authorities to Angolans – Roberto was entirely dependent on external backers for survival. Mobutu Sesse Seko of Zaire provided enlisted Zairian soldiers to swell the ranks of FNLA, China provided weapons and military instructors (Marcum, 1978:245–46) while the United States supplied the financial resources through the CIA.

Ultimately, however, FNLA's reliance on foreign help, even from a neighbouring country with close cultural and linguistic ties with the Ba- kongo community of northern Angola, further aggravated its political dif- ficulties. Outside the Bakong region of northern Angola, FNLA came to be increasingly regarded as a group of foreigners masquerading as a liberation movement. This suspicion simmered throughout the process of colonial disengagement leading to independence and was heightened by several events. For example, soon after the military coup of 25 April 1974 and as FNLA began to move troops from its main bases in Zaire into northern Angola, it expelled more than 60,000 Ovimbundu who had been working in the region's many coffee plantations (Marcum, 1978:246; Bridgland, 1987:108). This rekindled the memories of the atrocities commited against members of this community when Roberto's group initiated its anti-colonial struggle in northern Angola in 1962. The expulsion of these workers and the persistent harassment of mulattos, assimilados, and non-Bakongo residents of northern Angola contributed significantly to negative perceptions of FNLA while further poisoning an already difficult relationship among the liberation movements. Indeed, it was one more element in the complex mix of issues that led to the long and violent civil war.

In early 1975, FNLA made several moves that would further accelerate the onset of the civil war. Buoyed up by increased American help, FNLA attempted to establish a firm foothold in Luanda by acquiring a major newspaper and a TV station in preparation for what was expected to be a difficult electoral campaign. More ominously, FNLA moved into Luanda several hundred of the notoriously undisciplined soldiers from Zaire who, with little delay, proceeded to harass the civilian population and MPLA installations. Since MPLA had also been in even greater military disarray at the time of the coup in Portugal, it attempted to close the military gap vis-à-vis FNLA by creating "People's Power Committees", grass-root structures scattered around Luanda's peri-urban belt where the bulk of MPLA's supporters resided. These structures had important political and military roles. At the political level, they served as key channels for disseminating MPLA's political programme and were ideally suited for canvassing the local populations. But they also had a more menacing military component because MPLA transformed them into powerful paramilitary bases by arming its militants who ran them. For FNLA, these committees, not the recently returned MPLA leaders and their guerrillas, presented the greatest political and military challenge.

In the context of the zero-sum competition that had characterized FNLA-MPLA relations since the early 1960s, the "People's Power Committees" loomed increasingly larger for the survival or demise of the liberation movements in late 1974 and early 1975. In other words, MPLA's survival in the critical months leading to independence depended significantly on the strengths of these committees. Conversely, any FNLA hopes of controlling the capital city by independence depended on its ability to cage in, if not destroy, these same committees. FNLA's strategy of harassment culminated in the killing of 50 MPLA recruits in Caxito on 23 March 1975. However, FNLA's strategy backfired horrendously because, within months, MPLA's committees had sufficient means to drive FNLA out of the capital. By July 1975, MPLA was in sole control of Luanda having driven out its rivals using the same violent techniques – including attacking, killing and mutilating enemy recruits – that FNLA had first used. MPLA's keener sense of strategy had once again prevailed while FNLA would never regain its footing in Angola's deteriorating chaos.

After the collapse of the transition process negotiated at Alvor, Portugal, on 10 January 1975 and the onset of the civil war, FNLA attempted to reenter Luanda militarily before the date set for Angola's independence. Given its serious military shortcomings, partly a result of the severe purges in its military wing during the early 1970s, FNLA could only rely on Zairian soldiers on loan from Mobutu and an assortment of Western mercenaries. These foreign soldiers, however, lacked the conviction to engage in a fight to the death; their main motivation was the promise of money and Angolan loot. The military difficulties were compounded by FNLA's lack of political credibility in the capital region. Its relatively uncomplicated expulsion from the capital had confirmed its unpopularity among Luanda residents. Thus, initially alone, and later with the help of Cuban troops, MPLA was able to keep FNLA and its mercenaries at bay. Roberto's desire to play a central role in national post-colonial politics was irreparably and permanently frustrated. In fact, after failing both to take Luanda militarily and sustain its alliance with UNITA, Roberto returned to exile politics; this time without the help of his former benefactors – Mobutu and the CIA. He spent much of the civil war's first phase – 1976 to 1991 – in Paris while his political and military structures further disintegrated, resulting in massive surrenders to MPLA.

This second exile so weakened FNLA that it was ill prepared to take full advantage of the political opening in Angola that came as a consequence of the changes MPLA was forced to adopt in the early 1990s to ensure its own survival. For example, FNLA was unable to reestablish its relevance after MPLA and UNITA signed the Bicesse Accord in May 1991 – the first major attempt to end the civil war since it started in 1975. Although the Bicesse Accord ultimately failed to end the civil war, its implementation nevertheless involved a near complete dismantling of the one-party state apparatus.

Significantly, new political formations emerged, proliferated and created a vibrant, if ultimately ineffective, opposition to both the regime and UNITA rebels. Tellingly, FNLA was too weak politically to capitalize on this significant change in Angola's political life. Its electoral showing during the September 1992 polls was disappointing – it had not been able to break out of its regional confines. Clearly, most Angolans still associated FNLA with the aspirations of northern Angolans, not with a national political project. It currently exists moribund and divided. In 1999, two FNLA militants – Lucas Benghy Ngonda and Carlos Mendes – unsuccessfully attempted to wrestle party control out of Roberto's hands. They only succeeded in fracturing it, further threatening it with irrelevance and highlighting an internal crisis first dramatically exposed when, in 1964, Savimbi left Roberto's organization to create UNITA.

UNITA

By creating UNITA, Savimbi sought, first and foremost, to give a revolutionary political voice to the Ovimbundu – by far the largest ethno-linguistic community in Angola – of which he was a part. The Ovimbundu represent thirty-five to forty percent of Angola's population and dominate the areas with the highest population density in the country – the central plateau provinces of Huambo, Bie, and Benguela. Many Ovimbundu believed that, as the largest community in Angola, it was critical to have their own "liberation movement" to counterbalance the role and power of the movements representing the other two major ethnic communities. Thus, there was a strong ethnic rationale behind the creation of UNITA. This ethnic rationale notwithstanding, the birth and development of UNITA is inextricably associated with the determination and vision of one man: Jonas Savimbi. Early in his political career, Savimbi had been inclined to join Neto's MPLA because it had a progressive programme and he "did not want to be on the right wing" (Bridgland 1987:45). However, the dominance of mulattos in MPLA's leadership positions dissuaded the young nationalist leader from joining this already established political organization. In explaining his reasosn for not joining a mulatto-dominated MPLA, Savimbi argued that "it was very difficult for blacks to understand why mestiços should be leading a liberation movement to fight the Portuguese. It was not clear to us that mestiços were suffering in Angola; they were privileged people" (Bridgland, 1987:46). Although Savimbi did not say as much at the time, he was also deeply suspicious of the *assimilados,* i.e. Angolans who voluntarily or coercively were assimilated into a Portuguese way of life. He later suggested that mestiços and assimilados, "having bitten off a piece of the good life" (Bridgland, 1987:98) made selectively available by the colonial authorities, lacked both the legitimacy and the moral authority to lead the anti-colonial liberation struggle. Regrettably, this simplistic view of Angolan society – ironically heavily tinged with its own brand of racism and classism – imbued Savimbi's organization with a peculiar character that would eventually, like a deadly virus, corrode it from within and significantly contribute to its ultimate downfall.

After rejecting MPLA because it was dominated by mestiços and assimilados, Savimbi joined UPA on 1 February 1961 even though he had found Roberto to be an uninspiring leader who could not even adequately articulate the policy of his own organization (Bridgland, 1987:45). Perhaps due to this vacuousness within UPA, Savimbi rose rapidly through the ranks. By the time this organization initiated its military campaign against Portuguese colonialism on 15 March 1961, Savimbi had risen to the rank of secretary-general. In this capacity, he played an important role in the merger between UPA and the smaller PDA to create FNLA in 1962. A week later, after FNLA formed GRAE, Savimbi was given the foreign secretary post, the third most powerful position after president Holden Roberto and vice-president Emanuel Kunzika, the former PDA leader. But Savimbi eventually became disappointed with Roberto's autocratic leadership style and his keenness to fill the organization's executive posts with relatives and members of his community. He resigned from FNLA/GRAE in July 1964.

UNITA was created on 15 March 1966. A year earlier, after resigning from FNLA/GRAE in July 1964 due to profound differences with Holden Roberto, Savimbi travelled to China where he, along with several followers, received four months of training in Maoist guerrilla warfare at Nanking Military Academy. This short stint in China would profoundly shape the new organization's political and military character. Although UNITA would later be forced to compromise on Maoist principles of self-reliance and the guerrillas' organic relationship with the people, Savimbi at least insisted on keeping UNITA's leadership within Angola. There, Savimbi developed his own brand of autocratic leadership to build UNITA into a recognizable third force among the liberation movements. Beyond leadership style, Savimbi committed some of the very same errors that were at the base of his rupture with FNLA/GRAE and Holden Roberto. For example, UNITA never developed into an inclusive organization. Mirroring the FNLA's practices he criticized, individuals from Savimbi's Ovimbundu community dominated the organization. Moreover, as mentioned earlier, UNITA was overtly racist and classist in the sense that it sought to represented the majority rural African populations against white colonial domination and positioned itself as a direct opposite to the mulatto-dominated, urban-based MPLA. Ominously, Savimbi defined domination very narrowly by conflating class and race. Thus, he regarded both mulattos and assimilados as agents of oppression, indistinguishable from Portuguese settlers and their regime. As such, therefore, they constituted legitimate targets of the liberation struggle. Thus, in a very direct sense, the creation of this third liberation group complicated the anti-colonial struggle. It did not necessarily result in raising the anti-colonial forces'capacity to fight Portuguese colonialism in the various battlefields. Instead, it added new dimensions of division and animosity as well as new layers of violence to an already highly problematic liberation process. Ultimately self-destructive, this peculiar understanding of who was the enemy led UNITA to regard MPLA – a liberation movement dominated by mulattos and *assimilados* – as its natural enemies with horrendous consequences for post-colonial governance.

But in the mid-1960s, Savimbi appeared to present a fresh alternative to MPLA and FNLA. These two established liberation movements faced serious internal problems that were directly related to their respective visions of post-colonial Angola. For MPLA's Marxist revolutionaries, the key challenge resided not so much in establishing themselves in the "vanguard" of a barely existent proletariat as a first step to eventually replacing the colonial administration. As mentioned before, it resided primarily in their leadership's racial composition. For many Angolans who understood liberation in terms of a complete dismantling of the white man's colonial society, the presence of a large number of mulattos in leadership positions in MPLA foreshadowed an incompletely liberated post-colonial Angola. In the racial hierarchy of colonial Angola, mulattos occupied the intermediary position between whites on top and black Africans at the bottom. With the whites gone, black Africans feared that mulattos would occupy the dominant strata in post-colonial society and they would be relegated, again, to rural poverty. These perceptions were sufficiently crystallized that early in the liberation struggle FNLA indiscriminately attacked white/Portuguese and mulatto/MPLA targets. But FNLA had its own set of important challenges. Its political reach and military presence were restricted to the portion of Angola that was once part of the ancient kingdom of Kongo. Its "national" claims had very little resonance elsewhere in Angola. Moreover, MPLA succeeded in painting FNLA leader Holden Roberto as a CIA agent. By portraying Roberto as a stooge of the United States, MPLA further delegitimized Roberto's claims as a nationalist leader.

In creating UNITA, therefore, Savimbi wanted to offer a truly nationalist, progressive yet rural-based alternative to both MPLA and FNLA. As mentioned earlier, before UNITA was created in 1966, the majority Ovimbundu community did not have a liberation movement to call their own. Savimbi understood that, as the leader of a liberation movement representing the Ovimbundu, he would be guaranteed his place at the negotiating table whenever Portugal eventually decided to initiate a process of colonial disengagement. On this score, Savimbi was correct. But Savimbi also believed, incorrectly, that prominent positions for himself and for his organization were assured in post-colonial structures of governance so long as they were involved in, and somehow survived, the anti-colonial war. In other words, Savimbi's basic strategy was based on a false numbers' game – the Ovimbundu represented the majority, UNITA represented the Ovimbundu, Savimbi led UNITA, therefore he was destined to rule Angola. This strategically misguided calculation induced him into taking his organization down a path peppered with landmines – political and otherwise. Thus, UNITA rarely demonstrated great concern about the means used to arrive at the decolonization process and, for that matter, post-colonial power. All that mattered was to get there. This would lead the organization into several strategic blunders. Some were relatively inconsequential. Others, however, ultimtely led to its implosion.

Initially, UNITA opted for spectacular military actions for maximum publicity. Thus, in December 1966, after its first commanders returned from military training in China, UNITA mounted its first two military attacks against Portuguese targets. The first attack, personally planned and led by Savimbi, was against the small town of Cassamba in Moxico province. Cassamba was a soft target, "a small timber outpost" where Portuguese lumberjacks lived with their families and several hundred Angolans under the protection of "a couple of hundred Portuguese soldiers" (Bridgland, 1987:71). According to Savimbi's own account of the attack, "it was a disaster" (Bridgland, 1987:71). Against the advice of David "Samwimbila" Chingunji – a top military commander who also had received training in China – Savimbi led 60 poorly trained villagers on the Cassamba attack. The attackers were easily beaten back, suffering many casualties – not a single Portuguese was killed.

UNITA's wish to grab international attention would have to wait until Christmas Day 1966 when troops led by Samuel Chiwale, also trained in China, attacked Teixeira de Sousa (Luau), an important town at the end of the Benguela Railway. This was an important propaganda coup because it disrupted for a week the shipment of Zambian and Zairian copper to the Lobito port via the Benguela Railway. However, from a military perspective, the attack could not be considered a success inasmuch as UNITA – again using poorly armed recruits with little guerrilla training – lost half of its 600 fighters against six Portuguese killed, including the town's chief of secret police (Marcum, 1978:191–2). But, strategically, the negative consequences of this attack extended far beyond the casualty count. It led to UNITA being "outlawed in Zambia" (Bridgland, 1987:75) in early 1967. Given its dependence on copper exports through the Benguela Railway as a source of foreign exchange, Zambia could not be expected to tolerate UNITA's disruption of this critical commercial link. Zambia's actions against UNITA – perhaps as much as the organization's leaders' training in Mao's China – effectively forced UNITA to operate completely inside Angola. Initially, UNITA made a virtue out of this necessity by claiming that, unlike MPLA and FNLA who operated from bases outside the country, it was the only genuine liberation movement. But this bravado hid an untenable situation for UNITA. For the next two years, UNITA's main struggle was not against the Portuguese army – it was for its own survival.

By 1971, the Portuguese colonial army was in a position to eliminate UNITA's several hundred guerrillas that remained active in isolated pockets around Moxico region. However, the Portuguese army spared UNITA because "from a military point of view it was better to use them against the MPLA" (Minter, 1988:18). Minter quotes General Costa Gomes – commander-in-chief of the Portuguese forces in Angola from April 1970 through August 1972 and who later became President of Portugal after the 25 April 1974 coup – as saying that "it was understood that Portuguese and UNITA forces would not fight against each other. UNITA captured food and armaments from the MPLA, while the Portuguese gave them ammunition (not guns), as well as medical and school equipment. The area reserved for UNITA was the Lungue-Bungo river area, between Luso and Bie" (Minter 1988:18). Minter also reproduces documents indicating that Savimbi sought, and the Portuguese authorities seriously considered, the "reintegration" of himself and his group into "the national community" (Minter, 1988:83–85). In other words, Savimbi was ready to cut a political deal with the Portuguese authorities that would result in him being reassigned a position within colonial society.

The "gentlemen's agreement" between UNITA and the Portuguese colonial army lasted from 1971 until early 1974 (Minter, 1988:18), just before the military coup in Portugal. Savimbi's calculations, it would seem, were only accurate in the sense that UNITA did not pay a high political price for cooperating with the enemy. As he calculated, UNITA was given an equal place – along with the other two liberation movements and the colonial power – at the table where decolonization and the post-colonial frameworks were negotiated. But MPLA would never forgive UNITA for its treachery. In fact, for the next two and a half decades, both attempted to find ways to defeat each other.

Evidently, Andrade's admonition that only political-military coordination between the nationalist organizations, including "a single command over the maquis, could save Angola from a fratricidal war" (Marcum, 1969:220) was not heeded. Instead, the nationalist movements were divided as they negotiated the modalities of decolonization, especially the transfer of power, from Portugal. The resulting platform for power transfer, the Alvor Accord of 15 January 1975, further entrenched their historical divisions. The Alvor Accord succeeded in setting the date for Angola's independence – 11 November 1975 – and defined the parameters for achieving this target. It recognized the three liberation movements as "the sole legitimate representatives of the people of Angola" and stipulated that they and representatives from the departing colonial authorities form a transitional government to lead the colony to independence.

But the Alvor Agreement failed disastrouly because it was founded upon the erroneous premise that the nationalist movements would be willing to work cooperatively for the benefit of the soon-to-be independent state. Instead, shortly after it was signed, the agreement and the transitional government it brought into being were rendered irrelevant because MPLA expelled FNLA and UNITA from Luanda as the country descended quickly and irretrievably into civil war. True to form, the nationalist leaders, placed personal and group interests – not national aspiration – at the top of their political calculations as MPLA, FNLA, and UNITA engaged in a zero-sum fratricidal struggle for supremacy.

Beyond their ferocious domestic hostilities, the nationalist movements also ignored another of Andrade's warnings – not to bring the Cold War into Angolan politics "to avoid the complications of international intrigues" (Marcum, 1969:255) after the anti-colonial war had been won. For Angola, the consequence of failing to heed those warnings was a civil war with peculiarly escalating layers of violence. In the early stages of this internationalized civil war Cuban troops helped MPLA prevail over both UNITA, backed by a South African army lacking the political will to fight, and FNLA supported by a Zairian army lacking professionalism. Demoralized and humiliated for failing to install their respective allies in power, both the South African and the Zairian armies retreated within months of independence. However, independence and the defeat of UNITA/SADF and FNLA/Zairian armies in 1976 constituted a short pause in the civil war. It would continue with greater intensity, albeit now in the form of a protracted guerrilla war, proving that it was fundamentally a continuation of the unresolved struggles and contradictions within the anti-colonial movement pre-dating independence. In important respects, therefore, the roots of the extreme levels of violence registered after independence can be found in both colonial and auctothonous violence. However, the salience of an important new element – greater direct external participation in the conflict, a function of the prevailing bipolarity and superpower rivalry – also helps explain the nature of post-colonial violence in Angola. The next chapter looks at the external dimension of Angola's civil war in greater detail.

CHAPTER 3

External Interventions and
Internal Violence

Foreign interventions in Angola during the transition to independence must be situated within the broader Cold War struggle prevailing at the time. The existence of two superpowers engaged in an existential struggle of global proportions meant that changes of government in any unit within the international system involved potentially great geostrategic costs or benefits for the superpowers. This zero-sum calculus predictably led both superpowers and their allies to intervene around the world. The so-called third world, in particular, became "the terra nullius of geostrategic considerations" for the superpowers (Andreopoulos, 1994:192) because the outcomes of revolutionary struggles in countries like Angola had a direct impact on regional and global power balances (Falk, 1984:120). Thus, in important respects, superpower interventions in the third world were "the local reflection of global bipolar competition" (MacFarlane, 2002:38). But, since the global power structure severely constrained the superpowers from battling it out at the system's core, "the expression of the superpowers' global and systemic conflict was largely transferred to the periphery" (MacFarlane, 2002:38). Therefore:

> Intervention was not a matter of managing or resolving conflicts, defending human rights, or relieving human suffering. The aim was relative gain in the global bipolar struggle through the exercise of power in local conflicts and the internal affairs of targeted states, or the prevention of such gain by the other pole (MacFarlane, 2002:38–9).

In addition to the specific strategic nature of the bipolar rivalry described by MacFarlane, both Guelke and Bull suggest that intervention is an inherent and more ubiquitous feature of international society due to the fluidity of member states' tangible and intangible assets. Compelling strategic and economic reasons made Angola an irresistible target for international intervention. First, from an economic perspective, it is endowed with vast and valuable natural resources. Second, from the strategic perspective of regional and global powers, Angola was regarded as a potentially key player in Africa. Consequently, it became an important Cold War battleground in Africa.

But in 1975, Angola also highlighted some of the shortcomings regarding the applicability of international principles to embryonic states. In such cases, the rights and wrongs of foreign intervention could be debated from political, moral, and even military standpoints but hardly from solid normative foundations. Angola's tragedy started as a civil war within a political unit that was not yet an internationally recognized independent state and, as such, did not enjoy established protections under international law. Specifically, since it was not yet a sovereign state, Angola could not find protection within well-established international legal frameworks that forbid states from intervening in the internal affairs of other states. For all practical purposes, during the decolonization process, Angola was still a non-state actor with little international legal protection; it existed in a gray area where states-to-be have very limited recourse to international legal norms or security frameworks to defend themselves.

Concerning international interventions when the target is not yet a state, the UN Charter – a key source of international law on the subject – is "very silent" (Bull, 1984:21) partly because the complex processes of decolonization and state-building do not "fit easily" into the Charter's framework (Gray 3). Therefore, embryonic states have little international legal protection. Existing international norms pertaining to aspiring states are, at best, flimsy. First, the Declaration Regarding Non-Self-Governing Territories contained in Chapter XI of the UN Charter does not go beyond recognizing the interests of peoples living under colonial regimes as "paramount" while regarding the promotion of their well-being as a "sacred trust". Second, a key provision of UN General Assembly Declaration Resolution 1514 of 14 December 1960 regarding the Granting of Independence to Colonial Countries and Peoples affirms that "the subjection of peoples to alien subjugation, domination and exploitation constitutes a denial of fundamental human rights, is contrary to the Charter of the United Nations and is an impediment to the promotion of world peace and co-operation". But it does not provide protection against that subjugation, domination, and exploitation even for peoples who are on the verge of realizing their freedom through independence. Third, Article 1(1) of the International Covenant on Economic, Social and Cultural Rights adopted by the UN General Assembly as Resolution 2200A of 16 December 1966 states that "all peoples have the right of self-determination". However, it too does not provide would-be states with any legal foundation to fulfil their aspirations. In sum, the Charter and other key international legal documents do not adequately provide protection for entities that have not yet crossed the statehood threshold. In particular, international law generally fails to take into account the possibilities that the target of intervention could be a non-sovereign entity in the midst of civil conflict.

The haphazard process of decolonization provided optimal conditions for various foreign interventions as outside powers directly or indirectly committed military resources to affect the internal dynamics of the conflict in an attempt to help determine its outcome. First, profound fragmentation characterized domestic politics in the sense that the key domestic actors were unable to find peaceful means for managing the transition to independence as the colonial administration collapsed and, with it, law and order. The resulting chaos added instability to an already insecure region. To ensure survival, the domestic actors actively invited their respective foreign backers to intervene. Thus, at the regional level, two neighbouring states – South Africa and Zaire – carried out military invasions of Angola in support of UNITA and FNLA respectively. At the international level, the three-way fratricidal struggle provided opportunities for both the superpowers – as well as a sub-imperial power like Cuba – to intervene both directly and indirectly.

Foreign Interventions

South Africa

Decolonization of "Portuguese Africa" and the prospects of unfriendly governments in Angola and Mozambique posed an immediate and existential threat to the apartheid regime in South Africa. As Portuguese colonies, Angola and Mozambique constituted natural barriers shielding the last bastions of settler colonialism in Southern Africa. As independent states, they would become frontline bases for an expected nationalist onslaught against the racist regimes in South Africa and Rhodesia (now Zimbabwe). Such perceptions of insecurity explain, to a considerable degree, South Africa's strategic choices during Angola's decolonization process and, more specifically, its willingness to further provoke the international community's ire by invading Angola in an ultimately futile attempt to install a puppet regime in the former Portuguese colony before independence. Some economic dimensions of security also featured prominently in South Africa's decision to intervene in Angola. For Hallett (1978:349), "the basic reasons for South Africa's interest in Angola are easy to determine. With its oil, its diamonds, its coffee plantations, its promise of mineral and agricultural sources yet to be developed, Angola is clearly one of the richest of South Africa's neighbours." Besides, Angola had a well-developed infrastructure – at least by colonial standards – that included a system of paved roads, major ports, railways, and dams. In other words, a friendly post-colonial regime in Angola could enhance the apartheid regime's security by continuing to serve as a buffer against armed nationalist penetration and operations in South Africa as well as provide assistance to overcome the apartheid regime's increasingly untenable economic situation due to international isolation and seriously debilitating domestic structural problems. Angola, so the apartheid regime hoped, would be a critical piece of a South Africa-centred "co-prosperity zone" encompassing other bantustan(ized) southern African states.

For apartheid South Africa, then, the reasons for intervention in Angola were compelling on the basis of its survival calculus. In addition, the conditions for such intervention were ideal. As mentioned earlier, there was no specific international legal barrier against intervention. The decolonization process had not only led to civil war, it placed Angola on uncharted legal ground. Moreover, UNITA and FNLA – two of the groups engaged in the three-way civil war – had "invited" South African intervention to help them secure the military defeat of MPLA, their common rival. Critically, South Africa also had the means to intervene. Possessing Africa's most powerful army – a portion of which was stationed in Namibia, then called South West Africa, a territory that South Africa illegally occupied and Angola's immediate neighbour to the south – the apartheid regime could intervene militarily in Angola without major difficulties. And so, in June 1975, South African troops first entered Angola (Marcum, 1978:268). Ostensibly, their mission was to guard the hydro-electric schemes at Ruacana and Calueque on the Cunene River. These schemes provided electricity to and helped irrigate portions of Namibia. In addition to this "defensive" incursion to protect strategic interests in Angola, South Africa carried out several other minor military operations in the border region, allegedly to prevent penetration of SWAPO guerrillas into Namibia. But on 14 October, a South African armoured column began a deep penetration northward, routing MPLA forces as it move toward Luanda and helping UNITA recapture territory it had lost to MPLA in the early stages of the civil war (Marcum 1978:268). South Africa had clearly decided that, given the unavoidable security predicaments it would face with an unfriendly post-colonial regime in Angola, a pre-emptive invasion to alter the course of political developements in Angola was justifiable. Fortunately for MPLA, South Africa delayed making a final decision to invade and this postponement ultimately doomed the entire operation in the sense that the invading troops fell short of their goal of installing a UNITA/FNLA coalition in Luanda in time to receive independence from Portugal on 11 November 1975. The South African advance bogged down at the Queve River, 120 miles south of Luanda, too far to disturb, let alone impede, MPLA independence celebrations.

Although unsucessful from the apartheid regime's perspective, the South African intervention succeeded in significantly escalating the level of violence in Angola's civil war by introducing both sophisticated weaponry – including armoureded cars, tanks, large calibre cannons, helicopters, and fighter jets – and the qualified personnel to make full use of the weapons' destructive powers. Also, by rescuing UNITA from oblivion and continuing to support it as the rebel group opted to take to the forests and carry out a protracted guerrilla war after being defeated by MPLA, the apartheid regime ensured that the levels of violence in Angola would be kept at very high levels.

For more than a decade after South Africa's ill-fated invasion, Angola became a prime target of apartheid's "total strategy" – a set of political and military measures laid out in a 1977 Defence White Paper intended to prolong the life of the regime by enhancing its regional military reach – because, as South Africa had feared, the new Marxist regime allowed both ANC and SWAPO to set up military bases in Angola. Such bases were particularly important for SWAPO to infiltrate its fighters into northern Namibia. Equally troublesome for South Africa was the presence of thousands of Cuban troops as well as Soviet and other former eastern bloc military advisors in Angola. To counter the perceived threat posed by an unfriendly regime supported by important communist allies, the implementation of the "total strategy" relied heavily on special forces and covert operations. A unique feature of South African strategy to counter the "total onslaught" was the use of UNITA as a proxy army to weaken the Marxist regime in Angola, a strategy later employed with equally lethal effectiveness through RENAMO in Mozambique. In addition, South Africa conducted regular military invasions of Angola intended to weaken the new post-colonial regime, if not necessarily remove MPLA from power.

In all, SADF invaded Angola twelve times after 1975. These incursions were crucial for UNITA's development as a major military force. While SADF kept the government occupied, UNITA was also able to expand its guerrilla activity throughout most of the country forcing the MPLA government to become even more dependent on Cuban and Russian military assistance to remain in power. By the late 1980s and early 1990s, the survival of the regime required negotiating with the rebels. Such negotiations, however, would not result in an end to the civil war because of the diverging objectives of the parties involved: the government wanted to negotiate the incorporation of UNITA within its ranks while UNITA wanted to negotiate devolution of power and wealth. In the end, the externally-imposed and managed electoral process did not end the war. Dissatisfied with the results of the elections it lost in September 1992, UNITA returned the country to war. Although this time UNITA could not count on the support of South Africa, it believed that it still had the capabilities to bring the MPLA regime to its knees. UNITA's misguided strategy was based on two critical elements. First, its illegal trade in diamonds provided the rebels with large quantities of cash, thus lessening the need for external sources of funding. Second, they could still count on the support of an old enemy of the MPLA regime – Mobutu's Zaire.

Zaire

Of all the external players that intervened in Angola's decolonization process and beyond, Zaire was arguably in the best position to influence events in the former Portuguese colony. As discussed earlier, the deep historical ties that linked both countries served as an important basis for the support Zaire provided to FNLA's anti-colonial struggle against Portugal. FNLA was allowed to establish military bases in Zaire from which it mounted incursions into Angola. Zaire was also an indispensable conduit for American financial aid and Chinese military and diplomatic assistance to FNLA. Therefore, at the time of the 1974 coup in Portugal, FNLA's fortunes – especially its odds of becoming the government of post-colonial Angola – were inextricably linked to Zairian support. Zaire, in turn, had important reasons for supporting FNLA. An FNLA government in Angola would render the arbitrary colonial divisions meaningless. More pragmatically for Zaire, Angola's vast natural resources would provide added opportunities for grand corruption, if not regional economic development. In addition, control of the Benguela Railway – providing Zaire with an important outlet to the Atlantic – constituted a potentially rich prize.

Zairian motives for intervention also included a profound aversion toward FNLA's main rival – MPLA. This aversion was partly based on Mobutu's notions of African authenticity, views that contrasted with MPLA's embrace of African cosmopolitanism. Also important, within a Cold War context, Mobutu's Zaire – itself an unwavering ally of the US – regarded the Soviet-backed Marxist-Leninist MPLA with an overt hostility that could be traced back to Mobutu's difficult formative experiences during Congo's own traumatic decolonization process in the 1960s as he dealt with Katangan secessionists supported by the former Soviet Union. Many of these secessionists had found refuge in colonial Angola and were retrained and used by Portugal as special counterinsurgency troops. During the colonization process, this Katangan gendarmerie shifted allegiances to MPLA. This was only partly for ideological reasons. Basically, this shift was driven by the expectation that, after helping MPLA secure a victory over its rivals in Angola, the newly installed government in Luanda would return the favour by helping the Katangan secessionists conquer Katanga (now renamed Shaba), if not the whole of Zaire. This was a nightmarish prospect that Mobutu attempted to preemptively avert by supporting his FNLA proxy and cutting off MPLA's route to post-colonial power.

Like South Africa, in addition to apparent motives for intervention, Zaire also had the means. When the decolonization process began in Angola, Zaire's proxy FNLA army was clearly superior, at least as far as military resource endowment, to MPLA's military units. It had 4,000 guerrillas operating inside Angola and an additional 10,000 in Zaire (Stevens 140). Zaire was also channelling major external military assistance to FNLA. In addition to receiving American assistance for FNLA, in July and August 1974, Zaire welcomed 125 Chinese military instructors to train the Angolan rebels who were expected to constitute the core of a new post-colonial Angolan army. The Chinese instructors brought 450 tons of armaments with them. Extensive additional supplies were secured from Rumania (Stevens, 1976:141). In the unlikely event of ineptitude on the part of its Angolan proxy, even given this significant arsenal, close geographic proximity to Angola made direct Zairian military intervention a viable option. In the end, FNLA proved to be inept and the Zairian army directly intervened in Angola.

Once deployed in Angola, the Zairian army – much like its proxy FNLA which was soundly defeated twice in its attempts to capture Luanda – proved to be an ineffective military paper tiger with a greater inclination to loot than fight. Zaire initiated its direct military intervention in Angola in May 1975 when 1,200 regular Zairian soldiers moved across the Angolan border to prop up FNLA forces (Marcum 1978:259). This was followed by the dispatch of a commando company in July, an armoured-car squadron and two additional Zairian paratroop companies in August and, in September 1975, two more Zairian battalions (Davis, 1978:121). The Zairian army carried out a major offensive to take Luanda just prior to independence. But, ultimately, direct Zairian military intervention, while contributing to increased levels of violence, was no match for MPLA – now supplied with larger Soviet weapons deliveries and aided by Cuban troops. Met by strong MPLA resistance organized by Cuban advisors and supported by a barrage of Soviet 122-mm "Stalin's Organs" rockets, attack helicopters and light aircraft, the Zairian army and its FNLA proxy retreated haphazardly toward the border, looting and raping all the way back to Zaire while leaving behind huge quantities of American and other Western weapons (Marcum 1978:275). The failure to install FNLA in power did not deter Zaire from further involvement in Angola, even after the disintegration of its proxy as a fighting force soon after its defeat in 1975. Continuing Zairian intervention was partly as a response to MPLA's involvement in the two invasions of Zaire, from Angola, carried out by Katangan soldiers in 1977 and 1978. Partly as retaliation, but also conforming to its role as an important regional ally of the United States during the Cold War, Zaire intervened in Angola uninterruptedly during the 1980s. With FNLA defunct as a military force, Zaire became the main conduit for American covert and overt help to UNITA, its new proxy.

Major international and regional changes in the late 1980s and early 1990s – the end of the Cold War and the transition to a post-apartheid regime in South Africa – had left UNITA internationally isolated inasmuch as it could no longer count on substantial aid from its main American and South African backers. Thus, by the late 1980s, UNITA faced the real possibility of withering away as a major political and military force in Angola as had happened to FNLA in the late 1970s. UNITA's ability to survive into the 1990s depended, to a considerabl degree, on Zaire's willingness to assume the role of UNITA's main ally. What motivated Zaire's support for UNITA? First, as a Cold War ally of the United States, Zaire supported the "Reagan Doctrine" which included support for UNITA. In fact, Zaire became a key transshipment base for delivering American aid to UNITA. Second, support for UNITA was a way for the Zairian leadership to retaliate against the MPLA regime for allowing Katangan secessionists to invade Zaire from Angola on two occasions. The second invasion, in particular, seriously shook the Mobutu regime which was saved only by the quick military intervention of France, Belgium and Morocco with the logistic support of the United States. For Mobutu, Angola's willingess to serve as a base for the Katangan rebels' attempts to overthrow his regime constituted a direct threat that required a reciprocal response. In other words, the longevity of the Mobutu regime required a weak and unstable state in Angola. Since UNITA, if adequately supported, was willing and able to seriously weaken the Angolan state, it came to be regarded as a worthy recipient of Zairian assistance. But beyond the state security motivation, the Mobutu regime could use this relationship as yet another source for elite enrichment. Since the early 1980s, UNITA had been mining important diamond deposits in Angola. According to Global Witness, UNITA sold diamonds worth at least US$3.7 billion between 1992 and 1998 (Global Witness 1998:1).Until Mobutu's overthrow in 1997, these diamonds were transported via Zaire to international diamond marketing centres.

In the end, when the MPLA regime in Angola saw an opportunity to help permanently end the Mobutu regime it sent thousands of troops to support the rebellion that finally drove the Zairian dictator from power in May 1997. The fall of Mobutu's regime led to a significant improvement in the security of the post-colonial state in Angola. Now, it could focus its attention almost exclusively on finally decapitating its internal enemies. Within five years Savimbi would be killed. Both Mobutu's overthrow and Savimbi's demise were facilitated by America's new posture in Africa, especially regarding Angola, after the end of the Cold War. The United States was now primarily more interested in focusing on its participation in the development of Angola's vast energy resources than in regime change. This represented a major change in American policy.

The United States of America

In the mid-1970s, Angola provided ideal conditions for extending superpower rivalry to a strategically important region of the periphery. Two important reasons – oil and geopolitics – provided motives for American intervention in Angola. First, for several decades American oil companies had explored Angola's rich oil deposits. These companies were committed to staying, especially given the anticipated oil bonanza that was expected in the near future due to the continuing discoveries of bigger deposits. The United States was intent on keeping and expanding its presence in Angola's oil sector while, more generally, preserving Angola's links with the international economic system where it was expected to play a significant role in the global oil sector.

The second reason for American intervention was more straightfor-wardly geopolitical because, at the regional level, Angola could play a key role in accelerating the process of complete liberation of Southern Africa. Given the former Soviet Union's long relationship with MPLA, one of the main geopolitical incentives for American intervention was the desire to deny its main global adversary an easy victory in Southern Africa where the US had important strategic interests. These interests revolved around the fact that most of the West's oil supplies were carried in the shipping lanes in the Indian Ocean and around the Cape of Good Hope into the Atlantic. Consequently, the security of Southern Africa under pro-Western regimes featured prominently in American global security calculations. The United States feared that Soviet influence in Southern Africa would significantly alter those calculations in the sense that it could seriously imperil the free flow of oil to the Western alliance with disastrous economic consequences (Price, 1978:6). From this perspective, the US had little choice but to re-spond in kind to the Soviets' significant escalation in their global projec-tion of power.

But, in the wake of the American debacle in Vietnam, there was little inclination on the part of the US government to undertake direct military intervention in another distant third world country. There was nothing the US government "needed or desired less than another crisis in a distant con-tinent heretofore insulated from the Cold War and one likely to lead to an-other domestic controversy" (Kissinger, 1999:791). Indeed "US citizens and policymakers sought to prevent any repetition of such fiasco by imposing a number of important restrictions on US military involvement in regional third world conflicts" (Klare 36). The "Vietnam syndrome", however, did not prevent the United Sates from intervening in an attempt to stop the pro-Soviet MPLA movement from taking power in Angola. Given the po-litical realities militating against direct intervention, "Henry Kissinger and his colleagues devised what may be called the 'post-Vietnam strategy' of in-direct intervention" (Klare, 1989:37). Thus, the United States intervened in Angola indirectly because there was "no conceivable way" for it to intervene in post-colonial conflict in Africa "except by means of covert operation" (Kissinger, 1999:802) defined by the CIA as "clandestine activity designed to influence foreign governments, events, organizations or persons in sup-port of US foreign policy conducted in such a way that the involvement of the US Government is not apparent" (Weissman, 1979:263).

American activities to influence events in Angola were not new. They started soon after Angolan nationalist movements initiated armed struggle against Portuguese colonialism. By April 1961, the American embassy in Kinshasa (then Leopoldville) was in "close contact" with FNLA leader Holden Roberto (Weissman, 1979:277). For most of the liberation struggle, American support for the nationalist movement was minimal, with Roberto receiving only about US$10,000 a year, the minimum amount the CIA paid to its "intelligence collection" agents (Weissman, 1979:281; Rodman1994:167). Through Roberto, the US sought to "establish a claim for information and access to the group [its] intelligence agencies judged to be most likely to succeed" (Kissinger, 1994:795). However, this amount increased substantially after the 1974 military coup in Portugal and the start of the complex decolonization process. Roberto's yearly stipend was raised to US$300,000 on 22 January 1975 after the signing of the Alvor agreement (Kissinger, 1999:795). Through 1975, American covert action in Angola reached US$32 million to purchase weapons, "political action support" and propaganda (Weissman, 1979:283) mostly for FNLA but increasingly for UNITA as well. Thus, "American arms poured in on C130s from Zaire to the FNLA's staging centres at Ambriz and the former Portuguese airbase at Negage" (Marcum 1978:269). This effort, however, was inadequate to avert a major setback in American foreign policy in Africa.

Early US policy for post-colonial Angola, especially under the Nixon administration, was "a disaster" because it was "formulated and carried out without a good sense of regional possibilities, much less with a comprehension of the forces at work in Southern Africa and in Angola" (Bienen, 1980:33). Ultimately, Cold War calculation propelled the United States to intervene in Angola, as it had done before elsewhere in the third world and as it would continue to do in order to advance an American vision of how the international system ought to be structured. Often this American vision clashed with international norms regarding when force could be legally used. Thus, the US developed its own set of criteria to justify its use of force on the international stage. This included overthrowing a communist (or "procommunist") government or to prevent a communist (or "procommunist") government from assuming power, even if it was popularly elected or emerged as a result of internal forces (Henkin, 1991:55). As far as American foreign policy was concerned, the decolonization process was turning Angola into a communist state and thwarting this development became an important goal. For the US, the "red line was intervention from outside the continent and domination from Moscow" (Kissinger, 1999:795).

The goal of preventing a communist regime from installing itself in power in post-colonial Angola ultimately failed as American weapons and mercenaries were unable to catapult their UNITA and FNLA allies into power. American defeat, however, only temporarily halted American intervention during the Carter years. With the election of Ronald Reagan, the US adopted a pro-insurgency stance toward Angola. Generally, American pro-insurgency took the form of "paramilitary support for anticommunist guerrillas who [sought] to overthrow pro-Soviet governments in the third world" (Klare, 1989:41). In Angola, this pro-insurgency policy was implemented in a two-step sequence: first, by repealing the Clark Amendment to the Defense Appropriations Bill for Fiscal Year 1976 prohibiting US involvement in the Angolan civil war and, second, by securing congressional backing for support of UNITA. American pro-insurgency activities in Angola escalated significantly after the Clark Amendment was nullified in 1985. This repeal enabled the Reagan administration to renew American covert support of UNITA, providing the rebels with US\$15 million to US\$30 million a year in arms, medicines and food. Within the broad framework of the Reagan Doctrine and the regional focus of constructive engagement, the United States justified this funding in terms of UNITA's critical role in resisting the presence of the estimated 30,000 Cuban troops stationed in Angola.

The Reagan Doctrine was concerned, above all, with the moral legitimacy of American support for anti-Soviet insurgencies around the world (Kirkpatrick and Gerson, 1991:20). In particular, it targeted situations "where there [were] indigenous opponents to a government that [was] maintained by force, rather than popular consent; where such a government depend[ed] on arms supplied by the Soviet Union, the Soviet bloc, or other foreign sources; and where the people [were] denied a choice regarding their affiliations and future". The implementation of the Reagan Doctrine took the form of "a full-blown, global campaign" for providing overt American support for anti-communist guerrilla movements around the world (Crocker, 1992:290). As far as the civil war in Angola was concerned, the implementation of the Reagan Doctrine had an almost immediate impact both in terms of military and financial means supplied to the Angolan rebels. By the end of the 1980s, the annual infusion of American assistance to UNITA reached close to \$60 million (Schraeder, 1992:144). Buoyed up by both overt and covert American help, UNITA significantly escalated its operations in 1985. By 1988, UNITA – with the help of SADF – was able to survive a massive attack by MPLA troops and crack Cuban units at the battle of Cuito-Cuanavale. But given Cuba's determined willingness to deploy both troops and materiel to confront South African troops – for example, Cuba redeployed 15,000 troops closer to the Namibian border and introduced new weapons systems that for the first time since the beginning of the war ended South African air superiority – it could not be taken for granted that SADF would be able to save UNITA again from the predictable annual military offensives by the Angolan armed forces.

The battle of Cuito-Cuanavale affected all parties involved by demonstrating the unlikelihood that either side was in a position to achieve an outright military victory. For UNITA, Cuito-Cuanavale may have constituted an important symbolic, if not military, victory in the sense that it had again postponed it demise. But it also signalled MPLA's commitment to employ whatever means it could muster to destroy UNITA. Thus, the realities on the battlefield forced both parties to accept American pressure to negotiate a settlement of the conflict. The result was the New York Accord of 22 December 1988 calling for South African withdrawal from Angola and Namibia and Cuban withdrawal from Angola to pave the way for Namibia's independence.

The lessons of Cuito-Cuanavale were more easily grasped by outside forces – Cuba and South Africa – than by the internal combatants. For MPLA and UNITA Cuito-Cuanavale was inconclusive and, therefore, neither completely discarded the military option as a way to settle the conflict. In other words, for both, negotiations were simply a way to manage their respective immediate pressures: MPLA genuinely needed peace to avoid a collapse of the regime while UNITA was unwilling to upset its American allies especially because it had also convinced itself – in hindsight, with careless optimism – that it could win either though bullets or ballots. The latter was, obviously, the rebels preferred option. UNITA's decision to return to war after losing both parliamentary and presidential elections held in September 1992 reflects this group's preference for military options to settle essentially political matters. For example, after going back to war Savimbi admitted that one of UNITA's "greatest errors was to sign the Bicesse Accord in 1991" because "UNITA had everything to continue its unstoppable struggle" (Angola Peace Monitor Vol. II, Issue 7, 29 March 1996, p.3).

UNITA's bellicose attitude after the 1992 elections caught the United States by surprise. The Angola rebels, once regarded as one of the best examples of global "freedom fighters" deserving support from Washington, were now justifiably seen as poor losers in a democratic process backed by the United States. After UNITA's electoral defeat and its return to war, American involvement changed dramatically. The Republican administration of George H.W. Bush initiated a constructive relationship with the MPLA government which was further strengthened when Bill Clinton came to power in 1992. The new Democratic administration soon granted diplomatic recognition, albeit belatedly, to the post-colonial Angolan state. But this change in American involvement did not immediately and significantly alter the situation on the ground because, by the early 1990s, UNITA had evolved away from its dependent relationship vis-à-vis the United States into self-sufficiency, especially as far as financial resources were concerned. Control of diamond producing areas provided UNITA with the financial resources it required to gain this independence. UNITA could now use its own funds to purchase in the vast international arms bazaar the resources it needed to sustain itself and Mobutu's Zaire could still be used as a reliable conduit for this materiel into Angola. Thus, for much of the 1990s – including through the critical Bicesse peace process – UNITA was able to thwart the will of the international community for a permanent end to the post-colonial violence in Angola. The UN in particular, but also the troika of countries most deeply involved in Angola's peace process – the US, the former Soviet Union and Portugal – were unable to hold UNITA accountable to the commitments it had repeatedly made. Worse still, the Angolan rebels were able to cynically use the UN-led peace process as a period to regroup, reassess strategies, and rearm for a final military showdown with the government. By the early 1990s, after it had survived since independence with external help from Cuba and the former Soviet Union, toppling the government was no easy task.

Cuba and the former USSR

In 1975, faced with a real possibility of losing a power struggle with its rivals, MPLA sought foreign assistance from socialist bloc countries. Although several countries responded, decisive, direct and timely assistance came only from Cuba and the former Soviet Union. Like all the other countries that intervened in Angola, Cuba also had the motives and means to intervene. Cuba's reasons for intervention were mainly ideological. A leader among third world states with revolutionary regimes, Cuba was inclined to help establish a Marxist-Leninist regime in Angola and thus advance the cause of international revolution. Moreover, in Angola Cuba also saw an opportunity to humiliate the US – the superpower that had been hounding Fidel Castro since he successfully led the Cuban revolution in 1959. Economic reasons also featured prominently in Cuba's calculus since

Angola could eventually develop into an important trading partner able to supply Cuba with much needed oil. Finally, historical reasons – pertaining particularly to the slave trade – linked Cuba and Angola, even if mostly at the imaginary level. All these factors played a role in the decision to intervene. Regarding the means for intervention, Cuba had developed a strong military mainly due to the real and perceived threats emanating from the US Ironically, some of this military muscle was deployed halfway around the world to spoil American geo-strategic designs. Given the aforementioned reasons, Cuba responded positively to MPLA's request of March 1975 for help to counterbalance the foreign assistance being provided to its rivals. Initially, Cuba sent 230 military advisors to help train MPLA forces. However, in response to MPLA's growing difficulties, in early November 1975 Cuba mounted "Operation Carlota", a major airlift of combat troops to help MPLA stave off invading forces from Zaire and South Africa. By late 1975, Cuba had deployed 7,000 troops in Angola (Marcum, 1978:274), a number that increased to 11,400 by January 1976 (Stevens, 1979:144).

If Cuban troops played a key role in bringing MPLA to power, it was Soviet involvement – particularly in the form of military advisors and hardware – that ultimately ensured that victory. Cuban use of sophisticated Soviet weapons, including 122mm "Stalin Organs" rocket launchers as well as T34 and T54 tanks, provided MPLA with all it needed to prevail. After ensuring MPLA's victory, the former Soviet Union continued to provide the new regime with crucial sustenance in the critical first decade of its existence. But what motivated Soviet aid to MPLA?

Generally, post-Stalin Soviet leadership embarked on a strategy of "courting" the third world (Rubinstein, 1984:20). The means for this courtship often involved "direct military intervention on behalf of promising associates and prized clients". In the 1970s, this Soviet "courting" became markedly aggressive due to three important developments. First, the former USSR acquired the ability to project power globally. Second, it perceived the US as unable or unwilling to project global power in the aftermath of its defeat in Vietnam. Finally, there was an "increase in the opportunity factor" arising from regional instability and local actors' willingness to turn to the USSR for help to advance their own plans (Rubinstein, 1984:22).

More specifically, Angola represented a unique episode in the history of Soviet involvement in Africa inasmuch as never before had the former Soviet Union assisted an African liberation movement on "such a grand scale" (Stevens, 1976:137). The Soviets intervention provided MPLA with desperately needed financial, logistical, and training assistance (Rothchild and Hartzell, 1995:178) as well as invaluable political/ideological cover on the international stage. Clearly, from the Soviet perspective, Angola was a "promising associate" while MPLA was a "prized client". Thus, although the Kremlin attempted to play down its intervention in Angola to give the impression that its aid to the MPLA was no more than the legitimate continuation of a policy to support national liberation movements worldwide, Moscow clearly had more specific goals beyond ideological solidarity with MPLA. First, from a geostrategic perspective, an MPLA victory would allow the USSR to establish itself as an influential player in Southern Africa. For example, access to air and naval bases in Angola would enable the Soviet Union to more closely monitor, if not control, shipping lanes from the Persian Gulf to the West as well as other Western shipping in the South Atlantic. Second, within the complex geopolitical calculations of the Cold War, it would have been unrealistic to expect a non-interventionist Soviet posture when the US and China were intervening – albeit inadequately – to give a significant military advantage to FNLA and UNITA. For the Soviet Union, an FNLA-UNITA victory would be tantamount to victory for its main rivals – the US and China – and a setback for third world revolutionary forces. From the Soviet global perspective, MPLA's victory in Angola, much like the Vietcong's victory in Vietnam, would confirm the rapid decay of American imperialism. Therefore, for the former USSR, large investments to ensure MPLA's victory in 1975 were justified even when the ties that linked the Kremlin to the Angolan revolutionaries had been strained, and at one point severed, for much of the early 1970s due to increasing Soviet doubts both about MPLA's ideological commitments and its capabilities as a fighting force because of persistent infighting within this group. Third, Soviet help was also motivated by economic reasons in the sense that an MPLA victory would guarantee Russian access to Angola's vast natural resources and a potentially significant commercial partner in Africa. So, between March 1975 and January 1976 the USSR invested between US$100 and US$200 million in military aid supported by 170 advisors to ensure MPLA victory in Angola (Stevens, 1976:144). The Soviets introduced heavy military hardware thitherto absent from the civil war theatre, including T-34 and T-54 tanks, 100mm guns, 122mm multiple rocket launchers, amphibious vehicles, helicopters equipped with 20mm cannon and air-to-ground rockets, MIG-17, and MIG-21 aircraft (Stevens, 1976:144). By the 1980s, the Soviets had invested about $5 billion worth of military equipment in Angola (Vanemman, 1990:47)

The USSR remained highly committed to MPLA until the mid-1980s when its own internal crises and contradictions indicated an imminent collapse of the Soviet empire. By the late 1980s, as the Cold War entered its final thawing period – precipitated mainly by the impending implosion of the Soviet regime – Russian foreign policy in Southern Africa had shifted significantly and now rested on two main planks: support of negotiations as a conflict-resolution mechanism and the reduction of its commitments to satellite regimes in Angola and Mozambique (Kempton, 1990:545). This fundamental change forced MPLA to accept the political power-sharing framework for Angola that the United States – now the only remaining superpower – had insisted upon after MPLA came to power in 1975. External intervention would cease while internal parties – MPLA and UNITA – embarked on a peace process with United Nations (UN) assistance. Problematically, however, the UN presence in Angola was used by UNITA to continue its violent attempts to gain power for another decade. In other words, the UN presence in Angola during the 1990s delayed UNITA's ultimate demise for more than 10 years.

The UN

The UN was a key player in the international community's attempts to end the post-colonial violence in Angola. The world body's direct involvement in this process began on 20 December 1988 with the creation of the United Nations Angola Verification Mission (UNAVEM). This UN mission, an integral part of the international settlement that led to Namibia's independence, was set up primarily to monitor the withdrawal of the 50,000-strong Cuban military contingent that had been stationed in Angola. Upon this withdrawal – the main South African condition for disengagement from Namibia – hinged international efforts to bring peace to the region. UNAVEM was made up of 70 military observers and 20 civilian officials from ten countries[1] and was given a 31-month mandate, beginning with its deployment one week before the start of the Cuban withdrawal and ending one month after the completion of the withdrawal.

On 30 May 1991, on the eve of the signing of the Bicesse peace accord, UN Security Council Resolution 696 decided to "entrust a new mandate" to UNAVEM. The new mission, UNAVEM II, evolved into a 24-nation

---

1. Algeria, Argentina, Brazil, Congo (Brazaville), the former Czechoslovakia, India, Jordan, Norway, Spain, and the former Yugoslavia.

multinational force with the mission of monitoring the cease-fire between the Angolan government and UNITA.[2] UNAVEM II, which began its deployment on 1 July 1991, included 548 personnel and had a budget of US$132.3 million dollars. The UN personnel comprised 350 military observers and 90 police officers, 14 medical workers, and a 160-person support staff for administrative support. UNAVEM II military observers were given the task of ensuring that the provisions of the peace accord regarding the encampment of government and UNITA troops in their designated zones were respected. UNAVEM II was also deployed in 12 critical areas and had additional responsibilities for conducting patrols over the entire country. The 90 international police officers included in the mission were charged with ensuring the functioning of a new, integrated national police force.

On 24 March 1992, the UN Security Council unanimously approved the expansion of UNAVEM II and enlarged its mandate. A 400-person division was added to the existing mission to monitor and evaluate the operations and impartiality of the electoral authorities at all levels in preparation for the upcoming legislative and presidential elections. This division was expected to operate in all the 18 provinces of the country to monitor and verify the three main phases of the electoral process: the registration of voters, the electoral campaign, and the poll itself. An additional $18.8 million was allocated to the mission's budget.

In terms of both human and financial resources UNAVEM II was, at best, a diminutive reproduction of previous UN operations like those in Namibia and Cambodia in the sense that it lacked the financial and human resources as well as the international support to monitor and verify an extremely delicate transition to peace and democracy (Lodico, 1996:103). For example, in contrast to the UN role during Namibia's transition to independence, UNAVEM did not have to organize the elections. The UN stressed that the Angolan elections were essentially a national, sovereign affair. Therefore, the UN assumed the auxiliary role of merely observing the fairness and verifying the integrity of the elections. The more daunting task of organizing them was left to the Angolan state. This was expected of a country emerging from a devastating civil war that had crippled most of its infrastructure and from a regime generally regarded as both inept and corrupt whose very survival – both political and otherwise – depended on winning this zero-sum electoral contest at all costs. Predictably, therefore,

---

2. The original 10 UNAVEM members plus Canada, Egypt, Guinea-Bissau, Hungary, Ireland, Malaysia, Morocco, the Netherlands, New Zealand, Nigeria, Senegal, Singapore, Sweden, and Zimbabwe.

tension, fear, anxiety and ultimately violence filled the road from Bicesse to the first multi-party elections in Angola. Thus, the UN would not intervene to preventing armed UNITA cadres in civilian clothing from moving into towns across the country. Nor would it investigate widespread reports by frightened local people of large UNITA arms caches hidden in the forests. Moreover, the UN turned a blind eye to reports that UNITA's heavy arms had not been brought into its designated cantonment areas – they were kept in the forests with UNITA's best units. In other words, the UN in Angola was unable to defuse escalating tension ahead of the country's first multi-party elections and was caught completely unprepared to deal with both the pre-electoral clashes between Angola's former civil war enemies and the full-fledged post-electoral war that ensued.

In the final analysis, therefore, the failure to steer the peace process toward a sustainable transition to elected government and a democratic regime in Angola can be partly attributed to the UN and, by extension, to the international community (Lodico, 1996:103). This failure derived mainly from the mismatch between the role of the UN mission in Angola and the realities of the conflict. The stated goal of the UN mission in Angola was neither peacebuilding, peacemaking, peacekeeping nor peace enforcement. It was vaguely defined as "verification" and "monitoring". Consequently, UNVEM II was unable to act as a deterring factor within the framework of traditional peacekeeping, defined in the Galtungian way as keeping the antagonists away from each other through measures – such as monitoring the cease-fire, controlling buffer zones and military encampment sites, investigating arms flows – that could have prevented the resumption of fighting. UNAVEM II was equally ineffective in the critical area of peacebuilding in the sense that its mandate did not address the need to change the structures that had caused and sustained the war. Furthermore, at least as far as UNITA was concerned, it provided few realistic alternatives to war. Left to their own questionable political wills and within the context of a country physically destroyed and a society profoundly traumatized by a long civil war, MPLA and UNITA left vital features of the transition process – particularly the demobilization of the two armies and their fusion into a single, unified, non-partisan national army – unfulfilled partly as their own life insurance policies which, ironically, ultimately led directly to UNITA's demise. But this would not happen for another decade. In the meantime, several other UN missions in Angola could do precious little to help stop the violence unleashed by UNITA.

CHAPTER 4

UNITA's Insurgency

Mutations and self-mutilations

UNITA never recovered from its ill-fated choice to return the country to war in 1992. This decision marked the beginning of the end for this organization as an alternative to the MPLA regime by concluding the process of UNITA's decay in the civil war that had dominated Angola's post-colonial era. If UNITA's standard justification for its long insurgency – often inarticulately presented as a struggle against the governing elite's monopoly on power and wealth – rang increasingly hollow due to the rebels' own transformation into a criminal enterprise, the resumption of the war cemented the general view that Savimbi's group was the worse of the two evils. Indeed, as suggested earlier – and as this chapter describes in greater detail – UNITA's peculiar and self-destructive metamorphosis had begun decades earlier. Under Savimbi's erratic leadership, UNITA underwent a long period of political and military self-mutilation. This was primarily a result of the movement's inability to deal with several major and momentous crises that periodically shook its foundations. Throughout its history, UNITA invariably made strategic political and military mistakes when confronted with major challenges. The costs of such blunders varied in terms of impact and severity. First, as discussed in chapter 2, UNITA responded to its early isolation from external sources of support by developing a relationship with the very colonial forces against which it was purportedly fighting. Second, when faced with defeat in the civil war, it entered into an alliance with apartheid South Africa, one of the most despised and isolated regimes in the world. Third, after agreeing to participate in free and democratic elections – the culmination of an internationally-promoted peace process and an outcome the rebels had sought since the problematic decolonization process of 1975 – UNITA plunged the country back into war after its defeat at the polls in 1992. Finally, unable to cope with electoral defeat and staring at the prospects of a futile military attempt to dislodge MPLA from power, UNITA degenerated into a criminal insurgency.

This chapter, then, deals with the political economy of military violence and focuses on UNITA as its prime mover in an attempt to capture the complex metamorphosis of this rebel group. The chapter argues that, all along, UNITA was torn by severe schizophrenic drives – a major guerrilla army masquerading as a political party and a powerful grassroots organization as a veil for an armed personality cult. These untreatable maladies – particularly the militaristic and cultist traits – hindered UNITA's ability to play a constructive role in post-colonial politics and ultimately led to its downfall. UNITA's main strategy for taking power was fundamentally flawed inasmuch as it hinged on making the country ungovernable as a way of forcing major political concessions from the governing MPLA. However, by using indiscriminate violence, UNITA sabotaged its own goals. Although the government could be brought to the negotiating table and be forced into making major concessions, UNITA's violence – especially after the 1992 elections – frightened and alienated the majority of the population. Another dimension of UNITA's violence – regular internal purges – also frightened much of the rebel leadership into accepting the inertia of violence. Consequently, since its creation until Savimbi's death in 2002, UNITA was unable to make much-needed self-corrections at critical junctures.

The death of Jonas Savimbi provided UNITA with a unique opportunity to reinvent itself politically. But UNITA was unwilling to make a clean break with its problematic history as a first step to reinvent itself and opted for continuity with the leftovers of a nationally discredited leadership. For the first time in its history, UNITA had the freedom to reinvent itself – it was no longer a proxy in the hands of foreign forces nor was it an instrument of its leader's raw ambitions and peculiar whims. But, in the short run, reinventing UNITA was sure to be a complex and unlikely proposition involving, first and foremost, its transformation into an inclusive and democratic political party led by individuals capable of developing and articulating a new vision for the post-colonial state based on transparent, accountable, and people-oriented governance. The politics of opposition alone could not ensure UNITA's continuing relevance or popular support. But before dealing with the possibilities for reinventing UNITA, this chapter analyzes this organization's survival strategy – first as a proxy and then as a criminal insurgency.

Survival as proxy

The withdrawal of the invading South African troops from Angola in February 1976 after failing to prevent a post-colonial MPLA take-over left

UNITA virtually destroyed. But although MPLA had prevailed over invading armies and internal enemies – UNITA and FNLA – it was traumatized by the complex and violent birth of the new state. It was also cognizant of the fact that, surrounded by enemies like South Africa and Zaire it would remain indefinitely on life-support. Thus, after independence, the MPLA regime viewed its long-term security as being intrinsically tied to its ability to foster a friendlier regional environment. This, even more than ideological solidarity, led MPLA to actively support domestic opponents of the regimes in South Africa and Zaire. Thus, the new Angolan government provided open and unconditional military and diplomatic support for South Africa's ANC, Namibia's SWAPO and Zaire's FNLC. Both the South Africa and Zaire regimes responded by supporting their own proxies in Angola. With FNLA out of commission as a military force due to its implosion after failing to capture Luanda in 1975, UNITA became the proxy of choice.

South Africa's response to the perceived threats emanating from the new Angolan state came in the form of the so-called "total strategy". As mentioned earlier, this strategy involved a set of policies aimed at ensuring the survival of the apartheid system through a combination of reform and repression at home and coercive regional intervention. The main proponents of the "total strategy" argued that the source of instability and conflict – both inside South Africa and in the region – was neither apartheid nor colonialism but external intervention. Through this strategy, South Africa sought to force neighbouring states not to actively support the armed liberation struggle in South Africa and Namibia. Therefore, Angola became one of South Africa's principal enemies in the region due to its position as the main SWAPO sanctuary and an important ANC base. Its ideological orientation and the presence of thousands of Cuban troops on its soil only served to further underline its position as the apartheid regime's enemy number one in the region. Consequently, from the late 1970s through the 1980s, Angola was the brunt of the apartheid regime's total strategy. South Africa used two main instruments to threaten Angola's territorial integrity: first, frequent and well-planned military invasions deep into Angolan territory; and, second, the instrumentalisation of UNITA as a proxy in its regional destabilization policies. A defeated UNITA in the mid-1970s faced a situation peculiarly similar to its predicament a decade earlier when it had also faced extinction at the hands of the Portuguese army. Now, as then, willingness to accept a new proxy role ensured its survival.

Between its withdrawal in 1976 and its final disengagement in 1988, SADF carried out regular military operations in Angola. The duration of such actions, carried out under the pretext of responding to increased SWAPO attacks in northern Namibia from bases in southern Angola, varied according to the real objective of each mission. Thus, for example, missions to destroy SWAPO bases did not take as long as assisting UNITA. Incursions whose real objective was to aid UNITA were crucial for the rebels' development as a major military force. Although virtually destroyed by MPLA and Cuban troops in 1975–6, UNITA was reorganized into a significant military force by 1979. After 1980 UNITA was restructured "by the South Africans along the lines of a conventional army, with brigades (made up of several battalions), regular battalions (900–1,500 men), semi-regular battalions (300–500 men) and 'special forces' (small groups of a few dozen men normally used for sabotage operations)" (Conchiglia, 1990:45). Thus reorganized and revitalized, UNITA took advantage of South Africa's regular incursions to advance behind SADF, "liberate" territory, and defend it with weapons captured by the South African army. Thus, while SADF threats kept the government occupied, UNITA was able to expand its guerrilla activity throughout most of the country. In the process it seriously disrupted food production in rural areas, brought the vital Benguela Railway to a standstill, and threatened to disrupt onshore oil production and diamond exploration.

Seriously threatened, the MPLA regime sought to defeat UNITA militarily by mounting annual offensives against the rebels' main headquarters in the southeastern corner of the country. These massive military operations commenced in 1985 and culminated with major conventional battles for the strategic towns of Mavinga and Cuito-Cuanavale in 1987–88. Mavinga was especially critical as it represented UNITA's main defensive position north of the main headquarters at Jamba. In these offensives, MPLA was supported by large quantities of sophisticated heavy armaments from the former Soviet Union, including jet fighters, tanks, combat vehicles, helicopter-gunships, and air defence systems. In addition, it could also count on about 45,000 to 50,000 Cuban troops to supplement its own increasingly capable army. To save UNITA, South Africa deployed equally heavy and sophisticated weaponry, including 127mm multiple rocket launchers, 120mm mortars, G-5 155mm heavy and high precision artillery guns (with a range of 25 miles), tanks, armoured cars and combat troops like the notorious 32nd "Buffalo" Battalion. Likewise, the United States provided UNITA with significant military assistance including sophisticated Stinger missiles. Such assistance was decisive in thwarting MPLA's attempts, at the battles for Mavinga and Cuito-Cuanavale in 1987, to break UNITA's main line of defence before taking Jamba.

As discussed earlier, the battles at Mavinga and Cuito-Cuanavale clearly showed to both sides the futility of pursuing a military option. By the end of the 1980s, then, both MPLA and UNITA faced important pressures to find a political end to the war. In combination, apartheid South Africa's twin strategies toward Angola – regular military invasions and support for UNITA – convinced the Angolan government that a regional settlement with South Africa was in its best interest. Thus, MPLA accepted the Reagan Administration's "linkage" policy tying the withdrawal of Cuban troops from Angola to Namibia's independence on the basis of UNSC Resolution 435 of 29 September 1978. This resolution reaffirmed the legal responsibility of the United Nations over Namibia and approved a UN Secretary-General report containing a proposal for a settlement of the issue based on the withdrawal of South Africa's illegal administration from Namibia and the transfer of power to the people of Namibia. The New York Accord of 22 December 1988 was the culmination of this process. The Peace Accord signed by Angola, Cuba, and South Africa provided for the removal of Cuban troops from Angola in exchange for South African commitment to implement UNSC Resolution 435. Angola saw this accord as a major foreign policy victory inasmuch as it was expected to bring MPLA closer to finally achieving a measure of domestic security. The Angolan regime believed that full implementation of UNSC Resolution 435 (1978) would bring two important benefits. First, remove the South African threat from its southern border. Second, lead to the collapse of UNITA as a military threat because its main supply routes via Namibia would be cut off by a SWAPO-led government (Timsar, 1981:1). But the optimistic scenario whereby UNITA would disappear due to discontinued South African support did not materialize because UNITA was also a proxy within a wider global ideological war – an important instrument in the implementation of the "Reagan Doctrine".

UNITA and the Reagan Doctrine

By the late 1970s, a reorganized UNITA could serve important American security interests in Africa. Ironically, the re-emergence of UNITA in this role is partly the result of strategic miscalculations on the part of the governing MPLA on how best to enhance its own fragile security within a hostile regional environment. Seeing its security in terms of regional regime changes, as discussed above, MPLA encouraged and supported two invasions of Zaire by Katangan gendarmes that had been based in Angola since their defeat in Zaire's own turbulent transition to independence. These invasions seriously threatened the Mobutu regime as well as Western interests in Zaire. As expected, therefore, Mobutu's allies – including the United States, France, Belgium, and Morocco – promptly came to his rescue and quickly pushed the invading forces back to Angola.

The invasion of Zaire from Angola provided Mobutu and his Western allies with a rationale and justification for continuing intervention in Angola. Within a Cold War context, Angola's actions – whether or not they had been carried out with Cuban and Soviet consent or support – were seen as an attempt to expand the Soviet sphere of influence into central Africa. Consequently and predictably, the United States and its allies responded with massive military support for Mobutu. Even more significant for Angola, Western intelligence services accelerated efforts to provide training and weapons to UNITA via Zaire. This Western-Zairian-UNITA connection seriously weakened the new Angolan state and constituted a major threat to its territorial security, exactly the reverse outcome to what MPLA had sought for Angola in its early years of independence. In other words, in seeking its own security by attempting to induce regime change in Zaire, MPLA enhanced UNITA's relevance as a foreign proxy. Thereafter, UNITA became an important player in the southern African theatre of the Cold War, particularly in the context of implementing the Reagan Doctrine. As discussed earlier, this American relationship with UNITA lasted until the rebels' decision to return to war after losing both parliamentary and presidential elections held in September 1992.

Prelude to defeat

UNITA's electoral defeat in 1992 can be attributed principally to the rebel groups' internal idiosyncrasies. Specifically, Savimbi's paranoid and authoritarian leadership led to UNITA's propensity for self-mutilation. Permanently bleeding at the sub-leadership level, the party lacked sufficient flexibility to make fundamental self-corrections in the conduct of the insurgency. Ultimately, by emphasizing military over political means, UNITA alienated a significant segment of its traditional support base, with negative electoral consequences. But the internal factors that ultimately led to UNITA's decline and Savimbi's death were apparent from the initial stages of the anti-colonial struggle. Savimbi never succeeded in developing his organization into a liberation army. As such, its survival depended primarily on the degree to which its was useful as a tool in the hands of foreign powers – whether Portugal, South Africa, or the United States. This inability to transform itself into a liberation army had negative impacts on both the internal dynamics of the organization and, more generally, on the way the civil war was fought. UNITA, unlike classical guerrilla insurgents, did not adequately resolve the relationship between political ends and military means. This partly explains why Savimbi did not seem to grasp the fundamental contradictions inherent in his organization's problematic relationships with the Portuguese army and secret police during the liberation struggle and later with the South African apartheid regime and the CIA.

Above all, however, the character of Savimbi's leadership robbed UNITA of the flexibility it needed to face changing political circumstances both at the domestic and international levels. By the time of its defeat in 1976, UNITA was already in the advanced stages of its transformation from a rag-tag rebel group that had barely survived the anti-colonial armed struggle into a powerful fanaticized military organization with a political wing whose main functions were divided between enforcing the internal personality cult of its leader while wreaking havoc throughout the country. The first function – enforcing the personality cult – eventually led to the politics of fear as UNITA robbed most of its members of their basic sense of individual identity. Although initially many people filled UNITA's ranks voluntarily, exit was rarely an option. Given UNITA's military character, deviance was dealt with through severe punishment, especially against those members who were perceived by Savimbi as a potential threat to his leadership. Thus, Savimbi eliminated most of his party's most promising political and military cadres including Jorge Sangumba (foreign secretary), Pedro "Tito" Chingunji (foreign secretary and deputy secretary general), Wilson dos Santos (international cooperation secretary), Eunice Sapassa (president of UNITA's women's organisation), António Vakulukuta (UNITA's top Ovambu leader), Valdemar Chindondo (chief of staff), Jose Antonio Chendovava (chief of staff), and Mateus Katalaio (interior secretary), among others. Bizarrely, Savimbi did not just kill his close assistants; he also had all their families, including small children, killed. To instill fear in his followers, Savimbi often meted out punishment in public, ranging from beatings to a variety of the most horrific killing methods: burning at the stake, use of heavy vehicles to crush victims, smashing of the victims' children's skulls against trees, and death by firing squad. One infamous such episode took place at UNITA's former headquarters in Jamba on 7

September 1983. After accusing a group of women and children of witch-craft, they were burnt to death on a giant bonfire under Savimbi's personal supervision. This level of intra-party violence was symptomatic of a seriously dysfunctional organization. But it only represented the tip of a much larger structural problem that contributed to its electoral defeat.

Rebels in a ballot war

Beyond the leadership problems and concomitant intra-party violence, in the early 1990s UNITA faced serious structural challenges as it approached a new era of multi-party politics. For much of its post-colonial insurgency, UNITA attempted to cultivate the image of champion of peace, freedom and multi-party democracy. Thus, it attempted to present itself as the main catalyst for all the political and social transformations that took place in Angola culminating in the end of single-party politics. Ironically, UNITA was dreadfully unprepared for the new realities of multi-party politics because it was very slow in adjusting from war to peace, from a guerrilla group to a political party.

The complexities involved in UNITA's transformation from a guerrilla group into a political party were colossal, as Savimbi himself recognized. In a speech to his groups' 7th Congress, Savimbi acknowledged that "UNITA was not born as a political party, but as a military force with a political outlook" (VORGAN, 14 March 1991). Thus, the end of the civil war presented stark choices for UNITA: it could either seek alternative pretexts for continued fighting or reinvent itself to face a new political reality for which it was unprepared. Specifically, this involved organizing an inclusive political party, developing a coherent electoral strategy, and carrying out an election campaign with a viable alternative programme of government. In other words, UNITA cadres would have to do precisely the opposite of what their leader ordered them to do at the March 1991 Congress, i.e. "think politically in order to find the best way of fighting". But this was precisely the opposite of what UNITA needed because the new era of multi-partyism required rebels to develop winning strategies to struggle politically.

The political fight against the MPLA posed serious problems for UNITA inasmuch as the former clearly had some recognized advantages. Savimbi publicly recognized this at the 7th UNITA Congress when he pointed out that "the MPLA will benefit from certain advantages because it has been a politically inspired and motivated organization, whereas we have always been guided by our political thought but with emphasis on the armed struggle". Thus, belatedly, UNITA made an attempt to acquire a political outlook by seeking to adapt its structures to the new political conditions. Some changes were announced at the 7th Congress, held just before the signing of the Bicesse peace accord. Thus, UNITA kept the Party Congress as the supreme organ of its structure. This organ would meet every four years. The party also kept its Central Committee to represent various political, economic, and religious interests. But the Central Committee was relieved of all its decision-making powers and assumed a merely consultative role. UNITA's decision-making powers were transferred to the new Political Commission. In effect, the Political Commission thus gained all the powers that were once in the hands of the Central Committee and the Political Bureau. The latter was kept with the sole function of advising the party's president. UNITA's Executive Committee, or "government-in-waiting", was charged with the responsibility of executing the decisions of the Political Commission. These transformations in UNITA's internal structures, however, did not change the external perception as an extremist organization. The serious divisions that occurred within the organization soon after the signing of the Bicesse peace accord further reinforced this view. Two prominent UNITA figures – Tony da Costa Fernandes, who co-founded the movement with Jonas Savimbi in 1966, and Miguel N'Zau Puna, UNITA's deputy leader for nearly 24 years – defected on 29 February 1992. Both accused Jonas Savimbi of serious human rights abuses and corroborated allegations regarding the execution of prominent UNITA figures. The defection of Puna and Fernandes represented the first serious crack in UNITA's outward façade of unity. UNITA's legendary internal discipline, harshly enforced during the long years as a guerrilla group, could not have been expected to survive in an open political system. No longer virtually captive, many close Savimbi associates could now break away from UNITA's rigid society and integrate into the wider Angolan society even if the latter also showed signs of rot.

Significantly, in addition to corroborating information about the wickedness of Savimbi's leadership, Puna and Fernandes ominously publicized UNITA's lack of commitment to the peace process. The defections exposed for the first time the rebel group's intention to block moves toward a genuine democracy in Angola. Fernandes and Puna claimed that UNITA had devised plans to use military force to usurp power if it failed to win the 1992 elections. Tony Fernandes attested, for example, that Savimbi maintained a secret army in UNITA-controlled areas on the border with Namibia. Why would UNITA insist on pursuing a military path to power?

Throughout the years of insurgency, UNITA did not demonstrate that it was any better equipped to establish a new and improved form of post-colonial governance than MPLA. As described before, after losing a pre-independence power struggle with MPLA, UNITA returned to the countryside and waged a devastating guerrilla war with the help of South Africa and the United States. By the time the Bicesse accords were signed, the rebels controlled most of the southeastern portion of Angola. However, political participation in the areas controlled by UNITA was just as problematic as in government-held zones. Several reasons account for this situation. Although UNITA portrayed itself as a democratic organization, its practice suggested that this was a military organization masquerading as a political movement. Thus, UNITA created highly centralized and authoritarian structures both at the political as well as at the military levels. Peculiarly, its military structures dominated the organization in the sense that few civilians held leadership positions. For example, all the members of UNITA's Politburo and its Political Commission (the decision-making body) had a military rank. The primacy of the military over politics gave UNITA a particularly rigid and non-revolutionary character.

Second, open political competition with MPLA, within a multi-party system, was not UNITA's principal and optimal option. UNITA's preferred path to power involved military means. The political option was forced upon the rebels as a direct result of the major global and regional changes that took place in the late 1980s and early 1990s. The end of the Cold War and the collapse of the minority regime in South Africa threatened UNITA with irrelevance at the international and regional levels, even if not yet domestically. These momentous changes presented UNITA with important challenges. The rebels could no longer count on the generosity of external benefactors to ensure military survival, let alone victory. Thus, UNITA reluctantly joined an externally driven peace process aimed at ending the civil war. As expected, however, UNITA did not completely abandon its long-term goal of capturing power by force. But, paradoxically, the peace process opened significant military opportunities for the rebels who, deceitfully, used the lull in fighting to reorganize for a planned new phase of the war. Savimbi believed that the MPLA regime was irremediably debilitated by long years of economic mismanagement, internal squabbles, and civil war. Moreover, MPLA could no longer count on 50,000 Cuban troops that had kept it in power since independence. Cognizant of these regime weaknesses, UNITA guerrillas initiated their northward movement immediately after the signing of the Bicesse Peace Accord. The process of demobilizing excess government and UNITA soldiers as part of the peace process provided the ideal pretext inasmuch as both government and rebel troops were expected to assemble with their weapons at various pre-determined sites around the country. But UNITA did not send its best soldiers to the demobilization centres. Savimbi used the cessation of hostilities provided by the Bicesse peace process to move his best troops northward from southeastern and central Angola into the diamond producing regions of Lunda Norte, Lunda Sul, and Malanje. Such a move enabled UNITA to both offset the loss of American and South African support by controlling important sources of diamond wealth and also hide its crack troops to resume fighting in the event that they lost the elections.

During the 1992 elections, MPLA and UNITA counted on their respective traditional bases for support. UNITA confidently expected to win the election because the Ovimbundu – its main support base – represent the major ethnolinguistic group. UNITA, therefore, did little to attract other segments of the population, including those that were not traditionally associated with the two other major parties. In addition, Savimbi alienated urban segments of the population, especially white and mulatto, with threatening and racist rhetoric, including threats to remove them from their employment in state institutions. Unsurprisingly, Savimbi and his party lost the elections. In the presidential election, incumbent president José Eduardo dos Santos received 49.6 per cent of the vote compared to Savimbi's 40.1 per cent. MPLA won the parliamentary election with 53.7 per cent of the vote while UNITA received 34.0 per cent. Before a second presidential run-off election could take place, Savimbi claimed that the elections had been rigged and re-ignited the war. This was easier done militarily than politically. This new war emptied UNITA of whatever legitimacy it could still claim as a political force engaged in a struggle to induce fundamental positive changes in the country. Without this legitimacy, the post-electoral phase of the rebellion acquired all the traits of a criminal insurgency.

Aftermath of defeat: Criminal insurgency

Insurgency refers to a protracted political and military activity directed toward completely or partially controlling a state through the use of irregular military forces and illegal political organizations. Typically, insurgencies are triggered by chronic governmental ineptitude, corruption, and other forms of bad governance. More proximate causes often include governmental insensitivity and ineffectiveness in meeting popular demands. Insurgencies can be ignited either through repressive actions by the government or by calculated actions carried out by legal or illegal opposition groups. Insurgent movements use a variety of means to achieve their ultimate political goal of eroding governmental control and legitimacy. These actions can include guerrilla warfare, terrorism, and political mobilization (Snow, 1998:228). Most insurgencies have a dominant political character because they are often precipitated by real or perceived governmental breakdown manifested in unwillingness or inability to redress the demands of important social groups. In other words, where good government does not exist, insurgent movements appear and use warfare as a means to eliminate bad governance. In this sense, insurgencies traditionally have a Clausewitzian character inasmuch as military actions are subjugated to the political purposes for which war is fought. In addition, once initiated, the physical conduct of insurgency often requires the adoption of Maoist revolutionary strategy and tactics to overcome important initial military disadvantages. Specifically, the initial stages require considerable patience because governments are typically more heavily armed than insurgent movements. This important military disadvantage is often minimized through the adoption of a highly mobile guerrilla warfare strategy.

Guerrilla war refers to military conflicts using unconventional tactics. Historically, this has been the preferred tool of smaller and weaker insurgent forces involved in combat against much larger and stronger conventional armies. Guerrilla fighters are usually irregular forces who possess neither the weapons nor the training to engage in a conventional war to achieve their political objectives. The mismatch in military assets, however, is not always disadvantageous to guerrilla forces because guerrilla warfare is much cheaper to conduct. Also, guerrillas have an important advantage because they generally control the tempo of fighting: they choose when and where to strike. Unlike conventional wars, where the principal objective is the control of territory, guerrilla warfare seeks to undermine the exercise of central political authority within a country or region of a country. In this sense, although guerrillas may successfully control or even administer "liberated zones", control of territory is not their overriding objective. Their main objective is to induce the collapse of the central government by de-linking it from the countryside and its population and, ultimately, delegitimize it. These de-linking and de-legitimizing processes often build on incipient dissatisfaction with prevailing socio-economic conditions of decay caused by government incompetence, corruption, or both. The dissatisfaction with poor governance often facilitates revolutionary movements' attempts to win "the hearts and minds" of the alienated population with promises of radical reforms to eliminate real or perceived injustices. By building on the dissatisfaction of those segments of the population that feel ignored by the government, especially in the countryside, guerrilla movements are able to implant themselves in rural areas. Since guerrilla wars then become primarily rural military conflicts, the countryside is vital to most guerrilla strategies because it opens up possibilities for relatively secure bases of operations and reliable access to food. This is often a determinant factor for an eventual victory because, after achieving effective military and political dominance of the countryside, guerrillas can then move to encircle major urban areas and wear down government troops, a process that often lasts many years.

Predictably, therefore, most guerrillas wars are long-term, protracted conflicts of attrition that seek to wear down a much stronger conventional army. Unlike conventional wars where direct military contests between two opposing groups are the norm, guerrilla groups traditionally avoid direct military confrontations altogether. Instead, the preferred strategy involves weakening the opposing force psychologically and militarily through surprise hit-and-run operations against isolated military installations and poorly defended communication, power, transportation, and supply centres. The ultimate aim of the guerrillas is to weaken the central government in at least three ways – politically, militarily, and economically. First, at the political level, guerrilla activities can further alienate a rural population from the central authorities, especially when governments respond to such activities by mounting military counter-attacks that affect civilian targets residing within the guerrillas' area of operation. Second, guerrilla warfare presents governments with important military challenges. For example, guerrillas' ability to quickly submerge themselves among the population makes their detection by government forces highly unlikely. Thus, after starting operations in remote areas where government control tends to be at best tenuous, guerrillas are able to expand their areas of operation relatively quickly. Many guerrillas go as far as proclaiming "liberated zones" in areas where the central government loses effective political and administrative control as a result of guerrilla activity. Eventually, through a slow process of attrition, guerrilla warfare forces the concentration of government forces in larger cities while the insurgents are left to dominate increasingly larger portions of the countryside. Third, guerrilla warfare often succeeds because it is able to bring formal economic activity to a halt, especially in the countryside. The guerrillas' favorite soft targets include bridges, railway tracks, ports, airports, electricity and telephone lines, schools, hospitals, small-scale manufacturing enterprises, farms, etc. By constantly and relentlessly attacking such facilities, insurgents force the government to continuously spend limited financial resources to repair such infrastructure. Over long periods of time, this imposes unbearable costs upon a central government that must also spend considerable financial resources on the war effort. This is especially debilitating in situations like that of Angola after independence where the state was already highly unstable due to internal and external pressures.

For much of the 1980s, UNITA successfully used guerrilla warfare to further weaken the government at the political, military, and economic levels. The end of the Cold War, however, eliminated key conditions for a successful insurgency in Angola. One of these was that UNITA could no longer place its insurgency within a larger international ideological context – a critical element for sustaining external backing. Moreover, at the domestic level, the insurgency had also lost much of its support because the rebels abruptly reneged on the very key issues they were purportedly fighting for – democratic elections and the end of MPLA's monopoly on political power. To succeed in such altered conditions, therefore, renewed insurgency required an even greater Clausewitzian content in the sense that the population had to be convinced that a higher political goal existed to justify the suffering exacted by military actions. Problematically for UNITA, however, its insurgency had long abandoned the strategy of creating an intimate and reciprocal relationship between the political and military aspects of the war. In other words, the insurgents did not fight at the military level to achieve clearly discernible political objectives; war was not regarded as part of a broader contest for political support involving, first and foremost, winning "the hearts and minds" of the people. In fact, for UNITA in the 1990s, people came to be regarded as burdens, if not obstacles, whose elimination by military means was often justified. For example, by removing people from, say, diamond producing areas, rebels could enrich themselves without the political and administrative costs of governance.

After resuming the war, UNITA demonstrated neither the ability nor the inclination to bring new, more effective and inclusive forms of governance to Angola. More significantly, it was unable to articulate a coherent set of political objectives for the renewed fighting. Indeed, the insurgency had, more than ever before, acquired a uniquely criminal character. After returning to war, UNITA held fast to its strategy of rendering the country ungovernable to induce a regime implosion that would ultimately enable the rebels to achieve power amidst the anticipated chaotic state collapse. Thus, the rebels increased pressure on infrastructure targets, such as water and electricity, while continuing to attack small towns and villages throughout the country, resulting in countless civilian casualties and the displacement of 1.3 million people or ten per cent of the population. UNITA also stepped up terror actions against the population including the use of torture, summary executions, indiscriminate killing of civilians in operational areas, forced displacement, and continuous mine-laying. Peculiarly, for the first time since the civil war began in 1975, UNITA reversed its long-held practice of forcing people into its "liberated" areas. Instead, it pursued a policy of forcibly pushing civilian populations into government-held cities and towns to overwhelm already strained state infrastructures and thus demonstrate governmental incapacity to provide IDPs with the basic means to survive – i.e. food, shelter, clothing, water, and medical assistance – while also emphasizing the state's inability to provide security to its citizens because those relatively safe areas could then be bombarded incessantly and indiscriminately (Campbell 2000:151–53). UNITA, it appeared, could use conventional war to bring the government to its knees. However, as discussed below, the combination of popular alienation and the choice to pursue a conventional strategy ultimately led to UNITA's demise.

Expediting disaster: UNITA's conventional option

After losing and rejecting the results of the first multi-party national elections of September 1992, UNITA used conventional military tactics to overrun most government positions around the country and seriously threatened the capital city, Luanda. It would take the Angolan government about two years to beat back the rebels' pressure. By November 1994, Angolan government forces had captured Huambo, UNITA's main stronghold only days before the two sides were due to sign the Lusaka Peace Protocol to end the post-electoral round of fighting. Ominously, UNITA leader Jonas Savimbi did not personally endorse this accord. He retreated to Bailundo and Andulo to set up his new headquarters. Gaining control of these two strongholds now became a top political and military priority for the government for two main reasons. First, the government's post-electoral legitimacy rested heavily on its ability to fully implement the Lusaka Protocol which provided the government with both a mandate and a timetable to reestablish state authority in all areas still under rebel control. Second,

UNITA's headquarters were highly symbolic – Bailundo was regarded as the cradle of Ovimbundu nationalism while Andulo was Savimbi's hometown. But these towns were also significant from a military standpoint in the sense that they were the main nerve centres for UNITA's then impressive military machine. Andulo, for example, was the main operational centre supporting UNITA forces fighting on various fronts throughout the country. Equally important, their geographic position in the centre of the country was of particular concern for the government inasmuch as, from there, UNITA could continue to spread its operations around the country. By retaking Bailundo and Andulo, the government could force UNITA military forces to disperse into various unconnected regions thus making communication, coordination, and control as well as logistical support extremely difficult for the rebels. In other words, without its central headquarters, UNITA could not retain a conventional military posture. Conversely, from the rebels' point of view, this meant that Bailundo and Andulo had to be defended at all costs.

Initially, guided by the provisions of the Lusaka Protocol, the government embarked on an attempt to regain control over these two areas through negotiations. However, after four years of failed efforts, the government changed course. On the eve of its fourth Congress, the governing MPLA blamed UNITA's "warmongering wing" for obstructing the fulfillment of the Lusaka Protocol by refusing to demilitarize and thus preventing the government from reinstating administration in all areas of Angola. Therefore, it decided to discontinue talks with the rebels while condemning their leader as a "war criminal". The government promptly directed the armed forces to retake the two UNITA strongholds. At the time, however, UNITA was strong enough to withstand this offensive. In fact, buoyed up by new military equipment recently acquired with the proceeds of diamond sales, the rebels responded with military offensives of their own. After successfully stopping FAA's March 1999 offensive, UNITA escalated its military operations and brought them, as in 1992, closer to the capital city. Thus, on 20 July 1999 UNITA rebels mounted a daring and surprise attack on the town of Catete, just 60 km from Luanda. The rebels' movement towards Luanda had begun in Zenza do Itombe, Maria Teresa and Calomboloca. Catete represented a clear warning to the government that Luanda itself could be the next target.

UNITA's military and political calculations, however, reflected its continuing inability to carefully assess the realities on the ground or, worse, willingness to believe its own propaganda. This would, again, lead to major tactical errors for the rebels. For example, UNITA's pressure on Luanda could not be sustained for any prolonged period for three important reasons. First, FAA had significant concentrations of military power in the capital. Second, the civilian population in Luanda was heavily armed as a result of the government's distribution of surplus army rifles to its sympathizers in the aftermath of the electoral fiasco of 1992. Third, and most importantly, while UNITA was putting pressure on Luanda, FAA was fortifying its positions in the central highlands, in preparation for its long-delayed *cacimbo* (cold season) offensive against Savimbi's headquarters in Andulo and Bailundo. Tactically, instead of preparing to attack Luanda, UNITA was in a much better position to deny government troops the ability to mount the inevitable *cacimbo* offensive without much harassment. Specifically, instead of mounting a futile offensive against Luanda, the rebels were in a much better position to continue the sieges of Huambo, Kuito, Malanje and Menongue – all government-controlled cities where FAA would have to concentrate its forces in the central highlands before attempting to strike out and evict Savimbi's troops from their bases in Andulo and Bailundo as well as the diamond mines around Nharea. What led UNITA into such a tactical blunder?

First, UNITA had lost most of its top military leaders to the government in the context of the demobilization and reintegration processes stipulated by the Bicesse peace accords and the Lusaka Protocol. In 1990, on the eve of the failed peace process, UNITA had a sixteen-member top military command[1](UNITA, 1990). Of these top rebel officers, only generals Sapalalo (Bock), Dembo, and Kamalata (Numa) remained with Savimbi. In other words, UNITA could only count on mostly second-tier military officers. Many of those who had commanded the bulk of UNITA troops were, ironically, now commanding the very government troops that would pursue Savimbi to the death. Second, UNITA demonstrated an uncanny inability to properly interpret conflicting messages from senior FAA officers and members of the Angolan government regarding their perceptions and interpretations of the rebel military threat. Some FAA officers expressed overt pessimism about the government's prospects for defeating

---

1. Jonas Savimbi, Arlindo Chenda Isaac Pena (Ben Ben), Andrade Chassungo Santos, Altino Bango Sapalalo (Bock), Renato Sianguenhe Sakato Campos Mateus, Augusto Domingos Lutoki Liahuka (Wiyo), Peregrino Isidro Wambu Chindondo, Jeronimo George Ngonga Ukuma, Demostenes Amos Chilingutila, Geraldo Sachipengo Nunda, Antonio Sebastiao Dembo, Abilio Jose Augusto Kamalata (Numa), Carlos Tiago Kandanda, Jeremias Kussia Chihundu, Carlos Veiga Morgado, and Daniel Zola Luzolo (Mbongo-Mpassi).

UNITA. For example, in June 1999, in a report to the Angolan parliament, the army chief of staff, Lieutenant-General Jose Ribeiro Neco, admitted that "UNITA has the upper hand and the Angolan army is largely on the defensive" (Daley, 1999; McGreal, 1999). Even the Angolan president was publicly seeking support from his regional allies to deal with UNITA. Regardless of whether or not such signals where intended to confuse the rebels, they all reinforced UNITA's misperceptions of its own military capacity. UNITA exhibited this exaggerated sense of confidence when it claimed to control 70 per cent of the country in the semi-circular zone adjoining the Democratic Republic of Congo, Zambia and Namibia while "the regime control[led] only 30 per cent of the territory, mainly the coastal band about 100–175 km wide" (BBC, 31 August 1999). From this dillusional position of strength, UNITA leader Jonas Savimbi threatened to enter Luanda. In a letter to the ruling MPLA, he stated that "this time, UNITA may reach Futungo (the presidential palace) before the Angolan armed forces reach Andulo" (BBC, August 31, 1999). But government forces were not as unprepared as Savimbi envisaged. In fact, they were openly preparing for a decisive offensive against UNITA. For example, then Deputy Minister of Defense Armado Cruz Neto confirmed that FAA was "preparing for a decisive offensive against UNITA" and repeated his government's intention "to wipe out" the rebels (Xinhua 13 July 1999). Other senior FAA officers maintained that the government was "very close to cancelling UNITA's military advantage, especially in the area of long-range artillery" (BBC summary, July 21, 1999) that had been primarily responsible for UNITA's ability to block FAA's previous military offensives aimed at reoccupying Andulo and Bailundo in March 1999.

Self-deceivingly, until the eve of of their defeat in Bailundo and Andulo, UNITA rebels demonstrated a total disregard for the conditions on the ground and chose to believe only those reports that presented them as the stronger force. Thus, the rebels did not appear to fully appreciate the previously mentioned political and military factors driving MPLA's strategy. Consequently, they seemed both surprised by and unprepared for the scale of FAA's much anticipated offensive that began on 14 September 1999. According to UNITA's account, government forces supported by a "massive numbers of tanks, self-propelled artillery pieces, and MiG and Su fighter bombers", attacked on four fronts:

> Northern Front, from Uige towards UNITA-administered towns. Malanje Front, a two-pronged offensive from Malanje and Caculama, and from Malanje and Mussende towards Andulo. Bie Front, a two-pronged offensive from

Kuito and Chipeta towards Catabola; and from Camacupa and Vouga towards Andulo. Huambo Front, a two-pronged offensive from Mbave, and from Vila Nova and Chiumbo towards Bailundo (BBC September 19, 1999).

The government formally announced the capture of Bailundo and Andulo on 20 October 1999. The following day, Angolan television showed pictures of then FAA chief of staff, General João de Matos, in Andulo. Despite UNITA's deployment of some of its most experienced troops back to Andulo from the siege of Malanje for a final stand on the outskirts of this key rebel headquarters, the government advance was so powerful that Andulo was evacuated without heavy fighting. In the disorderly evacuation, the rebels abandoned large quantities of war materiel including heavy artillery guns and vehicles. They also abandoned other valuable possessions including their leader's white Mercedes limousine. As he moved east into Moxico province toward his last dead-end, Savimbi would not need such luxurious means of transportation. Savimbi was now moving on foot, heading back to where his journey had begun more than three decades earlier, taking UNITA into one last grand act of self-destruction.

The loss of Bailundo and Andulo affected the insurgency in several important ways. It was a major political and psychological setback for UNITA. It proved its inability to hold on to two key symbolic bastions. From a military perspective, the loss of the two towns threw the insurgency into disarray because it robbed the rebels of important command, control, and communication systems. Beyond these two factors, however, the demise of UNITA's insurgency can be attributed to Savimbi's fateful decision to de-emphasize guerrilla warfare in favour of more conventional military tactics to engage the government. This decision was inspired by the rebels' control of important diamond revenues that could be used to purchase vast quantities of war resources. However, the rebels seriously misjudged the degree to which control of significant diamond revenues could be translated into military and political power. In the end, diamonds did not prove to be a guerrilla's best friend.

Accelerating defeat: The role of illicit diamond revenues

For much of the 1990s, until the last phase of the war – i.e. from their eviction from Andulo and Bailundo in 1999 – the bulk of UNITA's resources were drawn mainly from mining and selling diamonds. This illegal diamond trade provided the rebels with about US$ 400 million to US$

600 million dollars per year in income (Global Witness, 1998; Dietrich, 2000:275; Campbell, 2000:163–65). UNITA's wealth came at a time when the acquisition of military means to support guerrilla wars had become considerably less complicated. In the post-Cold War era, diamond smuggling from rebel controlled areas took place within a context of unprecedented worldwide proliferation of light weapons. While during the Cold War the United States and the former Soviet Union often supported their respective clients with massive quantities of weapons, such support – whether to governments or liberation movements – took place mostly through "official" channels. In the post-Cold War era, however, many states and weapons manufacturers were eager to empty their warehouses and arsenals of weapons that were no longer needed either due to the end of the East-West rivalry or simply because they had been made obsolete by technological innovation. Places like Angola became irresistible markets for arms traders.

The relatively easy availability of both diamonds and weapons created a particularly nightmarish situation in Angola. UNITA used its considerable diamond revenues to evolve from a guerrilla group into a conventional army, with near catastrophic consequences for the government. But the availability of such enormous amounts of money also engendered premature overconfidence within UNITA, leading the rebels into committing major military and political errors. Specifically, control of diamond revenues led to an illusion of military capacity. This illusion, in turn, caused serious strategic and tactical miscalculations. The bottom line is that UNITA used its newly acquired wealth to transform itself too rapidly from a guerrilla group into a conventional army. Ultimately, UNITA's option to use conventional tactics of warfare – including the deployment of large infantry units, mechanized units, and heavy artillery – to face government forces proved fatal for the rebels. They were simply not ready to confront Angolan government forces in successive conventional battles. After all, since coming to power in 1975, the government had molded its own former guerrilla army into a powerful fighting force with the help of Cuba and the former Soviet Union. Although UNITA had important advantages – a plentiful supply of seasoned and fanaticized troops and, since the early 1990s, access to important sources of revenue – the rebels grossly underestimated the government's military advantages, particularly in the in air but also in artillery and logistics.

At the political level, UNITA's control of important diamond mines induced the rebels into committing significant blunders as well, especially after signing the Bicesse Peace Accord. For example, as argued above,

UNITA failed to build on its post-independence insurgency to position itself as the natural political alternative to the governing MPLA. Specifically, UNITA did not offer a clear programme to satisfy national aspirations for change, particularly in terms of good governance and respect for the fundamental rights of the citizens. Instead, its misplaced overconfidence led UNITA to underestimated MPLA's strong desire to stay in power and the regime's willingness to employ all available means to achieve this objective. Conversely, UNITA's relationship with the population grew increasingly hostile, even vicious. For the rebels – no longer dependent on the population for food and other necessities because such essential goods could now be purchased abroad with diamonds and flown into rebel controlled areas – people became both dispensable and disposable. Consequently, from a strategic point of view, control of resources, not people, became the rebels' primary concern. Tactically, this was consistent with a movement away from guerrilla warfare toward more conventional forms of combat to secure control of territory, especially diamond-rich territory.

UNITA used its substantial diamond revenues to undertake a fundamental military reorganization away from its traditional posture as a guerrilla army into a more conventional disposition in preparation for delivering a last victorious blow against government forces and finally seizing power. To this end, the rebels engaged in a major military procurement programme. The Fowler Report (UNSC 2000), prepared in compliance with UNSC Resolution 1237(1999) presented a detailed account of UNITA's activities in acquiring arms and military equipment. It established, for example, that UNITA used several international arms brokers as well as connections in several African states – especially Burkina Faso and Togo – to facilitate delivery of large quantities of weapons imported from Eastern Europe including "mechanized vehicles such as tanks and armoured personnel carriers, mines and explosives, a variety of small arms and light weapons, and anti-aircraft weapons, and a variety of artillery pieces" (UNSC, 2000: paragraph 48). This evidence corroborated previous reports that, between 1994 and 1998, UNITA had purchased military hardware from Eastern Europe, particularly Ukraine and Bulgaria, including about 50 T-55 and T-62 tanks; a significant number of 155-mm G-5, B-2, D-2 and D-30 guns; medium- and long-range D-130 guns; BMP-1 and BMP-2 combat vehicles; ZU-23 anti-aircraft weapons; and BM-21 multiple rocket launchers (Gordon, 1999). In the end, however, as discussed above, UNITA's attempts to topple the government through conventional means backfired.

In sum, UNITA's own errors ultimately contributed to the Angolan government's victories both in the political arena and on the battlefield. The rebels, on the other hand, were left with only one viable option – another return to guerrilla warfare. However, given the rebels' violent track record, the rural populations were particularly loath to aid them, making it impossible the return to the classic Maoist framework. Defeat, in such circumstances, was just a matter of time. It happened within two years of the fall of Andulo and Bailundo.

Post-Savimbi UNITA: Headless toward oblivion?

Savimbi's death punctuated the rebels' defeat. Headless without their creator, UNITA quickly accepted the government's demand for surrender. A formal cease-fire agreement – the Luena Memorandum of Understanding – was signed on April 4, 2002. The key provisions of this document, negotiated as a addendum to the Lusaka Protocol, included the quartering in several camps around the country of an estimated 70,000 UNITA troops and more than 400,000 members of their families before selecting 5,000 former guerrillas for integration into the National Army and the Police Force. The turbulent civil war thus ended with the quietest whimper. With MPLA clearly the victor, UNITA was faced with yet another existential challenge. At the political level, the government's magnanimous embrace of UNITA as "peace partner" quickly came to a predictable end as MPLA reverted to pointing to the war – and implicitly the rebels – as the main cause for critical problems of post-conflict governance (or lack thereof) and reconstruction confronting the country. UNITA, then, faced its not entirely undeserved scapegoat role while simultaneously taking tentative steps in a long process of adapting to fundamentally new and difficult realities. These realities included, first, the sudden disappearance of its main source of admittedly destructive energy resulting from the elimination of its founding leader and the collapse of the rebels' once feared military structure. Second and of critical importance for its long-term relevance, if not survival, UNITA faced the reality of urgently needing a genuinely forward-looking political strategy to recast itself as a force for positive national renewal – and thus alter the opposite perceptions prevailing in the country – as the first step toward recapturing its position as the natural alternative to the governing MPLA.

The basic issue of post-Savimbi leadership became particularly delicate because the party had been depleted of its leaders: some had been killed, many left the party, a few joined the government, while others completely withdrew from politics. In 1990, UNITA's leadership presented the following structure and composition: the president,[2] a ten member secretariat of the central committee,[3] a fifteen member command of the armed forces, a twenty member administrative council,[4] and a fourteen member external mission[5] (UNITA 1990). By the end of the civil war, the rebels' leadership had been almost completely decimated or neutralized either via internal purges or by government action: Savimbi was dead; of the ten-member secretariat of the central committee, only Alberto Mario Vasco Miguel (Kanhali Vatuva) and Armindo Moises Kassessa remained actively involved in the party. Most of the former administrative council members were either dead or inactive. Most of the key military leaders who survived the war have integrated into the national army. In fact, only the external mission survived the purges relatively unscathed and was thus in a position to produce Savimbi's replacement in the person of Isaias Samakuva. The new UNITA leader now confronted the delicate issues pertaining to how the immediate aftermath of the civil war impacted upon his organization. Specifically, he had to focus immediately on ways to help former UNITA guerrillas make the transition into civilian life and the problematic post-conflict relationship with the governing party – now victorious and emboldened and with a tradition of defining "partnership" with other national political forces in terms of co-optation, if not incorporation.

2. Jonas Savimbi.

3. Miguel Nzau Puna, Pedro Ngueve Jonatao Chingunji (Tito), Alberto Mario Vaco Miguel (Kanhali Vatuva), Smart Gaston Mandembo Chata, Eugenio Antonio Ngolo (Manuvakola), Armindo Moises Kassessa, Odeth Ludovina Baca Joaquim Chilala, Noe Kapinala (Andulo), and Isalina Kawina.

4. Jeremias Kalandula Chitunda, Elias Salupeto Pena, Jorge Alicerces Valentim, Tony Fwaminy da Costa Fernandes, Fernando Wilson Fernandes dos Santos, Aurelio Joao (Kalhas), Almerindo Jaka Jamba, Samuel Martinho Epalanga, Ana Isabel Paulino Savimbi, Nicolau Chiuka Biangu, Junior Agostinho Benguela, Henrique Afonso Raimundo, Lourenco Pedro Makanga, Teodoro Eduardo Torres Kapinala, Serafina Costa Pereira da Gama Paulo (Bebe), Judite Bandua Dembo, Georgina Clara Sapalalo, Germana Melita Malaquias (Tita), Alda Juliana Sachiambo, and Aniceto Jose Manuel Hamukwaya.

5. Armindo Lucas Paulo (Gato), Adolosi Paulo Mango Alicerces, Domingos Jardo Muekalia, Isaias Henrique Ngola Samakuva, Joao Miguel Vahekeny, Alcides Sakala Simoes, Marcial Adriano Dachala, Ernesto J. Mulato, Jose Jaime Furtado Goncalves, Honorio Van-Dunem de Andrade, Marcos Samondo, Abel Epalanga Chivukuvuku, Anibal Jose Mateus Candeia, and John Marques Gabriel Kakumba.

But UNITA's long-term survival as a viable political force under Samakuva depends only partly on how it deals with current challenges. Equally important is how it deals with its recent past. How can UNITA overcome its treacherous and violent history? Specifically, how can it overcome the stigma of its past choices, i.e. the relationship with the colonial regime and, later, with apartheid South Africa? How can it come to terms with the killing of hundreds of thousands of innocent Angolans, most of them Ovimbundu, the very people UNITA claimed to represent? How can UNITA come to grips with the fundamental issues of reconciliation, both national and intra-party? In other words, to move UNITA forward, Samakuva must seriously look at its past. UNITA must, minimally, undergo a period of reflective soul searching to ascertain the fundamental causes that led it to invariably opt for the path of self-destruction. This necessarily includes dealing openly and transparently with ethical and moral questions including the degree to which collective responsibility can be assumed for the violence and devastation that UNITA directed against Angola after independence. This process may produce a cathartic outcome to avoid a slow relegation to the margins of Angolan politics. Ironically, the governing MPLA is likely to work toward avoiding UNITA's final demise at all costs. Indeed, the "partnership" serves MPLA's political purposes brilliantly in the sense that compared to the governing party UNITA will remain the greater of the two evils for the foreseeable future. Thus, the governing party will retain UNITA as perpetual – and ideally comatose – scapegoat to blame for its own serious failings. This will indefinitely postpone the coming to terms with a basic post-colonial fact in Angola: while UNITA is the undisputed culprit for the physical violence and destruction that assailed Angola for its first twenty seven years as an independent state, the governing MPLA is primarily responsible for the structural violence that has permeated society, especially since the death of President Agostinho Neto in 1979. Thus, while many deaths, human displacements – both internally into the relative safety of increasingly overcrowded urban areas and externally into equally overcrowded refugee camps – can be attributed to UNITA's indiscriminate violence against civilians, a significant number of deaths occurred due to the lack of basic needs in government-controlled areas, far away from the war zones. Corruption and mismanagement, not just the war effort, caused many of those deaths.

CHAPTER 5

The Problematic Post-Colonial State

Angola is a fabulously wealthy African country endowed with abundant reserves of oil, diamonds, and other precious minerals. Paradoxically, this country is also consistently regarded as a problematic state. For more than a quarter century of civil war, the country tottered precariously on the edge of collapse. This situation of prolonged instability provided ideal conditions for rapacious national elites to pillage the country's resources, seemingly oblivious to the suffering of most Angolans. This chapter deals with a salient aspect of Angola's civil war, i.e., the interplay between violence and kleptocracy in shaping Angola's post-colonial political economy, by focusing on corruption. It argues that grand corruption is at the very centre of the political and economic activity that facilitates the grotesque enrichment of the highest circles of government while relegating the vast majority of citizens to increasing misery.

During the course of the civil war, the governing MPLA – once guided by Marxist-Leninist principles that initially frowned upon private enrichment and capitalist accumulation and severely punished corrupt "economic saboteurs" – abandoned most of its revolutionary ideals. Instead, a thoroughly corrupt system emerged where high officials, their entourages and families and friends have effectively appropriated chunks of the state as their private fiefdoms. In the process this small elite has grown spectacularly rich by embezzling significant revenues originating from the exploration of oil and diamonds while the vast majority of the population was forced to live precariously as double victims of physical violence and structural violence perpetrated by the rebels and state elites respectively. The end of the civil war in Angola exposed the magnitude of the physical reconstruction challenges facing the country. Now, in addition to this colossal and long-term national project, an equally important institutional rebuilding effort must be undertaken to construct the foundation for a vibrant post-conflict society. Specifically, post-conflict Angola must confront structural violence that thrived during the civil war. Unchecked, this form of violence – especially when it manifests itself as corruption – will frustrate the post-conflict physical rebuilding effort while producing powerful corroding elements throughout society thus ensuring continuing instability.

Corruption can take many forms – ranging from "petty corruption" to "grand corruption". Petty corruption refers to the taking of bribes, embezzlement, or other illegal uses of public office by ordinary government employees while grand corruption involves the misuse of public power and/or resources at the highest levels of the government. Both types of corruption are endemic in Angola where, at all levels of government, public officials have misused their positions for personal enrichment. Indeed, there is a direct correlation between the various types of corruption because, for example, the weak material base of ordinary public officials – an important cause of petty corruption – is partly a by-product of misappropriation of public funds at the highest levels of government. This misappropriation has two important effects. First, since little is left to trickle down to ordinary public officials, the latter resort to corrupt practices to ensure their own and their families' survival. Second, corruption at the highest levels has a powerful demonstration effect in the sense that, over a relatively short time, such practice is generally accepted as normal conduct with the only difference being in the scale of the abuse. Thus, for example, while the head of state can accumulate a significant fortune in donations from multinational companies doing business in the country, an ordinary clerk can only accumulate a few hundred dollars to facilitate the acquisition of permits. Regardless of the scale, however, the various types of corruption lead to a general abandonment of bureaucratic ethics and loss of trust in the government's ability to manage public funds in the public's interest. More importantly, especially as far as grand corruption is concerned, the capturing of resources at the highest levels means that those same resources become unavailable to the population in general to be used for poverty alleviation or wider developmental goals.

The era of people-focused policies that marked the leadership of Agostinho Neto (1975–79) has become a distant memory as the state he brought into being degenerated into a kleptocracy where oil and most other sources of revenue are controlled by the head of state and his entourage of political, military, and business elites while the general welfare of most citizens is largely ignored. The national oil company, the central bank, and the presidential palace now represent an opaque financial "Bermuda Triangle" where hundreds of millions of dollars are captured to sustain the vast patron-client network that sustains the regime or, more grossly, used by top government and party officials for a variety of personal ends. For example,

President dos Santos is believed to hold a significant portion of his personal wealth invested in Brazil, making him the 20th richest person in that country (Munslow, 199:563). Other members of the governing elite have benefited as well, albeit on a smaller scale, all protected "behind the façade of laws and government institutions" (Reno, 2000:434).

This collective graft and corruption at the top as well as the patron-client linkages they sustain provide some important clues for understanding the governing MPLA's metamorphosis – from doctrinaire Marxism-Leninism to kleptocratic capitalism – as a key survival strategy during the civil war in the sense that it was this control of revenues and their distribution among those who maintained the decrepit state structures that ultimately ensured its survival. It was also this control over resources that enabled MPLA to eliminate or co-opt possible challengers: FNLA in the early 1980s and UNITA in the early 2000s. Now, however, with the civil war over, sustainable peace in Angola will require the loosening of this elite's stranglehold on power and wealth. Ironically, this would require reversing this party's movement away from its original people-centred ideals. Although a return to Marxism-Leninism is neither practical nor desirable, MPLA's earlier focus on distributive justice must be recaptured to facilitate the attainment of economic development, social harmony, and political stability. Specifically, sustainable peace requires not only the abandonment of coercion and co-optation as methods of political management but also forgoing corruption as a form of elite aggrandizement. It requires an open and inclusive political framework and transparent financial management.

Corruption: Conceptual issues

Corruption is the intentional and improper use of public office for personal gain. This includes the taking of bribes, kickbacks, commissions, gratuities, or any other illicit remuneration by a public official to increase his/her wealth and/or status. Peculiarly in Africa, corruption is not generally seen as an abnormality. It is "commonplace" (Chazan et al., 1999:188); it is "the way the system works in the typical African state" (Diamond, 1987:581). Hope and Chikulo suggest that "although the incidence of corruption varies among African countries, ranging from rare (Botswana) to widespread (Ghana) to systemic (Nigeria), the majority of the countries are in the range of widespread to systemic" (Hope and Chikulo, 2000:1). Corruption has been endemic in Africa at the highest levels of government since independence. Thus, for example, in Ghana, Sub-Saharan Africa's first independent state, President Kwame Nkrumah is alleged to have accumulated more than $10 million (Nye, 1967:420) before being deposed in a military coup in 1966. The levels of corruption have significantly increased in many African countries since the hopeful years of Africa's independence decade of the 1960s (Mbaku, 2000:120). Since then, several African states – with Nigeria, Democratic Republic of Congo, and Angola providing extreme examples of patrimonial states – have been ruled by kleptocratic regimes. While "the scale of political corruption in many African states is by now legendary, and increasingly well documented" (Diamond, 1987:579), the impacts on society at large, especially in the realms of politics and economics are overwhelmingly negative (Chazan et al., 1999; Ayittey, 2000; Coolidge and Rose-Ackerman, 2000). In many ways, Africa is proving the correlation between levels of corruption and poverty, i.e. the higher the level of corruption, the higher the level of underdevelopment.

Yet, there is no universal agreement on the deleterious effects of corruption. In fact, some analysts (Leys, 1965; Bayley,1966; Nye, 1967; Bardhan, 1997) challenge the assumption that corruption is "invariably bad". For example, some argue that "corruption serves in part at least a beneficial function in developing societies" (Bayley, 719). In fact, while seeking "to dispel any impression that corruption is a uniquely Afro-Asian-Latin American problem", Nye suggests that corruption "has probably been, on balance, a positive factor" in the political and economic development of the former Soviet Union, the United States and Britain (Nye, 1967:417–8). However, echoing Leys, Nye argues that corruption is more prevalent in less developed countries due to several factors that condition their underdevelopment. These factors include, "great inequality in distribution of wealth; political office as the primary means of gaining access to wealth; conflict between changing moral codes; the weakness of social and governmental enforcement mechanisms; and the absence of a strong sense of national community". He suggests that corruption can be beneficial to political development – defined as the growth in "the capacity of a society's governmental structures and processes to maintain their legitimacy over time" – by contributing to economic development, national integration, and governmental capacity (Nye, 1967:418–9). First, in terms of economic development, corruption may, for example, be useful for capital formation, especially where private capital is scarce and in the absence of governmental capacity to accumulate capital via taxation. But, as Nye quickly adds, "the real question is whether the accumulated capital is then put to uses which promote economic development or winds up in Swiss banks". Second, corruption can lead to national integration, especially elite integration, by helping to "overcome divisions in a ruling elite that might otherwise result in destructive conflict" (Nye, 1967:420). As Theobald (1994:493) points out, "strategically placed elites and sub-elites are incorporated into the regime by the ruling individual or faction, through the judicious distribution of jobs, contracts, loans, development grants, useful information and other opportunities for self-advancement". Third, corruption may mitigate less developed countries' inadequacies in coping with change due to their limited structural capacity and institutional weakness.

But any potential benefits must be weighed against the negative effects of corruption. First, it represents an implicit acceptance of the state's failure to achieve its ultimate goals of societal betterment through legal means. Second, it involves potentially massive waste of resources in terms of increased administrative costs, time devoted to developing and maintaining corruption relationships and, more importantly, the wider benefits forgone due to corruptive practices. Capital outflows – the cycling of public funds out of the national economy and into foreign bank accounts – represent significant development costs for less developed countries already reeling from severe developmental challenges. Corruption also acts as a disincentive on investment and, therefore, negatively affects growth (Bardhan, 1997:1327–30). It may also lead to serious social and political instability – including military coups and possibly national disintegration – by lowering respect for public authority structures that are captured by a privileged and hegemonic group. Thus captured, the state is seldom able to deal evenhandedly with wider societal concerns. In other words, the majority of the population is marginalized and must endure as sideline spectators as the hegemonic group engages in the restrictive politics of dividing the spoils of power and wealth. The consequence of this marginalization is profound and long-lasting because it heightens self-centredness in individuals who now see corruption as an optimal path for social, economic, and political advancement. Thus, the (ab)use of public resources for private ends is inimical to broader national goals. For Theobald, "whether these ends are directed to rewarding supporters, buying off opponents, or straightforward personal accumulation or rentseeking, the general consequences for policy making, investment, public authority, the poor, democracy and overall development are decidedly negative" (Theobald, 1999:493). In Africa, the nefarious political consequences of corruption are such that it often threatens the state with collapse (Zartman, 1995; Theobald, 1999). As Hope and Chikulo point out, "by violating the public trust and corroding social capital, corruption has far-reaching externalities including the slow erosion of political legitimacy" (Hope and Chikulo, 2000:3).

Several factors contribute to the prevalence of corruption in Africa: the ruling elites' ability to exercise full and unchallenged control of state power, the central role of the state in processes of accumulation of power and wealth, a propensity toward centralized economic decision-making, the abandonment of the rule of law and the ethic of administrative competence, pathetic leadership, and an enabling socio-cultural normative environment (Hope, 2000:18–22). In addition, the exploration of Angola's vast natural resources – especially oil and diamonds – provided the governing elites with ample opportunities to steal.

Angola's wealth and poverty

Oil, diamonds and the rentier state

Oil and diamonds have dominated Angola's political economy since independence. The importance of the oil, in particular, cannot be overestimated. It was the single major exception to economic decline that followed the end of colonialism in 1975. In fact, in stark contrast to what has happened in the rest of the economy, the oil industry has flourished. Aside from a brief shutdown after independence, it has continued to operate normally, mainly due to the close partnership between the Angolan government and its national oil company, SONANGOL, and several major foreign oil companies – including ChevronTexaco, TotalFinaElf, and ExxonMobil – that have been instrumental in the successive discoveries of major oil fields off the Angolan coast.

The development of these fields has required the infusion of great quantities of foreign investment. Partly as a result of the need to maintain such high levels of foreign investment in this sector, the post-colonial state adopted a very pragmatic oil policy. Specifically, the new regime not only left intact the lucrative relationship Portugal had developed with the multinational oil companies, it sought to expand cooperation with foreign companies through the establishment of joint ventures and production sharing agreements. Joint ventures allow SONANGOL and its foreign partners to share both investment costs and oil revenues. Production sharing agreements require foreign companies to bear the full cost of exploration and development and be compensated with a share of the oil produced. By undertaking this pragmatic strategy, the Angolan government sought to minimize the costs associated with exploration, production, and development of the oil fields while maximizing benefits accrued through interaction with the major foreign companies in this field. In the process, however, Angola was unable to avoid becoming a classic *rentier* state.

The nature of Angola's rentier state is best captured by how important the oil sector has been since independence. It expanded almost without interruption during the civil war, partly as a result of the government's pragmatic policies for this sector and, more specifically, the attractive terms offered to multinational oil companies operating in Angola. Soon after its creation in 1976, and after acquiring 51 per cent of the Angolan assets of Gulf Oil and Petrofina of Belgium, SONANGOL conducted seismic surveys and divided the territorial coast into fourteen offshore blocks. It then proceeded to sell exploration rights to foreign oil companies. Subsequently, an additional twenty blocks were allocated. Currently, these companies help Angola produce more than 1 million b/d, a level expected to reach 2 million b/d by 2008. These estimates are based on the fact that current oil exploration has taken place primarily in shallow waters.[1] Recent explorations in deep and ultra deep water have yielded colossal deposits that are expected to make Angola one of the most important non-OPEC producers in the world.

If the rentier nature of the Angolan state is best captured by the growth of the oil sector since independence, the fact that oil accounts for 46 per cent of Angola's GDP, 90 per cent of its total exports and more than 94 per cent of government revenues provides a glimpse of this sector's importance as the regime's critical support pillar. Besides having acted to prevent a total post-independence economic meltdown, it enabled the government to find the funds it needed to finance the purchase of war materiel during the civil war. What was not spent on the war and did not disappear in the regime's vast patron-client network was allocated to current consumption. Consequently, the effect of oil on GDP growth has generally been limited partly because this is an enclave sector – i.e., it is isolated from other sectors of the economy. But its impact on overall socio-economic development has been further constrained by the government's own policy choices. For example, the government has maintained high levels of expenditure notwithstanding the fluctuations in oil income. This resulted in large budget deficits and a mounting foreign debt. Moreover, oil revenues led to a policy of real exchange rate appreciation. Thus, from 1975 to 1991, Angola's currency

---

1. Angola has divided its oil concession areas into three bands: shallow water blocks (up to 500 meters), deep water blocks (500 to 1,500 meters), and ultra-deep blocks (1,500 to 2,500 meters).

– the Kwanza – was artificially set at 29.9 to the US dollar. This favoured imports while further hurting other sectors of the economy, especially agriculture. Serious inflationary pressures also resulted from the government's heavy reliance on oil windfalls and its propensity to maintain both public expenditure and domestic consumption at unrealistically high levels. Plentiful oil revenues led to undisciplined fiscal and monetary policies particularly as far as the growth in the money supply was concerned. As a result, galloping inflation further eroded the already precarious living standards of most Angolans. With the end of the civil war, the government has an opportunity to finally use oil revenues more wisely toward alleviating some of the major economic difficulties facing the country. Indeed, the government can now count on additional revenues from diamonds.

Commercial extraction of diamonds in Angola began in 1913. Four years later, DIAMANG (Companhia dos Diamantes de Angola) was set up to carry out the mining operations. It did so, with considerable foreign capital, until independence. Soon after independence the new government moved to nationalize all DIAMANG shares held by the Portuguese government, representing 38 per cent of the total shares. The Angolan government's control over DIAMANG increased in August 1977 when 30.85 per cent of the shares in the company held by small shareholders – mostly expatriates who had fled the country at the beginning of the civil war – were also nationalized. The government's controlling share in DIAMANG rose to 77.21 per cent in December 1979, following the nationalization of the stock belonging to the larger Portuguese corporations. In April 1979, the Angolan government had passed the "General Law on Geological and Mining Activities", laying out the conditions for mining activities in Angola. In another decree, passed in 1981, the government created the state national mining enterprise ENDIAMA, to which the 77.21 per cent majority shareholding was transferred. This state enterprise subsequently acquired "the sole non-transferable rights for the prospection, research, surveying, exploitation, treatment and marketing of diamonds over the whole of Angola" (Helmore, 1984:531).

The Angolan government initially attempted to develop the diamond industry using the same formula that proved to be so successful in the oil sector. Thus, it divided known diamond fields into various blocks to be exploited under production-sharing agreements. Although major international diamond companies were granted permits, the continuing civil war and the government's inability to wrestle control of the countryside from UNITA rebels hampered the development of the diamond sector. Yet, even during the civil war years, Angola annually accounted for 5 per cent–8 per cent of the world's diamond production and exports (Premoll, 1992:32). But not all diamonds came under government control. For example, in 1999 Angola produced about US$ 600 million in rough diamonds. However, a considerable portion of Angola's diamond industry was illegally controlled by UNITA rebels who often used violence to dislodge an estimated 150,000 informal sector mine operators (*garimpeiros*) who working individually or in small syndicates, braved dangerous military conditions to illegally mine diamonds and smuggle them into neighbouring countries. In addition, small groups of FAA soldiers regularly participated in informal mining operations on behalf of their superiors (Dietrich, 2000:178). In sum, Angola's diamonds helped to fuel the war by providing the rebels with the means to prolong the conflict. They also provided members of the ruling elite with additional opportunities for illicit enrichment while much of the population remained mired in abject poverty. As Coolidge and Rose-Ackerman (2000:83) suggest, pervasive rent-seeking at the top of resource-rich countries' governing structures hinders, rather than encourages, growth. Angola is a case in point. Control of the state and a protracted civil war provided MPLA elites with enormous opportunities for self-enrichment while pauperizing the population.

Enduring poverty

The World Bank (2001:15) defines poverty as "pronounced deprivation in well-being" and suggests that it is "the result of economic, political, and social processes that interact with each other and frequently reinforce each other in ways that exacerbate the deprivation in which poor people live" (World Bank 2001:1). Angola's social indicators capture the extent of its citizens' deprivations. Although peace has given Angola its first real post-colonial chance to create the conditions for people-centered development, four years after the end of the civil war most Angolans are still desperately poor and their prospects for escaping poverty condition remain slim. Potentially one of the richest countries in Africa given its considerable resources and relatively small population, Angola has one of the weakest social indicators on the continent, placed near the bottom of the United Nation's Human Development Index – 160th out of 177 countries. Poverty affects 68 per cent of the population, half of whom survive on less than US$ 1/day, 50 per cent of the population live without sustainable access to an improved water source, 70 per cent of the population live without sustainable access to improved sanitation, the infant mortality rate is 154/1,000 live births, the under-five mortality rate is 260/1,000 live births. Life expectancy, unsurprisingly, is 40.8 years (UNDP). This picture, in and of itself, constitutes an indictment of Angola's governing elite. But the real measure of relative suffering it represents requires juxtaposing it with another set of images provided by the luxurious lifestyle of the ruling class. The coexistence of extreme displays of wealth and poverty and the growing gap between those with access to wealth and those who must endure deprivations and vulnerabilities while witnessing the illicit enrichment of the small ruling elite has become the defining feature of contemporary Angolan society. The rich own big mansions with water pumps and diesel generators, spend lavishly at trendy shops and restaurants, and have access to private schools and hospitals. MPLA's early revolutionary zeal has been forever lost and has been replaced by an equally zealous embrace of the immense wealth generated by oil revenues. What factors led the regime to abandon its pro-people approach to post-colonial development?

From revolutionary to rickety state: What went wrong?

Political dimensions

The major factors conspiring against the viability of the Angolan state were glaringly visible at the time of independence. Given the highly fractured nature of the anti-colonial movement – and the consequent inability to take advantage of the momentous changes brought about by the collapse of the colonial regime to unify the liberation groups – the unresolved problems that marred the liberation struggle were brought unchecked into the realm of post-colonial politics with calamitous consequences. As discussed above, the three liberation groups by-passed most avenues of peaceful conflict resolution and each attempted to usurp the political power left up for grabs by the precipitous disintegration of the Portuguese colonial empire. At independence Angola had essentially three governments: MPLA backed by Cuban troops controlled Luanda, the capital, and little else; UNITA controlled Huambo, the second largest city and several southern provinces with South African help; while FNLA, supported by Zairian troops, was holding on to the northern provinces. The divisions fed during the anti-colonial war had come home to roost. In the early stages of this internationalized civil war MPLA and its foreign allies prevailed over its internal enemies and their foreign allies. However, independence in 1975 and the defeat of UNITA/SADF and FNLA/Zairian armies in 1976 constituted but a short pause in the civil war. It would continue with greater intensity, albeit now in the form of a protracted guerrilla war that would undergo several mutations before it finally ended 27 years later.

Although the importance of these unresolved contradictions in explaining the length of the civil war cannot be minimized, there were several other factors that complicated MPLA's initial "victory" and made the establishment of a fully functioning and inclusive state highly problematic. These initial difficulties were visible soon after the euphoria of independence subsided. As the political and military dust from the struggle for independence settled, a significant gulf between the new regime and society became apparent. This schism was the result of various domestic conflicts related to class, race, ethnicity, and overall inability to fully cope with the administrative challenges of post-colonial governance that resulted, to no small extent, from the precipitous departure of the settler population that had formerly controlled the economy and dominated colonial society. This destabilizing exodus notwithstanding, MPLA's major post-colonial challenges were primarily political. In a classic example of "statist" approaches to African development in the 1970s, the post-colonial policies implemented by the new regime were invariably injudicious in the sense that they emphasized an exclusivist vision of politics where the victorious political party attempted to represent the diverse aspirations of a highly fragmented society – both horizontally, in terms of ethnicity, region, class, race as well as vertically within the various ethnic groups, regions, classes, races, etc. The choice of an exclusivist model of politics – partly a reflection of MPLA's own ideological foundation – contributed significantly to Angola's post-colonial predicament because it induced the governing party into assuming the sole responsibility for building a new state. Granted, in a situation of civil war, MPLA had very limited options other than to rely on those segments of the population that responded to MPLA's commitment to "People's Power", i.e. to provide hope for those who had been disenfranchised by the colonial rulers while securing popular support for the installation of a new order.

The idea of "People's Power" combined Soviet rhetoric, neo-Marxist theories of development and underdevelopment, and revolutionary experiences of other third world countries. It was seen as a way of preventing FNLA and UNITA – which MPLA regarded as "agents of Imperialism" – from implanting in Angola the neo-colonialism and dependency that characterized the relationships between many African countries and the West. More theoretically, by devolving power to the people, MPLA hoped to carry out a fundamental and revolutionary transformation instead of simply replacing the colonial elites with indigenous elites without significant changes in the socio-economic order. In reality, however, this new framework for building a post-colonial state did not produce the results envisioned. The repressive colonial order was not replaced by people-centred institutions and governance. Instead – as elsewhere in one-party Africa – the new order became characterized by excessive centralization of power, elite privilege and extravagance, kleptocracy, repression, and widespread economic collapse outside the oil and diamond sectors.

This emphasis on post-colonial politics does not seek to downplay the impact of colonialism in Angola. But although the colonial legacy can be cited as a plausible justification for the missteps involved in building a new state, such argument has important shortcomings. First and foremost, the early blunders resulted from a series of fundamental misconceptions, including the false impression that the many and complex political problems the post-colonial state inherited from the long colonial overlay – particularly the critical questions relating to how individuals with multiple identities and groups with unfulfilled political aspirations ought to relate to the new state – could be solved by instituting a one-party regime. Second, a further misconception rested on the belief that new institutions, upon which the post-colonial state would be erected, could be swiftly knocked together. The handful of committed revolutionaries that undertook to create the new state soon realized that theirs was an extraordinarily complex task, particularly since those skilled Angolans who did not belong to the governing party were excluded from any relevant participation in the erection of this embryonic state. Thus, the government became overstretched – unable to fulfill the expectations of a populace emerging from colonial oppression – and, therefore vulnerable to accusations of incompetence. Even worse politically, this systematic exclusion of non-MPLA members from important position within the new state – even if only in symbolic roles – made the governing party appear illegitimate to a significant portion of the population, especially those individuals who supported the two defeated liberation movements. In other words, unwittingly, MPLA's policies after independence created the important disconnection between state and society that endures until today.

This disconnection became apparent shortly after independence. Widespread mismanagement led to acute economic problems including severe food shortages, forcing the government to use rationing cards and causing many citizens of the new post-colonial state to look fondly to a recent past when, in spite of the colonial oppression, food was more easily available to them. What further widened the gap between state and society, even in the early years after colonialism, was people's realization that post-colonial hardships were being borne differently by the various segments of society. Specifically, while the general population suffered the consequences of government ineptitude and mismanagement, the governing elite began to exhibit signs of corruption and to operate in ways similar to the settler elite it had replaced in terms of its exclusivist exercise of political power and control over the state's financial resources for their own aggrandizement, not national development. Predictably, many Angolans also deeply resented the fact that, even after independence, European descendants could still live comfortably – now as members of the ruling elite – while the majority of the population suffered the consequences of the regime's reckless economic policies. This dissatisfaction caused major dissension even within the ruling party and was an important factor in the bloody coup attempt led by Nito Alves, the powerful and popular Interior Minister, on 27 May 1977. Although the coup was crushed with the help of Cuban troops it marked the end of the initial revolutionary euphoria that drove MPLA's attempts to deconstruct the colonial system and create a new revolutionary state in its place. Significantly, in the aftermath of the coup, MPLA became a more exclusive, secretive and less accountable organization. The hunt for the coup organizers provided an ideal opportunity for the governing post-colonial elite to rid itself of those MPLA members who – whether sympathetic to the coup plotters or not – defended a people-centred approach to post-colonial politics. Thus, besides the coup leaders, tens of thousands of mostly MPLA sympathizers – some of the few educated Angolans who remained in the country at the time – were killed. Additional steps taken by MPLA to regain its political balance further accentuated the cleavage between state and society. For example, the governing party underwent a "rectification campaign" which ensured that only chosen militants, not just sympathizers, could qualify for positions of relevance within the state apparatus. In effect, a few hundred individuals literally controlled the state with only themselves to ensure their own accountability. This, of course, did not happen. On the contrary, corruption as a way of political life set in as those chosen few governing party members quickly evolved into powerful patrons in an extensive patronage system greased with vast sums of oil money.

Oil-induced corruption within the MPLA regime deepened after the death of Agostinho Neto in 1979 and the coming to power of José Eduardo dos Santos. No longer restrained by Neto's authority and prestige and without effective institutional mechanisms above the party to ensure the accountability of its leaders, the new elite began to brazenly use state resources – especially oil money – for their personal enrichment. Not incidentally, this post-Neto period coincides with the development of Angola's "Bermuda Triangle" into which considerable revenues vanish to be used as a key tool in the patronage system that is largely responsible for maintaining dos Santos in power. As Le Billon explains, control over oil revenues allows the Angolan presidency:

> ... to sustain a clientele beyond the military apparatus, building a degree of legitimacy among those rewarded and allowing support or resistance to reforms, according to short-term expediency (Le Billion, 2001:64).

Some international attention has recently been directed to this issue. For example, the World Bank (http://www.worldbank.com/ao/reports/2003_Angola_tss.pdf, p.6) has recently reported that "severe weaknesses in Angola's fiduciary framework have led to the occurrence of very large unexplained discrepancies in the country's fiscal accounts, varying from 2 to 23 per cent of GDP between 1997 and 2002". The report states that, for example, in 2001 the total estimated unexplained discrepancies – the difference between recorded inflows and recorded outflows – was more than $900 million, about 10 per cent of the country's GDP. As mentioned above, this situation has prevailed in Angola for at least the last two decades and has been sustained mainly for the benefit of the governing elite, especially the small clique comprising the president's family members, close political and business associates as well as former officers in the military and security structures.

Corruption has become such a way of life for the elite that some of its more powerful members no longer make an effort to conceal or deny its existence. Indeed, the small ruling class is increasingly willing to display its luxurious life-style amidst widespread misery. As a result, most citizens – destitute and helpless – now regard the elite's grip on the state as a nightmarish throwback to colonial times when power, prestige, and privilege were closely associated with class and race. Unfortunately, this particularly vicious type of predatory post-colonial state is likely to endure. As Diamond (1987:582) argues, "political corruption is essential to the survival of this clientelistic system, not only because of the huge and increasing scale of patronage resources required to maintain lengthening and proliferating lines of clientage, but also because clientelism can only function if office-holders are free to allocate political resources and goods to their clients irrespective of rules that demand distribution by impersonal, bureaucratic criteria". In Angola, the governing elites were particularly efficient in allocating these political resources and goods among themselves. Thus, for example, they have a near monopoly on state contracts, acquired most recently privatized state assets, and have sought to control most channels to the international economy. This unabashed control of state resources for private gain has infused the upper strata of society with a markedly decadent character: high levels of luxury consumption (largely produced and purchased abroad), favouritism, nepotism, and an arrogant disdain for the plight of the many. Once an important regime survival strategy, elite corruption has become a way of life.

In sum, the current problematic state of Angola's body politic is partly a result of the growing disconnection between the state – controlled since independence by a political party which, in turn, is controlled by an exclusivist and rapacious elite – and a society severely weakened by the colonial experience and devastated by a long civil war. The early post-independence hopes that MPLA would make good on its promises to govern as a "movement of the masses" gradually succumbed to the realities of corrupt elite governance where members of the new ruling class uses its superior education, political skills, and economic power to take control of the governing party and other sources of state power. Instead of building on the connections with workers and peasants initiated during the anti-colonial struggle, the new ruling class grew increasingly detached from the common citizen and – not unlike the settler elite it replaced – used the repressive means of the state to preserve its privileged political status and enhance its control over growing oil revenues while society's main demands were left largely unattended. Angolan society – emerging from a bruising encounter with colonialism whose last years involved repression and war – was unprepared to find peaceful and constructive alternatives to post-colonial violence. As a result, a widespread sense of powerlessness set in as the average citizen's life became consumed with the essential tasks of survival – i.e., the search for personal security and other basic needs. Since, given its capture by the new elite, the state acquired traits of violence – both physical, as administered through its security apparatus, and structural due to growing corruption and unaccountability – most segments of society were inclined to disengage from political activities thus further widening the gap between state and society.

Economic dimensions

As discussed above, many of the unique distortions characterizing the Angolan economy and society today can be attributed to the length and nature of the Portuguese colonial presence as well as to Portugal's own position as a peripheral player in the global political economy. In particular, the reliance on forced labour and foreign capital for Angola's colonial "development" had lasting negative consequences. The main consequence for Angola, beyond the variety of social traumas caused by the reliance on forced labour for much of the colonial overlay, was that much of its productive labour was relegated to activities that created few, if any, opportunities for accumulation of capital by the local, non-settler populations. Portuguese settlers were the key intermediaries of foreign capital and owned the plantations and, later, factories while colonial labour laws ensured a reliable supply of low-cost labour. Unsurprisingly, therefore, at the time of independence, Angolans owned little capital. Equally deplorable, as a society, newly independent Angola lacked a critical mass of individuals with the skills necessary for capital accumulation at the level to sustain a viable economy. Furthermore, since colonial Angola was little more than a rich source of imperial wealth, Portugal did not undertake to create an indigenous institutional framework for managing a modern economy. Thus, at independence, Angola lacked the expertise and the institutional framework to erect a viable economy with the capacity to meet its citizens' aspirations for material well-being. In addition to these factors, however, post-colonial policies contributed significantly to the rickety nature of the new state.

Post-colonial policies

After winning a power struggle against its rivals, MPLA undertook to build a post-colonial "socialist" Angola. A new constitution was drafted, subordinating state organs to the ruling party. Thus, the basic decisions concerning the organization of the economic system – from economic strategy to the choice of instruments for its implementation – were made by the governing party. It was the party, therefore, that adopted centralized planning, large-scale nationalization of productive enterprises, and strict state control of economic activities as key policy measures designed to help Angola establish a socialist economic system.

A National Planning Commission was established soon after independence as an organ of the Council of Ministers to "coordinate planning at all levels and directing activities in almost all sectors of the economy" (World

Bank, 1991:8). By 1978, state monopolies had been established in foreign trade, banking, and insurance. Furthermore, the widespread nationalization of enterprises after independence provided the state with a virtual monopoly in most other productive sectors of the economy, including coffee and diamond mining.

At its First Party Congress in 1977 MPLA reviewed the country's economic performance since independence and concluded that the drive towards building a socialist economy should be accelerated through improvements in centralized planning and supervision of the economy, continuing nationalizations and confiscations, and the establishment of rural cooperatives (MPLA 1977). In 1980, three years after Neto's death, MPLA held an extraordinary Congress. Besides confirming the position of José Eduardo dos Santos as its new leader, this Congress also attempted to come to grips with the immense difficulties of undertaking a fundamental restructuring of the economy away from its colonial character and hinted at some of the critical problems ahead. Thus, while announcing that progress had been made on the road to creating structures for building a socialist society, it also recognized that faster progress had been hampered by delays in drawing up the all-important national plan. Without the plan, the MPLA Congress concluded, the state could not re-establish links between industry and agriculture and thus reduce rural-urban migration. Furthermore, MPLA admitted that it had not yet instituted a "rational system of production" and the economy was beginning to suffer serious inflationary pressures since the total amount of wages paid to workers far outstripped the total volume of production. Also worrisome for MPLA, agricultural units under state control only produced 12 per cent of the total food needs of the population and 15 per cent of the raw material requirements for industry (MPLA 1980).

The Second MPLA Party Congress in December of 1985 reaffirmed Angola's choice of socialist development and adopted the national plan as the main instrument of economic management. It recognized, however, that the economic results achieved in the first ten years of independence had not been entirely satisfactory. The Congress indicated that important changes were needed in economic policy and called for an improvement in the methods of socialist planning. All institutions created in the post-colonial period would thenceforth be designed to comply with three principles: unified management, centralism, and planning. Through "unified management" the governing party attempted to safeguard its role in directing all facets of the country's economic life – from central to local levels. This was further reinforced by the principle of centralism ensuring that all decisions made at the top party and government levels would be implemented by lower units. Third, through planning, MPLA attempted to harmonize the economic system by defining national priorities and ensuring inter-sectoral as well as inter-regional cooperation while identifying the most efficient uses of scarce factors of production.

The bureaucratic-administrative structures created on the basis of these principles confronted severe problems including high levels of inefficiency and a culture of dependency. Given the omnipresence of the party, all authority was subordinated to its political power. Consequently, little or nothing was decided at the lower levels without proper consultation and approval from the overseeing party and government departments resulting in very slow decision-making and implementation of policies at all levels. Moreover, the new Angolan state, not unlike its colonial predecessor, was being erected on a mound of regulations and government interventions in the main areas of economic policy including price controls, licensing, investments, banking, and so on. The resulting bureaucratic structure of economic management was, at best, rigid, complex, and distorted. Thus, despite a vibrant oil sector, Angola's economy remained comatose for much of the post-colonial era. Beginning in the mid-1980s, the Angolan government undertook major restorative efforts to nurse its economy back to health with mostly disappointing results.

Economic reforms

Given the nature of the colonial economy it inherited, independent Angola was expected to face serious economic challenges despite its significant natural resource endowment. In fact, the experience of other resource-rich countries in the South had demonstrated that in the absence of robust societal structures and effective government policies, abundance of natural resources could exacerbate the symptoms of colonial underdevelopment. In Angola, the post-colonial economic challenges were amplified by the long civil war. The war had two major impacts on the country. Beyond widespread destruction of both human lives and physical infrastructure, it facilitated the onset of a culture of corruption and unaccountability. The governing MPLA adeptly portrayed the threat against its regime as a threat against the state itself. Consequently, it was able to successfully stave off criticisms of its governance failures by shielding itself behind the cloak of national security. Concealed behind this veil for more than a quarter century, the regime remained unaccountable for its failures in the post-independence attempts to provide alternatives to the colonial political economy. The war became the ultimate exculpator. Even more astutely, as the ruling regime came to terms with its own failures, the war became a source of both political capital and enormous financial rewards. Now the regime could justify its existence primarily as the defender of the citizens against murderous UNITA rebels. While UNITA's actions against defenceless civilians consistently provided the regime with ammunition to credibly justify high military expenditures financed by increasing oil revenues, those same expenditures provided vast opportunities for diverting public funds into the bank accounts of high level political and military figures of the regime.

The civil war also enabled the regime to carry out major shifts in economic policy without fear of political consequences. By the mid-1980s, the economy was on the verge of collapse. Economic activities in all sectors outside the oil enclave suffered dramatic declines due to a combination of factors including the mass flight of skilled Portuguese workers, the difficulties arising from the introduction of central planning, and the rising intensity of the civil war. The economic pain was felt mostly in the form of hyperinflation and through rationing of essential goods. In addition, the government had to contend with severe balance of payment deficits caused by collapsing exports, a result of both declining economic activity and the arbitrary setting of foreign exchange rates at artificially high levels.

If precarious domestic conditions pointed to the necessity of rapid reform, a changing global environment facilitated the probing of possibilities for such reforms. Ironically, Angola's main patron, the former USSR, was also confronted in the mid-1980s with difficult choices regarding ways to rescue a collapsing economy. In many respects, therefore, Gorbachev's rise to power in the former Soviet Union in 1985 and the belated attempt to rescue a moribund Soviet economy, provided the necessary inspiration, if not ideological justification, for the MPLA's own attempts to restructure Angola's economy. But there was another unavoidable reality. A sharp drop in oil prices in 1987 severely shook the fiscal foundation of a government almost totally dependent on oil revenues. That drop in oil prices, combined with a rise of war related expenditures, forced the Angolan government into a period of deficit spending for more than a decade. Given the quickly deteriorating military and economic conditions in the 1980s, the regime was faced with two options for initiating the unavoidable transformation process. The first option was mainly political and involved ending the war through a peace process involving constitutional changes leading to free multi-party elections. The second choice involved liberalizing the economy. Either choice, whatever the priority, would go a long way to strengthening the regime.

The first option was not particularly appealing to the ruling class because it might take the form of a national constitutional assembly, as in other parts of Africa, with the authority to restrict or take away some powers of the regime. Furthermore, if the government allowed itself to become one of various participants in the peace process, its power and legitimacy would be diluted by the structures emanating from civil society to oversee the transition to peace and democratic government. This would prevent the government from taking full credit for the anticipated peaceful settlement of the civil war and reaping the political benefits in a future multi-party election. Second, popular dissatisfaction with the regime was attributable mainly to the economic system's inability to produce goods and services in sufficient quantities and adequate quality to meet domestic demand. As a result, Angola opted to implement structural adjustment programmes ahead of political liberalization.

To counter immediate economic difficulties and with an eye to beginning to address the wider structural dysfunctions in the economy in anticipation of admission into the IMF and the World Bank, in 1987 the MPLA government introduced its first IFI-inspired, if not yet prescribed, structural adjustment programme. The *Programme for Financial and Economic Reorganization* (Programa de Saneamento Económico e Financeiro – SEF) was designed to transform Angola into a market economy. This overly ambitious goal could not realistically be met both due to the non-existence of the critical institutional and legal environments that would make such transition possible and the escalation of the civil war that made such radical transformations even riskier politically for president dos Santos. In the end, other than convincing the IFIs of its commitment to change – and thus winning membership of these institutions – SEF was an unmitigated failure.

After SEF's demise, Angola implemented a series of other adjustment programmes, all ambitiously designed and poorly implemented. Not surprisingly, much like the original programme, most attempts to reform Angola's economy failed. In 1990, a year after joining the IFIs, Angola introduced the *Programme of Action for the Government* (Programa de Acção do Governo – PAG) aimed mainly at controlling inflation through strict monetary policy and a currency change. But, given the political context

– imminent peace with UNITA and the prospects of the first multi-party elections in the near future – the government was unwilling to take the short-term political risks inherent in fully implementing a programme that included freezing 95 per cent of the value of all bank accounts! Consequently, PAG was abandoned in 1991. In the decade between the Bicesse peace process of 1991 and the end of the civil war in 2002, the government implemented several other adjustment programmes: *Programme for Economic Stability* (Programa de Estabilização Económica – PEG) of 1993; *Economic and Social Programme* (Programa Económico e Social – PES) of 1994 and 1995; *Programme "New Life"* (Programa Vida Nova – PNV) of 1996; and *Programme for Medium-Term Economic Stability and Revival* (Programa de Estabilização e Recuperação Económica de Médio Prazo – PEREMP) of 1998. The common feature of all these programmes is that they all ended without success.

Aimed at arresting and, more optimistically, reversing, the decay of its ailing economy through a series of liberalizing mechanisms, SAPs proved highly problematic in Angola, as elsewhere in Africa. Specifically, measures to liberalize the economy through privatization, currency and exchange rate reform produced mixed results and succeeded mainly in entrenching the elite's stranglehold on the economy. This was particularly the case with the policy of privatizing public assets. The MPLA regime skilfully used privatization as a means of transferring the ownership of public enterprises into the hands of top officials as well as their families and friends in the party, government, and the military. Thus, privatization primarily benefited those already close to the centre of a complex patrimonial set of relationships lubricated by oil revenues. Using oil revenues, these individuals could then "buy" newly privatized assets. This was the main "success" of SAPs in Angola. In most other respects, attempts to undertake a transition from a planned to a market economy through SAP-inspired policies have thus far resulted in failure. For example, under PAG, the government introduced measures aimed at price liberalization, currency reform, and exchange rate reform. However, as Aguilar (2003:4) notes, "failure to rein in the fiscal deficit and its monetization meant that hyperinflation quickly eroded much of the gain in competitiveness resulting from the devaluation". Furthermore, liberalization was attempted within inhospitable administrative and legal environments – i.e., bureaucratic red tape and ownership rights legislation – that constituted important barriers to entry. For example, currency reform was haphazardly implemented and involved little more than hastily issuing new bank notes and freezing bank deposits. Many individuals whose deposits were frozen were unable to convert their old money.

What explains the problematic implementation of reforms in Angola? A basic explanation must take into account the difficulties inherent in making a transition from an underdeveloped economy wrecked by war – still exhibiting many vestiges of a colonial economy and the debilitating effects of central planning – into a functioning market economy. Second, major structural deficiencies have always been at the root of Angola's inability to properly design and implement workable reform packages. For example, although the Angolan government includes three key economic policy bodies – the Ministry of Planning, Ministry of Finance, and the Central Bank – they function within an environment characterized by their lack of decision-making power. A parallel government – comprising the president and a handful of trusted aides – makes all key policy decisions with negligible oversight from a weak legislative branch. Within a governance system where much political and economic power is concentrated in the hands of the President, decisions by this virtual parallel government trump all other decisions. But, problematically, since the presidential aides are not formally part of the governing structure, they are rarely held accountable for policy failures. In other words, government officials charged with implementing policies designed by others are also the scapegoats of choice when those policies invariably fail. However, since high government officials owe their lucrative positions to the President and his aides, most ministers are unwilling to raise issues that may provoke the ire of the President and his men. The result is an institutional culture that both abhors delegation of authority and, in turn, avoids responsibility for implementing policies. Together, these peculiarities of governance enhanced the civil war's destabilizing effects.

CHAPTER 6

War Termination as Survival Strategy

At the end of the 1980s Angola faced a crisis in different areas – military, political, social, and economic – that hampered the state's ability to carry out many of its basic functions. The civil war had paralyzed the state, rendering it inoperative inasmuch as its reach and authority outside the capital and a handful of major cities was tenuous, resulting in its incapacity to provide security – let alone law and order – to many of its citizens. Indeed, the state had not yet been able to implement its own system of laws throughout the country because it was being challenged by UNITA. This was all compounded by the fact that the initial authoritarian character of the post-colonial state led to the subduing of civil society, thus stifling citizens' ability to create, aggregate, and articulate demands that might have provided alternatives to the problems facing the new state.

These domestic problems were heightened by the dramatic changes at the international level in the late 1980s and early 1990s. Most important of all, the end of the Cold War and the disintegration of the Soviet Union had an immediate effect on Angola both in military/security and economic terms because the former Soviet Union was no longer there to provide military hardware and training to counter UNITA. Combined with a worsening domestic situation, the changing international environment led the governing MPLA to abandon both ideology and dogma to survive, this time with Western assistance. MPLA also understood that in light of the momentous global changes that had recently taken place, Western countries were more likely to support the regime if it undertook fundamental processes of political and economic liberalization. The simultaneous implementation of structural adjustment measures and the peace processes can be best understood in terms of the dual sources of pressures – internal and international – threatening the MPLA regime at the beginning of the 1990s and not necessarily as a reflection of its sudden realization of the virtues of sharing power and wealth. In fact, especially as far as the political dimension was concerned, there was little inter-elite good will to serve as the basis for a lasting settlement to the civil war. The governing party did not trust

UNITA and, therefore, was not ready to regard the rebels as equal partners in a newly liberalized political system because this might provide them with a platform to win politically what they were unable to win on the battlefield. This lack of trust was fueled, in no small part, by many within MPLA who were not willing to share power with an opposition group that had been a proxy of South African and American destabilization policies during the Cold War. In the end, most within MPLA understood that regime survival required fundamental transformations at many levels. This chapter suggests that the democratization of the political system, including the peace processes it undertook to bring the rebels into it, were calculated moves that ultimately ensured continued MPLA hegemony.

Political reforms: Ensuring regime survival through "divide and conquer"

Angola formally became a multi-party state on 11 May 1991 with the passing of the Law of Political Parties. This milestone followed the ruling party's shedding of Marxism as its guiding ideology in April 1991 in anticipation of the imminent signing of a peace accord with UNITA that would allow for the rebels' transformation into a political party and compete in the country's first democratic elections. The Law of Political Parties constituted a major victory for the governing MPLA in the sense that – by accepting one of UNITA's long-standing demands of democratization – the regime clearly demonstrated that it was not afraid to move its contest with UNITA into the political arena. In fact, MPLA aptly used the Law of Political Parties to significantly weaken UNITA by bringing into the same arena many other political formations that could complicate UNITA claim to be MPLA's only real opposition.

The Law of Political Parties placed minimum requirements on groups aspiring to become a party. Those requirements simply included a membership list of at least 3,000 nationals over the age of 18 of which at least 140 members resided in 14 of the country's 18 provinces. By requiring a relatively low membership, the government intended to facilitate the emergence of various political parties. In practice, however, the new law divided the opposition. As expected, more than 30 political parties emerged soon after the proclamation of the new law of which 18 were legalized by the Supreme Court. An important motivation for the creation of new political parties included significant material rewards offered by the government, i.e. monies, cars, houses, and other material means to carry out political work.

Given the conditions of widespread poverty prevailing in the country, and since the bar for the creation of new political parties was set relatively low, the establishment of political parties often constituted an irresistible vehicle for improving its members' economic lot. In many important respects, therefore, the emergence of many political parties in Angola after the end of the one-party system had as much to do with financial incentives as with the desire to create a truly democratic system. The centrality of non-political inducements was reflected in the financial scandals that beset many of the new parties. While most were dealt with internally, others were made public. The Angolan Liberal Party, for example, publicly expelled its president for diverting party funds and property to personal uses (RNA, 14 September 1992).

Generally, however, in terms of availability of resources the new parties could not compete with the more established traditional parties. The governing party, for example, not only had better organization and more financial resources, it retained a tight grip over the media and took full advantage of radio, newspapers and the state-run television station to get its message to the electorate. In sum, the governing party's strategy to remain in power as it opened up the political system involved using material inducements to divide and distract its new opponents while focusing primarily on its main traditional foe, UNITA. MPLA's method of choice for disarming UNITA – both as military and political threat to its regime – involved a protracted peace process designed to ultimately bring the rebels into a democratized political arena where, nevertheless, the rules of the game were set by the governing party. Unsurprisingly, UNITA under Savimbi was reluctant to accept this approach to peace.

Bumpy road to peace

Forced by the mounting domestic and international pressures, the MPLA regime made several attempts, beginning in the late 1980s, to achieve a negotiated settlement with the UNITA rebels to end the civil war. This negotiated approach to end the war failed for several reasons. First, the Western-oriented "winner-takes-all" framework was highly problematic as a basis for resolving a conflict with such high political and symbolic stakes. Also problematically, the peace processes mainly emphasized divisions of power – i.e., the division of government posts between the warring forces – while mostly ignoring important questions regarding division of wealth and economic opportunities between the established governing elite and those who had had spent the better part of a generation fighting to overthrow the system but who now desired a fair share of the national cake. In addition, equally important and potentially explosive issues like land redistribution were not adequately addressed within the peace frameworks to end the war. In other words, attempts to achieve peace in Angola focused mostly on the political elements of a more complex political-economy equation. Indeed, the complexities of the peace being sought ultimately determined that it would be achieved on the battleground, not at the negotiating table. The following sections review the main political attempts to end the civil war in Angola that took place in New York, Gbadolite, Bicesse, and Lusaka. It seeks to explain why they all failed and why what was secured at Luena is negative peace.

New York

On 8 August 1988, Angola, Cuba and South Africa issued a joint statement in Geneva declaring that "a de facto cessation of hostilities is now in effect" in the conflict in Angola and Namibia. On December 22, the three countries signed a historic agreement in New York, committing themselves to the phased withdrawal of 50,000 Cuban troops from Angola over a period of 27 months in return for the implementation of the UN plan for Namibia's independence. The accord marked the culmination of eight years of mediating efforts by former US Assistant Secretary of State for African Affairs, Chester Crocker, and was heralded as a major diplomatic coup for the Reagan Administration. However, for many others, it represented the end of a sad chapter in Africa's modern history and a case study of belated superpower efforts to support the resolution of regional conflicts. Although the agreement facilitated the transition of Namibia to independence, it did nothing to hasten the resolution of the civil war in Angola itself. The "New York Accords" did not even mention UNITA, the guerrilla movement supported by the United States and South Africa, that had been waging a debilitating war against the Angolan government and which controlled more than a third of the country. What explains this omission? The negotiations leading to the signing of the accords were conducted along two tracks. Track I focused on issues related to the removal of Cuban troops from Angola in return for South African withdrawal from Namibia to pave the way for its independence. Track II entailed national reconciliation between UNITA and the MPLA government in Angola. Both tracks were to be pursued simultaneously. However, the parties involved in the negotiations leading to the New York Accord regarded the question of UNITA and more general issues of national reconciliation for Angola as, essentially, an internal matter. Therefore, little or no pressure was put on MPLA and UNITA to settle their differences within the framework of the negotiations for regional peace. Moreover, since the Reagan Administration expected that reconciliation between UNITA and MPLA was inevitable after Cuban withdrawal, little pressure was put independently on the rival parties to settle their differences.

Along with the United States, African leaders were also pushing for a negotiated settlement that would bring together the two warring factions in some form of coalition or national government. Despite regional and international diplomatic pressure, the agreement on the withdrawal of Cuban troops did not lead to an end to Angola's conflict. In fact, there was little predisposition on the part of the warring factions to settle the conflict simply through political means. The government did not plan to undertake a peace process that entailed sharing power with UNITA. At a state banquet for visiting former Malian president Mousa Traoré, Dos Santos declared that "Angola does not accept pressures from wherever they may come, which aim is the formation of a so-called coalition government" (*The New York Times,* 19 September 1988, p. A3). For the government, negotiations with UNITA would be contrary to the constitutional principles prevailing in the country at the time. Angola, the Angolan president declared, "is a one-party state and so the acceptance of such a political organization [UNITA] is out of the question" (Reuters, 1 October 1988). Instead, dos Santos insisted that his government's "national harmonization" policies – including clemency to reintegrate into Angolan society former members of UNITA who surrendered – would eventually resolve the conflict. This position reflected the view that UNITA was not a legitimate political force because it was a puppet of outside forces, namely South Africa and the United States.

The government planned to take critical steps to end the civil war only after a broader regional peace agreement was achieved because the MPLA leadership believed that since its armed forces were far superior to UNITA, once foreign forces were out of the Angolan battlefields it could finally deal a fatal military blow to the rebels. In other words, the problem was South African assistance to UNITA. Resolving this issue by forcing South Africa to disengage militarily from the region within the framework of Namibia's independence would accelerate the internal peace process in Angola because UNITA would be so weakened that it would not be in a position to demand negotiations with the government. If UNITA refused the government's harmonization policies, there was a real possibility that it would be annihilated.

The "problem with South Africa" was settled on 13 December 1988. Angola, Cuba, and South Africa signed the "Brazzaville Protocol" pertaining to the withdrawal of Cuban troops from Angola and implementation of the UN plan for independence of South African-ruled Namibia. This involved both South Africa withdrawal from Namibia and, equally critical for the Angolan government, a halt to all support for UNITA. To coincide with this major event, Dos Santos announced that his government would promulgate a law granting amnesty and commute death sentences to political opponents who renounced violence, turned themselves in to the authorities, agreed to respect the country's laws and Constitution, and pledged allegiance to the governing MPLA. With a regional peace plan in place, MPLA was convinced that UNITA would shortly cease to exist through a combination of political and military action. Without South Africa's support UNITA would have to rely almost entirely on support from the United States now channeled almost exclusively through neighbouring Zaire.

The Angolan government seriously miscalculated the importance of this new supply route and the rebels' own resourcefulness. In fact, the US did considerably raise the level of its involvement in the Angolan conflict by replacing South Africa as the main UNITA supporter. Washington was not yet ready to abandon UNITA until the Angolan government agreed to reach a political settlement. Assistance for UNITA at this critical phase was supplied via six American military bases in Southern Zaire. The opening of the supply routes through Zaire coincided with joint American-Zairian military maneuvers – code-named Flintlock 88 – in April-May 1988. In addition to providing training for Zairian forces, these maneuvers also included the refurbishing of a major air base in Kamina to serve as the hub for secret CIA operations to supply arms – including sophisticated "Stinger" anti-aircraft missiles – to UNITA. Furthermore, the arms and equipment used during these military maneuvers were left behind and given to UNITA, thus upgrading its logistics and infrastructure for a new phase of the war. Afterwards, the US continued to provide support to the rebels in order to counterbalance what the United States State Department characterized as "the vast amount of assistance coming from the Soviet Union to the other side" (*The New York Times*, 26 May 1988, p. A10). Thus, contrary to the outcome expected by MPLA as a result of South Africa's disengagement from Angola's civil war, American backing enabled UNITA to intensify its military operations throughout the country, especially in northern regions close to the Zairian border. The overall American objective was to exert unbearable pressure on the MPLA government to persuade it against the military option to end the conflict. The attempt to reach an agreement at Gbadolite is an indication that the Angolan government understood the new dynamics of the conflict brought about by heightened American involvement

Gbadolite

On 1 March 1989, President Dos Santos announced a "peace program" whose implementation would start on the following April 1 – to coincide with the start of the UN's plan for the independence of Namibia. This program called for:

a. An end to interference in Angola's domestic affairs by South Africa, the USA, and their allies;

b. Respect for Angola's constitutional laws, including the maintenance of a one-party political system;

c. Application of active political and military measures to end the subversive war;

d. Amnesty within the framework of the policy of clemency and national harmony;

e. Voluntary reintegration of all Angolans in an effort of national reconstruction in accordance with their capacities;

f. Special treatment in the case of Jonas Savimbi;

g. Support from the international community for social reintegration and national reconstruction programs.

Dos Santos also announced that, to expedite the achievement of peace, his government was prepared to host a summit to be attended by all neighbouring countries. By the time eight African chiefs of state – from Congo, Gabon, Mozambique, Sao Tome e Principe, Zaire, Zambia, and Zimbabwe – gathered in Luanda on 16 May 1989 to discuss ways to end the war, the Angolan government was ready to present a peace plan that explicitly and for the first time used the term "national reconciliation" and suggested the possibility of a direct dialogue between the warring parties. But the new MPLA peace plan still envisaged "exile" for UNITA's leader Jonas Savimbi, "integration" of UNITA into the MPLA, and "respect for the Constitution" of the People's Republic of Angola. UNITA objected vigourously to these terms on three grounds. First, by stressing the indivisibility between UNITA and its founder: "UNITA and Dr. Savimbi are one and the same thing" (VORGAN, 29 September 1989). Second, UNITA viewed "integration" as a means of submerging its members in the MPLA, a concept viewed as inconsistent with the goal of national reconciliation and political pluralism. Finally, UNITA regarded "respect for the Constitution" as tantamount to acceptance of the existing one-party, Marxist-Leninist state. Despite these differences, however, intense diplomatic pressure prodded the two warring leaders to come face-to-face at a summit of 18 African heads of state organized by former Zairian president Mobutu on 22 June 1989 at Gbadolite retreat to help settle the Angolan conflict. In the end, this summit accomplished little of substance. A number of contentious issues – including the specific political and military mechanisms to end the war such as exile for rebel leader Savimbi, integration of UNITA members into MPLA structures, and respect for the existing Constitution – were discussed without being resolved.

Gbadolite failed for several reasons. First, from the Angolan government's perspective, external forces evidently played a key role. The MPLA regime accused the United States and South Africa of pressuring the rebels to reject the peace plan proposed by the African heads of state at Gbadolite. According to the government, "Savimbi had initially expressed full agreement with the [peace] program, but a few days later, because of US and South African pressures restricting his behaviour, he backed down and has been rejecting the Gbadolite principles ever since" (ANGOP, 23 September 1989). This explanation, however, does not fully address the crux of the matter, i.e. that Savimbi was unlikely to abandon his life-long quest for personal power and a dominant position for his group within Angolan politics. Savimbi himself characterized such suggestions as "silly" and wondered why UNITA, which had never been stronger militarily and politically, should "surrender to the Luanda government in negotiations what the government could never obtain on the battlefield?" He also stressed that UNITA had not fought "first against Portuguese colonial rule and then against the Soviet and Cuban-backed regime, only to throw up its hands in surrender" (*The New York Times*, 30 October 1989, p.A19). Savimbi was neither ready nor willing to comply with the African heads of state's proposals submitted to him at Gbadolite. He went to the summit mainly to enhance his international public image. His was a sophisticated attempt to discard the negative images associated with him – traitor, puppet, bandit, etc – and use the international media's spotlight to project a new image of nationalist leader and peacemaker.

Second and most importantly, Gbadolite failed because the two warring factions had diametrically different views of what peace entailed. MPLA approached the peace process with magnanimity and envisaged war termination as "harmonization" mainly in terms of implementing its policy of granting clemency and integrating the rebels into the post-colonial structures it had designed. In other words, MPLA saw itself, prematurely, as the winner. UNITA, on the other hand, defined peace in terms of fundamental political changes including the establishment of a government of national unity, free and fair elections, and a constitution allowing for a multi-party democracy. The rebels saw themselves as an alternative to the ruling MPLA, not a vanquished army. The next attempt to reconcile MPLA and UNITA took place two years later at Bicesse.

Bicesse

The storms before Bicesse

Undeterred by the failure at Gbadolite, President dos Santos opted for a two-pronged strategy to deal with UNITA. First, at the political level, dos Santos produced yet another peace proposal which, for the first time, opened the door for UNITA members to become independent legislative candidates. He also opened the door for the creation of independent associations with a social or cultural character. This meant that, although UNITA could not participate in the political process as a political entity, MPLA no longer insisted that UNITA members be integrated into the existing one-party political structures. Furthermore, UNITA could continue to exist as a social or cultural association while its members participated in the political process. UNITA, as expected, rejected this proposal, arguing that it "represent[ed] a setback in the efforts in search for peace in Angola" and maintained that "there is no other way out for Angola other than ceasefire, direct UNITA-MPLA negotiations, free elections, multi-party democracy and gaining national reconciliation in the country" (VORGAN, 9 January 1990).

To force UNITA into his co-optation plan, the second leg of Dos Santos' post-Gbadolite strategy included, at the military level, the launching of a major offensive – code-named Last Assault – against the rebels in the Cuito-Cuanavale area in an attempt to take Mavinga and open the way to an attack on Savimbi's headquarters at Jamba. The government would then, finally, be in a better position to dictate peace on its terms. But American help would once again enable UNITA to stop a large-scale government offensive. Once more, the US was not willing to abandon UNITA before a political settlement had been reached. Consequently, it significantly increased military and logistical support for UNITA to enable the rebels to thwart the government offensive. In addition, the US publicly warned the Angolan government that "attempts to crush UNITA militarily are futile" (Inter Press Service, 2 February 1990). The American military and diplomatic support allowed Savimbi to claim in early April 1990 that his forces had beaten back the government offensive. The significance of this major success by both UNITA and its American allies was underscored by former US Assistant Secretary of State for African Affairs Herman Cohen's assertion that the Angolan government seemed to have been "blunted and defeated by UNITA" (Reuters, 13 January 1990).

For its part, UNITA continued to combine military and diplomatic pressure to seek a political solution. While making the threat of waging "a nationwide war, regardless of the consequences" (VORGAN, 1 February 1990), Savimbi was seeking the help of the former colonial power, Portugal, to help pave the way towards a rapprochement between UNITA and MPLA. Savimbi argued that "the Portuguese have a better understanding of Angola" and thus were better suited to "discreetly find ways of making Angolans understand each other" (VORGAN, 1 February 1990). To set the stage for direct negotiations with the Angolan government, UNITA offered an immediate cease-fire and agreed to recognize the Angolan state on the basis of the Alvor agreements (VORGAN, 8 April 1990). The Angolan government responded positively to UNITA's offer by dropping the long-standing demand regarding Savimbi's exile as a precondition for peace. In fact, the Angolan government now declared that Savimbi "deserved special recognition" (Inter Press Service, 12 April 1990).

What accounted for these dramatic changes in both antagonists' positions? Principally, they can be attributed to the new relationship between the United States and the Soviet Union. This post-Cold War relationship constituted the basis upon which solutions could be sought for regional conflicts like Angola. Now no longer adversaries, the former Soviet Union and the United States could jointly press MPLA and UNITA to begin direct talks on national reconciliation. Not insignificantly, the United States also dangled important carrots – diplomatic recognition and help for Angola to join the World Bank and the IMF upon successful completion of a peace agreement leading to elections – which helped steer MPLA to the negotiating table. Thus, on 25 April 1990, the Angolan government announced its intentions to initiate direct contacts with UNITA. The rebels reciprocated with two significant gestures. First, it recognized President dos Santos as the head of state, and proposed a three-month cease-fire to "give the peace process yet another chance", and declared its intentions to cease "all hostile propaganda against the Luanda government and its leadership, with the exception of objective criticism of that government's social and economic programs" (VORGAN, 1 May 1990). Second, UNITA recognized the MPLA government as "legitimate until elections are held" (VORGAN, 13 October 1990).

The newfound moderation of both sides' positions facilitated the holding of several exploratory meetings. These meetings, however, emblematic of much of the relationship between the two sides, were characterized by friction and confrontation. The government wanted to extract three basic concessions from UNITA at the exploratory talks: first, agreement on a formula whereby UNITA would stop receiving military aid from the United States and other countries in exchange for the government's suspension of all arms purchases from the Soviet Union and other countries; second, an immediate cease-fire to allow the free movement of people and goods, the creation of a climate of peace and stability, and the implementation of a program for the general elections process; and, third, the disarming of UNITA as a first step for the eventual creation of a national army. UNITA, however, believed that the government was not negotiating in good faith and accused it of "inflexibility" and attempting to "prolong the war situation while seek[ing] ways to implement its macabre plan to keep the Angolan people under MPLA subjugation" (VORGAN, 4 December 1990). UNITA was distressed with what it regarded as procedural and other major deficiencies at the talks. The procedural matters troubling UNITA were related to the composition of the government's delegation: it was composed of low-level officials and the government showed a propensity to change the head of the delegation at the last minute, thus necessarily changing "the complexion of the talks" (VORGAN, 30 August 1990). UNITA was also disturbed by more substantive issues including the government's refusal to officially recognize UNITA as a political opposition party as well as its demands that UNITA clipped its military wings as a pre-requisite for participation in the democratic process.

The seemingly intractable barriers separating the warring factions in Angola were again set aside due to direct intervention by the United States and the former Soviet Union who conveyed to those they backed their intention not to provide additional military and financial aid to prosecute the war. Both Washington and Moscow had found a mutually acceptable moment to collaborate on settling the Angolan war. The Bush administration was keen to resolve third world conflicts hindering steady improvement in American-Russian relations while the leadership in the Kremlin was eager to end financially draining involvements in overseas wars like Angola. Unsurprisingly, therefore, the US and the former Soviet Union collaborated not just in bringing the warring sides to the negotiating table but also in helping them draft the main documents that constituted the basis for negotiations in subsequent meetings between UNITA and the government. These documents on political principles and technical-military issues were based on five principles:

a. Angola will become a democratic and multi-party nation;

b. The international community ought to guarantee a cease-fire;

c. There should be free and fair elections in Angola, verified by the international community;

d. The signing of a cease-fire should be preceded by an accord on the date for free and fair elections; and,

e. All military assistance from abroad would stop once a cease-fire accord has been signed (RNA, 23 January 1991).

An agreement on these principles by the United States, the former Soviet Union, and Portugal compelled the Angolan government and UNITA to make further concessions prior to signing a peace accord. Thus, UNITA dropped its longstanding demand to be included in a transitional government and agreed to integrate its military forces into a single national army before elections. The MPLA government was also forced to make several dramatic concessions including dropping its demand that Jonas Savimbi should go into exile during the transition period, acknowledging UNITA's right to exist as an opposition party, agreeing to allow the development of a multi-party system and, accepting the principle of free and fair elections following the signing of a cease-fire. The stage had been set for the Bicesse peace accords between the Angolan government and UNITA.

The Bicesse peace accords

The Bicesse peace accords covered various important legal and organizational aspects for the transition to peace and elected government in Angola, including: cease-fire monitoring, disengagement of forces and their concentration in designated areas, formation of a national army, mechanics of the electoral process, and election monitoring. More specifically, they included four documents dealing with the cease-fire, the fundamental principles for peace in Angola and the formation of CCPM, the main concepts for resolution of outstanding questions between the government and UNITA and, finally, the Estoril Protocol dealing with matters regarding the elections, the CCPM, internal security during the transition period to elections, administrative structures, and the creation of the unified armed forces.

1. The cease-fire accord. The peace accords define the cease-fire as "a cessation of hostilities between the government of the People's Republic of Angola and UNITA, aimed at bringing peace in the entire national territory". The two parties agreed that the cease-fire would be "total and definitive" and would guarantee the free movement of people and goods throughout the entire country. The accord included commitments by the two parties to cease all movement of troops or armed groups, all attempts to militarily occupy new positions, all military maneuvers aimed at transporting military material, and all violent actions against the civilian population. The political control of the cease-fire would be the responsibility of both the government and UNITA and would be exercised through the CCPM. The UN would be invited by the government to send monitors to help both sides. The cease-fire accord included the undertaking by both sides to end all hostile propaganda both within the country and from abroad. It also obligated both sides to abstain from acquiring lethal material. The United States and the former Soviet Union informed the Angolan government that they would support the implementation of the cease-fire by ceasing to provide lethal material to either side as well as encouraging other countries to do likewise.

In terms of its implementation, both the government and UNITA committed themselves to "strict compliance" with the accords as well as all future rulings emanating from the structures created to oversee the cease-fire. Implementation of the cease-fire also included freeing all civilian and military prisoners of war with the assistance of the International Committee of the Red Cross. To successfully implement the cease-fire accord, and on the insistence of the international community, the Angolan government and UNITA reached agreement on a set of "fundamental principles" that would secure the establishment of peace in Angola and devised a framework to settle all outstanding questions.

2. The fundamental principles. The fundamental principles for the establishment of peace in Angola were essentially a number of concessions by both sides to create the political climate necessary to effectuate the transition to a multi-party regime. Thus, the recognition by UNITA of the Angolan state, President José Eduardo dos Santos, and the government until elections were held constituted a major political victory for the governing party in the sense that it provided it with legitimacy. In turn, UNITA gained the right to freely carry out and take part in political activities under the terms of the revised constitution and relevant laws on the creation of a multi-party democracy, after the signing of a cease-fire.

The fundamental principles for the establishment of peace in Angola also made provisions for the holding of talks between the Angolan government and all political forces with a view to learning about their views on the proposed constitutional changes as well as cooperation from all political parties in order to draft laws to speed up the electoral process; the holding of free and fair elections after the registration of voters and under the supervision of international observers who would remain in Angola until they confirmed that the elections were free and fair and the results were officially announced; and respect for human rights and fundamental freedoms, including the right to free association. The mechanics to guide elections, the CCPM, the administrative apparatus, and the creation of the unified national army were established in the Estoril Protocol.

3. The Estoril protocol. The holding of free elections had been a consistent UNITA demand since the breakdown of the decolonization process in 1975. In fact, the governing MPLA's refusal to hold elections was used by UNITA to legitimize its guerrilla war. The Estoril Protocol laid the framework for the first post-colonial electoral process. A key element of the protocol was the agreement granting all political parties and interested persons an equal right to organize themselves and participate in the electoral process. Furthermore, it ratified the "observer" countries' proposal that elections should be held in the period between September 1 and 30 November 1992. The Estoril Protocol also validated the creation of the CCPM, conferring upon it the mandate of exercising comprehensive "political control of the cease-fire process" and guaranteeing the "strict compliance of the political and military understandings" inherent in the application of the peace accords. Finally, it established the criteria for the creation of a national nonpartisan army before the election date. The accord provided for an end to the fighting from midnight, 15 May 1991 and a formal cease-fire signing on

May 31. Elections were scheduled for September 1992. On 31 May 1991, Angolan President José Eduardo dos Santos and UNITA leader Jonas Savimbi signed what was supposed to be a historic peace agreement formally ending Angola's civil war.

Implementing Bicesse

1. Shaky start. The implementation of the Bicesse accords was, to say the least, very problematic. Both UNITA and MPLA, it seemed, were not able to overcome the inertia of violence acquired through the long years of civil war. Thus, UNITA undertook to undermine the power of the MPLA regime during the transition process through an intense campaign of political violence. For example, it ordered its members to carry out "a persecution campaign against former state security members" of the old regime (RNA, 4 October 1991). In Lobito, this led to clashes between UNITA soldiers and city residents. In Huambo, UNITA occupied several government buildings and evicted entire families from their homes (RNA, 4 October 1991). It also prevented the holding of several demonstrations in support of peace by MPLA supporters.

The MPLA reacted to UNITA's actions by claiming that they were intended to create "psychological conditions of terror and fear" (RNA, 4 October 1991). But the conditions of terror and fear were more than just psychological and were not restricted to the civilian population. For example, angry airmen burned down the regional UNITA offices in Lubango in retaliation for the murders of four air force officers blamed on UNITA. Yet, UNITA considered itself the victim, not the cause, of political violence perpetrated by the governing MPLA. In a communiqué issued by the Chief of General Staff of its military wing, UNITA announced that the organization's assistant secretary-general, Col. Pedro Makanga, had been assassinated on 29 September 1991 while traveling by road to Luanda to attend a meeting of the UNITA leadership. The communiqué claimed that there was proof that Col. Makanga's assassination was the work of forces in the service of the MPLA and linked it to the "provocative behaviour" in every province of the country. UNITA maintained that the assassination was "intended to sabotage the peace process" and vowed not to "remain silent in the face of continued violations and provocations" (VORGAN, 5 October 1991). On 23 October 1991, UNITA again accused state security agents of having murdered the Deputy Communications Minister's chief of staff for being a UNITA sympathizer. UNITA also claimed that the government was transferring state security officers to the police force in order to commit further atrocities.

For its part, the MPLA accused UNITA of infiltrating armed men into urban areas to launch terrorist operations against government officials as well as armed forces and state security officers. In Bié province, for example, a UNITA youth gang called "007" allegedly attacked anyone wearing an MPLA t-shirt. Also in Bié, UNITA captured 11 members of the presidential guard after seizing and burning three of their vehicles. UNITA claimed that these soldiers, who had landed in Bié minutes before an aircraft transporting Savimbi was due to arrive, were planning "an attempt on [Savimbi's] life" (RNA, 23 September 1992).

The rise in pre-electoral political violence can be attributed to several factors including the central government's weakness – an ironic result of the peace accords which did not clearly define the roles of the government and the institutions created to manage the transition process. Thus, for example, the government was largely unsuccessful in re-establishing its authority in those areas of the country previously controlled by UNITA. Furthermore, the institutions created and legitimized at Bicesse – CCPM and UNAVEM – were unable to resolve the disputes that emerged regarding the government's attempts to extend its control throughout the entire country. The Peace Accords rested on the crucial assumption that both sides would cooperate in its implementation since, at least overtly, all wanted peace. Instead, UNITA took full advantage of the prevailing situation – including a weak government, a dysfunctional CCPM, and an ineffective UNAVEM – to further strengthen its own positions partly by preventing the government from extending its administration to areas it had lost during the civil war. Ironically, the UN unwittingly facilitated UNITA's strategy of keeping tens of thousands of peasants under its control as captive voters, instead of allowing them to return to their villages under the terms of the peace accord, by supplying the rebels with substantial quantities of food.

The Angolan government was not allowed to start the process of bringing UNITA-controlled areas under its control until six months after the signing of the peace accord. UNITA finally agreed that the government had the right to appoint administrative officials throughout the entire country but reserved the right to also appoint some of its own people to local government bodies. In practice, however, UNITA did not allow the extension of government authority into the territory it previously controlled. On the eve of the election, UNITA still militarily controlled 52 districts with an estimated population of one million persons. According to government estimates, this ensured 30 or 40 uncontested UNITA seats in the 220-seat parliament.

But there were other factors contributing to political violence. The demobilized soldiers from both armies retained many of their weapons due to the haphazard way in which the demobilization process was conducted. In many cases, soldiers simply did not report back to their barracks once the cease-fire was signed. Thus many angry and penniless FAPLA soldiers resorted to stopping traffic and rushing onto airplanes to return to their homes. Only a relatively small number of FAPLA soldiers were officially demobilized. Most simply abandoned their units and looked for the fastest way home only to be faced with severe economic hardships. With few jobs available, many of these demobilized soldiers resorted to crime as a way to survive. Since there was little distinction between the economic and political elites, many common crimes acquired a political connotation during the explosive pre-electoral period.

The government responded ambiguously to mounting political instability. While President dos Santos vowed never to permit "anarchy, chaos and violence to replace the civic state", he also acknowledged that his government was acting "in an extremely calm and thoughtful manner in light of the abuses, crimes and affronts that have been committed against peace and the people". For dos Santos the (in)action of his government was justified because it was facing "temporary situations typical of a delicate political process of national reconciliation" (RNA,10 November 1991). Basically, MPLA believed that UNITA was attempting to scuttle the entire process for fear of being defeated at the polls.

2. The electoral process. The government announced that, in compliance with the peace accord, general elections would be held in September 1992. Before this happened, however, it argued that certain minimum conditions should be met including, first, the confinement of all government and UNITA troops by mid-December 1991; second, the resolution of all prevailing shortcomings concerning the extension of state administration to areas still under UNITA control; third, the approval of the legal framework for the holding of elections – the electoral law, the law on international monitoring of general elections, the law on the right of political parties to radio and television time, the law on the creation of the news media council, and the law on the registration of commercial radio stations – and, fourth, approval of the law on the review of the constitution, and the law on political parties and government assistance to political parties (RNA, 10 November

1991). Although these legal steps were intended to open the political arena to the entire society, they served mainly to legalize UNITA's participation in electoral politics while also enhancing the governing party's claim to be the key architect of the democratic reforms and thus strengthen its chances of electoral victory.

UNITA intended to take full advantage of these changes. Savimbi was convinced that he would win the presidential elections and his party would have the majority in the future National Assembly. After all, UNITA perceived itself as the main force behind the withdrawal of Cuban troops from Angola. Savimbi not only expected the electorate to reward UNITA at the polls, he also believed that Angolans would punish the governing MPLA for its corruption and inability to manage the economy for the public good. MPLA was just as certain of winning the elections. Dos Santos, for his part, believed that the electorate would reward him and his party for having defended the people and the country's territorial integrity, after installing democracy and a market economy and achieving peace.

3. Elections. The elections in Angola were "an exercise in make-believe" in the sense that many of the fundamental pre-conditions stipulated in the peace accords were not fulfilled by the time the polls were held. First and foremost, the peace accords had failed to create a peaceful climate for political discourse and intercourse. In other words, having been denied victory on the battlefield, the two main opponents were attempting to win the civil war at the ballot box. Both sides still had armies and UNITA still controlled the territory it occupied during the civil war.

These factors notwithstanding, and given the mounting international pressure to adhere to the electoral schedule, the electoral process went ahead. The first phase of the election process involved voter registration. All nationals over the age of 18 could register and receive a voter identification card. An estimated 4,828,468 Angolans, or 92 per cent of the adult population, registered to vote. At the end of voter registration UNITA claimed that it was "not pleased that the government in power should impose [upon] the National Electoral Council rules of the game which prevented the registration of 500,000 Angolans of voting age" and warned that it would only accept the results "if the elections are free, fair and clear" (RNA, 26 August 1992). Furthermore, it stated that the government no longer possessed "the monopoly of force to manipulate events in our beloved fatherland as it did in 1975" (RNA, 26 August 1992). UNITA's message was unambiguously threatening and bellicose leading many politicians to believe that post-electoral war was inevitable. Savimbi did little to allay the fears of a post-electoral debacle. In fact, he seemed to anticipate it by claiming that if UNITA lost the elections it meant that they had not been free and fair.

The elections were held, as scheduled, on 29-30 September 1992. On 3 October, as voting returns continued to show Savimbi trailing in the country's first democratic elections, he accused the governing party of fraud and threatened a resumption of the civil war if he and his party lost. Savimbi accused the MPLA of wanting "to cling to power illegally with tooth and nail, by stealing ballot boxes, beating up and deviating polling list delegates and distorting facts and numbers". He went on to say that "it is the duty of us, freedom fighters, those who through their blood and sweat brought about democracy to this country, to tell you that the MPLA is not winning and cannot win". He then warned that, if UNITA lost the election, it might be forced "to take a position that could deeply disturb the situation of this country" (*The New York Times*, 3 October 1992, p.15). He meant war.

UNITA and its allies did, in fact, lose the election. The National Electoral Council published the election results on 17 October 1992 after investigating UNITA's claims that the elections were fraudulent. The official results confirmed that the presidential election was a two-way contest between President dos Santos and Savimbi. The incumbent received 49.57 per cent of the vote compared to the rebel leader's 40.07 per cent. Since both candidates failed to win at least 50 per cent in the first round, a runoff election was needed. Regrettably, the resumption of the civil war after UNITA refused to accept the election results prevented the second round from ever taking place. For the legislative election, the 18 parties fielded candidates for the 220-seat National Assembly. Unlike in the presidential contest, the ruling party achieved a convincing majority in the legislative elections. MPLA received 54 per cent of the vote and 129 seats in the National Assembly. UNITA trailed with 34 per cent of the vote and 70 seats. The next three parties with the highest number of votes (FNLA, PLD, and PRS) failed to receive 2.5 per cent of the popular vote and elected 6, 5, and 3 members of the National Assembly respectively. All the other parties failed to reach 1 per cent of the vote and each elected a single parliamentarian.

As expected, UNITA claimed that the results were fraudulent. Savimbi not only accused the MPLA of rigging the vote, he also described the National Electoral Commission as a puppet of the government and dismissed the views of the nearly 800 international observers who affirmed that the elections had been generally free and fair. Although President dos Santos declared that "no one can question the justness and neutrality in the counting of votes", (RNA, 8 October 1992) six opposition political parties – AD-Coligação, CNDA, FNLA, PDA, PDP-ANA, and PSDA – joined UNITA in claiming that "the electoral process was on the whole characterized by massive, systematic and general fraud and irregularities, thereby ceasing to be credible" (VORGAN, 16 October 1992).

4. Elections as prelude to war. Although Savimbi claimed, and many of his supporters still claim, that Angola's first multi-party elections were fraudulent, a more likely reason for the result can be found in the parties' approach to the elections, their respective strategies and how their messages were delivered to the electorate as well as the personality of their leaders. Although from the outset, each side believed that its victory at the polls was certain, MPLA and President dos Santos conveyed the image that they deserved to win while UNITA and Jonas Savimbi portrayed themselves as a party that could not lose. President dos Santos and MPLA ran a campaign whose main themes stressed stability and unity for Angola's fractured and traumatized society emerging from a costly civil war. Their campaign also exploited the fears of many Angolans, particularly urban dwellers, that Savimbi was a racist power-hungry human rights violator whose victory would throw Angola into a period of witch-hunting and general instability. This was made all too easy by Savimbi's own aggressive, arrogant and threatening demeanour. Savimbi failed to make the leap from authoritarian guerrilla leader to a post-civil war statesman capable of placing the national interest above his personal and party ambitions at a time when most Angolans desired national reconciliation above all else. His use of inflammatory rhetoric and veiled threats against MPLA members and sympathizers, people from ethnic groups other than his own as well as whites and mixed race Angolans, alienated an increasing number of people. By contrast, dos Santos cultivated and marketed the image of a soft-spoken, well-educated family man gently leading his country to a new and prosperous future.

At election time Angolans faced two equally bad choices: the governing party, once avowedly Marxist-Leninist which for many years was sustained by Soviet and Cuban support and whose economic mismanagement had brought the country to the brink of collapse or UNITA which fought a vicious war that had ravaged the country. In the end, Angolans voted not so much for President dos Santos but against Jonas Savimbi. Many people were simply not convinced that Savimbi would not continue behaving as a guerrilla if elected president.

As Savimbi had promised, UNITA rejected the validity of the results sanctioned by the United Nations and other international observers, declaring that massive fraud had taken place. Subsequently, it militarily occupied large portions of the country, including areas where it had never operated before. The government was caught by surprise: it had demobilized most of its troops. By contrast, UNITA – in a gambit reminiscent of events following independence in 1975 – was now poised to take the capital city. Fighting for control of Luanda began on October 30. After several days of intense fighting the government prevailed. Several senior UNITA officials, including its vice-president Jeremias Chitunda, were killed. The Bicesse Peace Accords had collapsed and, once again, Angola reverted to full-scale civil war. But this time around, the two combatants did not attract or need direct external intervention from foreign armies. The government's control of the oil resources and UNITA's control of some diamond mines provided both with sufficient domestic revenues to prosecute the new phase of the war.

Assessing Bicesse

Bicesse was expected to end one of Africa's longest-running and bloodiest conflicts and to mark a new beginning for a devastated country. On the surface, most conditions seemed ripe for a political settlement. After sixteen years of civil war, the conflict had reached a stalemate in the sense that the government lacked the wherewithal to defeat UNITA while, similarly, the rebels could not realistically expect to violently remove the government from power. Beyond the stalemate, there were further reasons, at both national and international levels, compelling the two belligerents to sign the peace accords.

At the national level, important segments of society – especially religious groups – exerted mounting pressure on the governing party to end the war. Sixteen years of civil war preceded by fourteen years of liberation war against the Portuguese colonial/settler occupation had brought Angola to a virtual political and economic dead-end with profound social impacts. Most Angolans, including those in government, feared that a continuation of the civil war represented an irreversible path toward the precipice while peace provided an alternative, even if not unproblematic, path. Besides this, as far as the key antagonists' perceptions of each other were concerned, the political battle could be won more easily than the military conflict.

From the governing MPLA's perspective, the long military stalemate, compounded by the autocratic style of leadership of Jonas Savimbi, had led to major internal squabbles and divisions within rebels ranks that could be usefully exploited. Typically, Savimbi dealt with internal dissent by physically eliminating his challengers – real or imagined. This brutal method of "problem-solving" led to the killing of UNITA's best and brightest political and military leaders and resulted in fear and political alienation within UNITA ranks, thus weakening the organization. This penchant for regular self-mutilation on the part of the rebels did not go unnoticed by MPLA. As it prepared to engage UNITA politically, the governing party was confident that, having eliminated some of its key political and military figures, UNITA no longer constituted a credible national political alternative. In fact, the governing party confidently believed that given the rebels' record of violence – both within their organization and throughout the country – they would be perceived more as a terrorist group without a political platform than a political party capable of leading the country out of its many and severe problems. Also, UNITA's longstanding alliance with apartheid South Africa – whose armed forces devastated the southern part of Angola through military incursions in the 1970s and 80s – could be used by the governing party to discredit the rebels and further reduce their political appeal. Furthermore, the MPLA counted on the possibility of capitalizing on Savimbi's negative image, especially among the urban population.

Conversely, UNITA also saw serious handicaps on the side of the governing MPLA party. Throughout the civil war, UNITA sought to paint it as a band of "communist lackeys" who needed direct foreign military assistance – mostly from Cuba and the former USSR – to hold on to power. Economic mismanagement and widespread corruption could also be highlighted to discredit the MPLA's post-colonial rule. For UNITA, then, the government was on the verge of collapse and was under immense pressure to negotiate an end to the war. Therefore, UNITA miscalculated that the country was ready for a change of government. In sum, beyond changed circumstances, political misperceptions helped drive the two historical rivals to sign the peace accords.

Notwithstanding these compelling reasons to sign a peace agreement, critical elements for sustainable peace were missing. First, neither side was on the verge of victory or defeat. In fact, a military stalemate had prevailed for some time, suggesting that there would be no winners or losers on the battlefield – at least not in the short run. Without an outright military victory to facilitate the imposition of a peace framework upon the vanquished, sustainable peace would have to be based on trust. Unfortunately, this critical element was also missing.

MPLA did little to hide its profound mistrust of Jonas Savimbi due to his alliance with Portuguese colonial authorities and with apartheid South Africa after independence. Similarly, UNITA did not trust the MPLA regime which it regarded as a mulatto-dominated party that governed on behalf of powerful coastal elites and not in the interests of the majority. Both parties' behaviour during the pre-electoral period reflected this profound animosity. For example, it was this lack of trust that led to the attribution of exceptional powers to CCPM. Since UNITA did not find the MPLA government to be capable of managing the transition process transparently, it pressed for this commission to act as a virtual parallel government to prevent perceived MPLA manipulation of the process. Lack of trust also reflected itself in the security arrangements enacted by both parties. Although a significant portion of the national army underwent an informal demobilization after the cease-fire, the MPLA government kept its well-trained secret police intact and created an additional rapid-reaction force, "the ninjas". The government largely ignored UNITA's demands for those "special forces" to be placed under CCPM oversight. But UNITA had safety mechanisms of its own. Most important of all, it refused to allow the government to extend its administration over territory under rebel control. In addition, UNITA did not disband its army nor did it give up its weapons. In sum, since neither party could achieve major immediate gains through war, they opted to use the Bicesse process as a continuation of the war by other means.

Inter-party dynamics also conspired against a sustainable peace. The urbane MPLA leadership was politically and culturally miles apart from the Maoist UNITA leadership. The multiracial MPLA grew out of urban anti-colonial organizations which found inspiration in Western models of post-colonial development while UNITA was a peasant-based Afro-centric movement that found inspiration in pre-colonial cultural and political memories. Also pertaining to inter-party dynamics, their respective leaders' personalities posed a problem for national reconciliation, making it particularly difficult and traumatic. Savimbi's abrasiveness contrasted with President dos Santos' quiet, self-effacing – even if equally ruthless – personality. Savimbi's behaviour over the years convinced the MPLA leadership that they would be in mortal danger if their nemesis ever achieved national power. His personality even rendered the notion of power-sharing – i.e., the Vice-Presidency for Savimbi – very unpalatable. These issues alone would seriously imperil the sustainability of the Bicesse process. In addition, there were also important structural impediments.

1. Dysfunctional structures. The bulk of the implementation tasks for the Bicesse peace process rested on the CCPM which included government and UNITA representatives as well as observers from the United States, the former Soviet Union, Portugal and the UN. Regrettably, this structure was incapable of managing a peaceful transition to the elections. In fact, it could not prevent the peace process from beginning to unravel soon after the signing of the accords.

The first major problem encountered concerned the release of government prisoners by UNITA. The government claimed that, in compliance with the peace accord, it had released the first 107 UNITA prisoners. The prisoner releases would be reciprocated by both sides until they were all freed. UNITA refused to reciprocate, claiming that the government POWs were "at liberty in Jamba" (Reuters, 25 July 1991) and therefore there was no need to provide for their transportation out of the remote UNITA headquarters. Both the government and the International Committee of the Red Cross disputed this assertion on the grounds that, under the peace accord, prisoners had to be transported to their place of choice to be deemed free. The dispute over POWs held by UNITA continued and was never fully resolved during the pre-electoral transition period. Although UNITA claimed in November 1991 – six months after the signing of the peace accord – that it had fully complied with the provisions concerning POWs' release, the government was able to present a list of 4,649 who were still being held (RNA, 5 August 1992). UNITA viewed this as an "abusive position" and accused the government of viewing all people residing in rebel-controlled areas as prisoners (VORGAN, 9 August 1992). Besides the row over the release of POWs, the peace process was seriously tested from the beginning by claims and counter-claims of cease-fire violations and political intimidation. There was little surprise, therefore, when less than three months into the implementation of the peace accord, UNITA withdrew from the CCPM accusing the government of bad faith. According to the rebels, their specific reasons for withdrawal included:

a. President dos Santos' "dishonesty" was endangering the entire peace process;

b. The Ministry of State Security was unleashing its "murderous wrath" against UNITA soldiers and sympathizers throughout the country;

c. The Angolan government was delaying the release of UNITA POWs and declined to disclose the exact number of UNITA members detained in its prisons (VORGAN, 10 September 1991).

UNITA demanded that several conditions be met before it reconsidered its participation in the CCPM, including a reduction of crimes committed against UNITA members and soldiers, total compliance with the confinement program for government forces, setting of an election timetable, impartiality of the UN verification and monitoring mission, police neutrality, and free movement of people and goods throughout Angola (Radio Renascença, Lisbon, 11 September 1991). Although UNITA returned to the CCPM shortly afterwards, this body had lost most of its effectiveness. Without a strong mechanism to manage the transition process, the country completed its descent into political turmoil characterized by intimidation and violence. As a crucial mechanism for the transition process, the CCPM was poorly designed in the sense that many of the problems it had to face were not anticipated by the signatories of the peace accord. Thus, many "weaknesses" that were detected in the functioning of the Commission's verification and control organs – particularly in the working methods that could permit a "more dynamic interaction" between the verification and control organs at the central and local levels (RNA, 19 September 1991) – could not be modified due to the relatively short transition period. In addition, the architects of the transition process had not additional structures – like, for example, a national sovereign conference – to help handle important challenges not contemplated in the accords.

2. *No national conference.* The MPLA government refused to call a national conference to work out the ground rules for the transition process to elections. The governing party dismissed the calls from emerging opposition parties to convene a national conference on the grounds that it was both unnecessary and dangerous to the peace process. In several African countries in the late 1980s and early 1990s, national conferences were held as a result of popular pressure aimed at changing existing political systems. But, for the MPLA, Angola had witnessed a totally opposite situation; i.e., it had been the governing party itself that took a leading role in changing the political system. The MPLA maintained that the convening of a national "sovereign" conference would necessarily lead to the dissolution of the existing legislative body, the People's Assembly. Moreover, in the words of President dos Santos, "the sovereign conference will be the parliament to be elected by the Angolan people" (RNA, 10 November 1991). Instead, the governing party opted for the creation of a national consultative mechanism consisting mainly of representatives of emerging political parties to examine legislation already submitted to the People's Assembly.

The governing MPLA did not intend to devolve power to a national conference because that would be tantamount to giving up important levers of state power. Ironically, UNITA was equally disinterested in a national conference. Savimbi regarded such conferences as "civilian coups d'etat" (RNA, 1 November 1991). This bombastic rhetoric hid more pragmatic considerations inasmuch as UNITA was not interested in diluting its role as the main opposition by participating in a national conference with about two dozen other recently formed parties. Although Savimbi had argued that all parties had the same rights and UNITA wanted to "establish a dialogue with them", he did not hide his belief that there were essentially two groups of political parties: first, the traditional parties that had been formed decades earlier to fight colonial rule and, second, the *"partidecos"* or insignificantly small parties created to take advantage of the new era of multi-partyism. Implicit in this argument was the suggestion that those parties that had fought against the settler regime had greater political legitimacy. They also had greater resources – both financial and military – that made them more competitive, coercive, and therefore more likely to win elections. For Savimbi, the *partidecos* were simply irritating encumbrances and so would a national conference be. Ultimately, Savimbi failed to recognize that the sustainability of the embryonic democratization process, including the narrower peace process, required not only greater participation from civil society – through political parties, for instance – but also the creation of innovative structures like national conferences to manage political power during the critical transition phase. This would have minimized the importance of creating a depoliticized and unified national army to guarantee the sustainability of the democratization and peace process.

3. No national army. The creation of a national, unified army posed important challenges for both UNITA and the government. For UNITA – a guerrilla army camouflaging as a political party – the creation of a national army that included its military wing would have required it to shed its military character and undergo a fundamental transformation into a real political party. Paradoxically, however, without the ability to command thousands of men under arms, and without time to fully reinvent itself before elections, UNITA faced very bleak prospects at the polls and beyond. Aware of this predicament, Savimbi attempted to keep UNITA's armed wing intact by strongly arguing that his troops could become a key foundation of the national army because "it would be a mistake to entrust the defence of Angola to FAPLA troops" (VORGAN, 14 March 1991). Unsurprisingly, the governing party was just as unwilling to contemplate entrusting its security to an army composed mainly of former UNITA troops. Instead, it preferred to proceed with attempts to establish a new army as defined in the peace accords.

Under the peace accord the two sides were expected to create a new 50,000-person army from their estimated 250,000 troops and demobilize excess personnel before elections. However, from the start, the process of assembling government and rebel troops was very slow, resulting in considerable delays in the establishment of the new national army. The slowness was caused by lack of food, transportation, and other logistical elements in the areas where the troops should have been confined. In a report to the Security Council, the UN Secretary General pointed out that two and a half months after the assembly of troops was supposed to have been completed barely 60 per cent of the troops declared by both sides had been encamped. The report declared that this undermined confidence and imperilled the implementation of various other aspects of the peace accord.

UNITA claimed that it had concluded the process of confining its troops to UN-controlled assembly areas just before the 15 November 1991 deadline stipulated by the CCPM. UNITA noted, however, that the government was not complying with the peace accords because it had not only failed to confine its troops but also transferred many soldiers into the police force to avoid demobilization (VORGAN, 18 November 1991). By UNAVEM's count, a total of 95,634 troops (68,666 government troops and 26,968 from UNITA) were in 45 assembly areas, compared with the projected total for all assembly areas of 165,440 troops (115,640 government troops and 49,800 UNITA troops.)

By early April 1992, it became clear that the provisions of the Peace Accords regarding the formation of a unified national army would not be met. Given the slow pace of implementing some of the crucial aspects of the Peace Accords, the UN and the foreign powers involved in overseeing the application of the accords all but gave up on attempts to meet the stipulated schedule for demobilization and form a unified army before elections. The British, Portuguese and French officers in charge of forming the new army had only succeeded in creating a unified command structure on paper (*The Washington Post*, 11 April 1992, p.A14). Thus, in a move that would prove fatal to the country's immediate stability, the parties involved undertook to make the first serious revision of the Peace Accords. The government and UNITA decided to hold back on their initial pledge to demobilize all their soldiers or integrate them into the new national army. UNITA decided to keep at least 15,000 soldiers in reserve while the government kept about 33,000 including 6,000 in the air and 4,000 in the navy. A month before elections only about 25 per cent of the combined soldiers had been demobilized and a mere 12 per cent of the national army had been formed. It was becoming clear that, at election time, Angola would not have one army, but three – the embryonic national army, FAPLA, and FALA.

Pressured by the international observers to the peace process – US, the former Soviet Union and Portugal – the government and UNITA agreed to officially disband their armies on 27 September 1992, just 48 hours before the start of the elections in Angola. However, the unity of the new armed forces only lasted a week. UNITA withdrew from the country's newly formed joint armed forces, FAA, on 5 October 1992, to protest alleged fraud in the elections. The vicious cycle of war and destruction was about to enter a new and more violent phase that lasted for another ten years, pausing only for the lull provided by the short-lived peace accord of Lusaka

Lusaka

The Lusaka Protocol of 15 November 1994 essentially committed the Angolan government and UNITA to conclude the implementation of the 1991 Bicesse Accords and to respect the institutions resulting from the 1991 elections as a way to achieve lasting peace and national reconciliation. Thus, the various documents (annexes) that made up the Lusaka Protocol – dealing mainly with military/security and national reconciliation issues – did not go much beyond a reaffirmation by both sides that they would accept previously agreed upon principles and the institutions that resulted from their implementation. Thus, at the military/security level, the Lusaka Protocol made provisions for the re-establishment of the cease-fire, withdrawal, quartering and demilitarization of all UNITA military forces, disarming of civilians, and the completion of the formation of FAA. In fact, as far as military/security issues are concerned, the similarities between Lusaka and Bicesse are striking. Annex three of the Lusaka Protocol spells out several "specific principles relating to the reestablished cease-fire" including – in addition to the bilateral and effective cessation of hostilities, movements and military actions "in situ" throughout the national territory – the setting up of UN verification and monitoring mechanisms; withdrawal and quartering of all UNITA military forces and armaments; UN verification and monitoring of all FAA troops and armaments; repatriation of mercenaries who had fought in Angola; and, free circulation of persons and goods. Annex four established the principles and modalities for completion of the formation of FAA. Here, again, the Lusaka Protocol basically follows the Bicesse blueprint. In fact, it explicitly states that "the composition of the Angolan Armed Forces will reflect the principle of proportionality between Government and UNITA military forces as provided for in the Bicesse Accords".

In political terms the Lusaka Protocol too does not stray away from Bicesse. In other words, it did not include innovative approaches to cement national reconciliation even if only by adopting successful regional models like South Africa's Truth and Reconciliation Commission. Instead, Lusaka wishfully established that national reconciliation depended on the political will of both the government and UNITA "to live together within the Angolan constitutional, political and legal framework" while "accepting the will of the people expressed through free and fair elections and the right to opposition". But the entire process of national reconciliation hinged on "respecting the relevant provisions of the Bicesse Accords". In fact, so as to emphasize the continuity with Bicesse, this clause appears throughout the Lusaka Protocol. Thus, instead of articulating the key principles upon which national reconciliation could be based – ethnic tolerance, respect for the rule of law, political inclusiveness, devolution of power, and so on – Lusaka mainly restated Bicesse while making the necessary adjustments to reflect changes on the ground experienced since the signature of the previous accords. Thus, the Lusaka Protocol made provisions for the filling of the 70 UNITA seats in the National Assembly and the granting of "privileges and benefits" as well as "special security arrangements" for UNITA leaders installed in office in the various political, military, administrative, and diplomatic structures of the state. But it remained mostly silent on the critical issues of what cathartic mechanisms would be developed whereby a post-colonial, post-conflict society could begin the process of cleansing itself and attempt a fresh start. All the signatories of the Lusaka Protocol could offer was an understanding that "on the day on which the Lusaka Protocol is initialed, the Government and the leadership of UNITA shall each issue a statement on the importance and meaning of pardon and amnesty". The expectation that two statements, however well drafted, could constitute the foundation of a complex process of reconciliation was at best unrealistic.

Equally unrealistic was the call for the completion of the electoral process with the holding of the second round of elections while not even addressing the fundamental reasons for the "post-electoral crisis". What new element would induce Savimbi to play the game by post-Lusaka rules?

Other than the tilting of the balance of forces on the ground in favour of the government, there was little else to coax Savimbi back into the political arena because the rules of the political game – i.e. winner-takes-all – remained the same. In other words, if Savimbi did not like Bicesse he was unlikely to embrace Lusaka. To succeed – i.e. to achieve lasting peace and national reconciliation – Lusaka would have to produce an imaginative political framework involving, for example, a radical devolution of powers to various sub-state levels of government or the provisions for changing the Law of Political Parties to allow for the emergence of purely regional parties that could contest for seats in the National Assembly. For Savimbi, Lusaka represented death by cooptation. Ultimately, he preferred death by other means.

Luena

After Savimbi's death on 22 February 2002, a decapitated UNITA had few viable options to continue a guerrilla war. Besides, by then, this once powerful guerrilla force had been severely battered into a dead end since losing its headquarters at Bailundo and Andulo in 1999. That successful FAA offensive forced the rebels to rethink their overall military strategy. As a result of this reassessment, UNITA decided to go back to its roots – both geographically and tactically. Thus, Savimbi moved his troops to Moxico – where he had formed UNITA more than three decades earlier – to reinitiate a classic guerrilla war. But three decades had robbed Savimbi and much of his group's leadership of the necessary agility to successfully conduct a guerrilla war. Now, Savimbi was no longer able to fully disperse his troops into small guerrilla bands because his own safety and that of his top aides required considerable concentration of resources – both troops and materiel. In addition, FAA continued its unrelenting pursuit of Savimbi after dislodging him from Bailundo and Andulo. Through "Operation Restauro", FAA was determined to prevent Savimbi from reestablishing guerrilla bases in the Moxico province. Consequently, the Angolan armed forces were willing to use a variety of methods – from heavy bombing to the depopulation of the target areas – to frustrate Savimbi's plans. By the end of 2001 Savimbi was left with two basic options: surrender or death.

For a leaderless UNITA, surrender was the best option. The modalities for UNITA's extinction as a military force were negotiated in Luena through the "Memorandum of Understanding Addendum to the Lusaka Protocol for the Cessation of Hostilities and the Resolution of the Outstanding Military Issues under the Lusaka Protocol" which, after being duly signed by both sides in Luanda on 4 April 2002, marked the end of the civil war.

Through the Memorandum of Understanding, both the government and UNITA committed themselves to fulfil their obligations under previous peace agreements – i.e. Bicesse and Lusaka – as well as respect the "Constitution and all other legislation in effect within the Republic of Angola". Another key element of the Memorandum of Understanding is national reconciliation. Unfortunately, like Lusaka, it still defined national reconciliation mainly in terms of amnesty. Thus, under the terms of the Memorandum of Understanding, the government undertook to approve an Amnesty Law "covering all crimes committed in conjunction with the armed conflict". In other words, there would be no sober introspection about the fundamental causes of the conflict, i.e. what triggered it, what sustained it, how it affected the country and its peoples, how to handle issues of culpability, whether anyone would be punished for war crimes, what mechanisms would be introduced to avert the possibility of future civil wars, etc. Such questions, it seemed, had been buried with Savimbi.

In addition to amnesty, the government also committed itself to absorb about 50,000 former UNITA military personnel into FAA and the national police "in accordance with existing vacancies". Excess military personnel would be demobilized and reintegrated into civil society. For the first time since independence, Angolan society would no longer be hostage to war. This is a critical first step on the long road to peace.

The road to positive peace: Challenges ahead

The end of Angola's long civil war will not automatically usher in sustainable and positive peace in the absence of an open and flexible power-sharing framework that is able to reconcile the different political aspirations within the country. Since independence, control of political power has been restricted to the hands of a single political formation. Now, with the end of the civil war, there is willingness on the part of the governing MPLA to magnanimously share power with other political formations, including a demilitarized UNITA. Problematically, this power-sharing formula does not appear to involve much more than an attempt to establish a coalition of elites. Two main problems are immediately discernible. First, the elites' pact will be necessarily lopsided in favour of the winning side in the civil war. Therefore, this pact retains a high degree of imbalance especially given the improbability of transcending destabilizing elements – regionalism, ethnicity, and corruption, among others – within the current political framework. Second, this pact is exclusive in the sense that it does not provide open access to all extant or would-be elites, let alone the average citizen. The excluded segments of society – whether ethnonational groups or socio-economic classes – will continue to see violence as a viable means to induce regime change, if not gain political power. Sustainable peace requires, minimally, embracing the politics of inclusion as national policy. Regrettably, this has eluded Angola since independence. The major participants in Angola's post-colonial saga sought, first and foremost, to annihilate or seriously debilitate the opposing side both at the political and military levels as a pre-condition for peace. As the review of failed peace processes presented above illustrates, this approach was inherently flawed because it neglected the non-political and non-military dimensions of positive peace.

Positive peace for Angola must be based on a careful and introspective assessment of the roots and dynamics of the conflict to ensure that the devastation it caused will never again befall the peoples of Angola. Facile explanations that attribute the length and severity of the war to one person may obfuscate the complexity of the conflict. Other factors including identity, fear, greed, equity, and so on are all legitimate points of entry for analysis and may provide important clues for understanding Angola's long post-colonial war. This is a prerequisite for finding adequate mechanisms to help a deeply scarred country begin to heal itself. Sustaining positive peace will also require a colossal effort in political reconstruction aimed at strengthening deficient state structures and institutions to improve their transparency with the ultimate objective of promoting good governance as the general basis of a stable political order. Ultimately, good governance is the best guarantee that potentially destabilizing post-conflict difficulties can develop into full blown crises.

CHAPTER 7

Post-Conflict Challenges
Identity and governance

Twenty-seven years of civil war postponed the materialization of the post-colonial state-building project in Angola. For much of the post-independence period, the state was unable to perform basic functions of governance particularly in rural areas. The end of the civil war provides Angola with the hitherto critical missing ingredient for building a strong state. The absence of war, however, does not suddenly eliminate other major hurdles to healthy post-colonial state building. As argued elsewhere, the civil war and the related post-colonial crisis of governance resulted from the major nationalist groups' inability to find mutually acceptable ways to share power and wealth after the collapse of the colonial regime. In Angola, the fact that in addition to important ideological differences these nationalist groups also represented major ethno-linguistic groups as well as classes, regions, and races greatly complicated the post-colonial state building project.

The inability to share power and wealth in the post-independence period had historical roots. It was a direct result of the major divisions among the main nationalist groups that participated in the anti-colonial war of liberation. But these cleavages were only partly the result of deep animosities caused by ideological differences reflecting Cold War allegiances – i.e. the Marxist MPLA was supported by the former Soviet Union while FNLA, and later UNITA, were supported by the United States. Basically, what divided the nationalist groups was their inability to move beyond their national identity differences. Some elements of their identity, like ethnicity, predated colonialism while others like region and class were exaggerated, if not created, by the colonial regime. Tragically for Angola, these differences were left unresolved and allowed to simmer during the anti-colonial struggle. In addition, the anti-colonial war also showed that two of the major liberation movements – FNLA and UNITA – could not claim to have "national" representation beyond the Bacongo and Ovimbundu groups respectively. Ethnic/regional identity was also important for MPLA, the movement that traditionally eschewed a discourse based on racial, ethnic, regional, or class identity. In the aftermath of the anti-colonial war and as the three movements became involved in the civil war, MPLA's base of support around the capital city – which rested heavily on ethnic, regional, and class appeal – enabled it to successfully evict its rivals from Luanda in time to receive independence from the departing colonial authorities. In important respects, therefore, MPLA's ability to prevail over its rivals in the crucial months both before and after independence can only be partly attributed to the external support it received from Cuba and the former Soviet Union. The internal support it received from its Kimbundu constituency around Luanda was just as critical for its ascent to and permanence in power. Using the "people's power" committees and other party structures it had established in the capital region, MPLA was able to arm a significant number of mainly Kimbundu civilians who helped ensure that UNITA and FNLA soldiers and militants were driven out and kept out of Luanda in the critical formative period of the post-colonial state. A similar episode occurred in the aftermath of the 1992 post-electoral fiasco when MPLA supporters helped drive UNITA and its sympathizers from Luanda, killing hundreds of non-Kimbundu persons in the process.

Beyond these episodes, the Kimbundu group has ensured MPLA's continued rule in more basic ways by consistently supporting the regime even when its increasingly corrupt governance negatively affected all citizens, including the Kimbundu. The patron-client networks that distribute the vast oil wealth do not necessarily have a dominant ethnic character. They are mostly based on personal friendships connected to the main centres of wealth and power, i.e. with individuals in the presidential entourage as well as tight political and military-security circles around the president. Since many of these individuals are from the Luanda area there emerged a natural overlap between access to power and wealth and ethnic/regional origin.

Given the minimal, direct material benefits accrued to the Kimbundu as a group as a consequence of their support for the MPLA regime, a more important reason for this group's support must be sought elsewhere. This critical support can best be understood in terms of the Kimbundu's own sense of identity. As mentioned earlier, the first European explorers to arrive in Angola found complex processes of state formation underway. As in many other parts of Africa, these pre-colonial processes were carried out mainly along ethnic lines. The colonial presence halted such processes and, by forcibly including within their colonial possessions different ethnolinguistic groups with different histories and aspirations, colonialism set the stage for very complicated processes of state-building in Angola as elsewhere in Africa after independence. Independence provided the opportunity for aspiring pre-colonial nations like the Kimbundu to claim their political, economic and cultural stakes within the new post-colonial state. Since FNLA and UNITA derived their support almost exclusively from the dominant groups in the northern and southern parts of Angola – the Bacongo and Ovimbundu, respectively – it is not surprising that the Kimbundu mainly support MPLA whose leadership included several of their group's most prominent members. Similarly, for MPLA, pragmatic considerations pertaining to regime survival made Kimbundu support indispensable. This relationship between MPLA and the Kimbundu contributed to the strong ethnic overtones the civil war acquired as it metamorphosed from a conflict based on the ideological differences among the major politico-military forces developed within the Cold War context into a conflict where the key factors included the political economy of ethnic identity. In addition to being primarily a conflict over control of important natural resources like oil and diamonds, Angola's civil war also became a conflict where a powerful force, claiming to represent the largest ethnic group, the Ovimbundu, attempted to redress the perceived unfairness of a system where power and wealth were divided along ethnic lines and where one ethnic group in particular, the Kimbundu, was portrayed as the primary beneficiary of MPLA rule.

In retrospect, the civil war provided both MPLA and UNITA with opportunities to use the politics of ethnic identity for different, yet equally destructive, purposes. For MPLA, informal ethnic networks kept it in power even after suffering two apparently crushing setbacks: neither the collapse of the USSR, its main external ideological and military supporter, nor the near implosion of the domestic economy outside the oil sector, significantly eroded its power base. Regrettably, this power base had to be perpetually greased with the vast oil revenues controlled, without being accounted for, by the regime. This fostered a culture of corruption. UNITA, on the other hand, succeeded in using ethnic politics to rally and sustain popular support among the Ovimbundu. By highlighting Kimbundu overrepresentation within MPLA's state apparatus, UNITA consistently characterized failure of governance in conspiratorial terms – as a conscious effort by MPLA to deny other ethnic groups a slice of the country's wealth. Thus, UNITA could justify the use of military means to redress the inequitable distribution of power and wealth. This fostered a culture of violence.

Given its central importance, therefore, the lense of ethnicity provides important additional insights for understanding Angola's recent past and perspectives for post-conflict governance. One of the central arguments in this chapter is that ethnicity in Angola remains a formidable and easily ignitable force. However, this force does not necessarily have to be destructive because its power can be harnessed for more positive and constructive ends, including the long-delayed post-colonial state-building project. Unless such new and more positive forms for managing ethnicity are found, peaceful governance in Angola will remain highly problematic. The "conscious management of regime structures with a view to enhancing the legitimacy of the public realm", as Hyden (1992:7) defines governance, cannot possibly be achieved in situations where, given their identities and allegiances – primordial or otherwise – significant segments of the citizenry question the legitimacy of the processes for distributing power and wealth within the post-colonial state. What is needed in Angola where ethnic identity remains a defining trait for many citizens is a new political architecture that takes into account ethnic differences and the need to undertake an equitable division of power and wealth within a decentralized, democratic state. This is a necessary first step in a long process to liberate society from a destructive brand of ethnic politics that, in Angola, has helped to foster twin cultures of corruption and violence.

This new architecture must move beyond the Westphalian blueprints that, alas, continue to dominate much of the political discourse in Africa. Although states will retain their importance in Africa, if less so elsewhere, their primacy in the African context cannot be at the expense of the sub-state entities that constitute them. Particularly in Africa, where the Westphalian model was introduced simultaneously with colonialism, the centrality of nations and ethnic groups cannot be dismissed as more stable and citizen-centred political structures are devised.

Ethnic identity and the African post-colonial state-building project

Ethnicity is an amorphous notion that originates from the Greek word ethnos meaning a group or people characterized by common descent. The term has come to denote a "condition of belonging to an ethnic group, the sense of ethnic identity felt by the members of an ethnic community" (Davies, 1996:80–1). Like many other social phenomena, ethnicity and ethnic identity cannot be considered in isolation. They must be understood in conjunction with other equally crucial and related notions like ethnic groups and, more broadly, nations. Schermerhorn (1970:12) defines an ethnic group as:

... a collectivity within a larger society having real or putative common ancestry, memories of a shared historical past, and a cultural focus on one or more
symbolic elements defined as the epitome of their peoplehood. Examples of
such symbolic elements are: kinship patterns, physical contiguity (as in lo-
calism or sectionalism), religious affiliation, language or dialect forms, tribal
affiliation, nationality, phenotypical features, or any combination of these. A
necessary accompaniment is some consciousness of kind among members of
the group.

Unlike Schermerhorn, Hutchinson and Smith (1996:6) de-emphasize the
connection with the "larger society". They prefer the term ethnie or ethnic
community to define "a named human population with myths of common
ancestry, shared historical memories, one or more elements of common
culture, a link with a homeland and a sense of solidarity among at least
some of its members". That the cultural undercurrents of these definitions
are not accidental for the contemporary usage of ethnicity as an important
variable to understand complex social phenomena is associated with the
anthropological works of Geertz and Barth.

Geertz emphasized primordialism and proposed that ethnicity is beyond human control because it stems from a natural division of human
beings into distinct groups, i.e., people are born with an ethnic identity
– a set of fundamental endowments and identifications which every individual shares with other members of the ethnic group – that include blood,
language, religion, and social practices (Geertz, 1963b:109). This is not an
unproblematic view of ethnicity because, as Davies (1996:82) points out, it
"disregards factors like the individual's social, economic and political circumstances and suggests an identity not based on a sense of rational interest, but a sense of self based on emotional ties and emanating from natural
affinities of kinship and language". Part of the difficulty in Geertz' argument is that it seems to suggest that individuals are somehow trapped into
the communities and identities into which they are born and are unable to
transcend them. Barth's anthropological view of ethnicity emphasizes its
contextual, circumstantial, and situational dimensions. For Barth (1969),
identity – including of the ethnic dimension – is a product of particular
economic, political, and social conditions and is determined by the context
in which an individual finds himself/herself. From this perspective, ethnic
identity is adaptive and voluntaristic (Davies, 1996:82).

A.D. Smith later broke the primordial/situational polarity by stressing
the historical and symbolic attributes of ethnic identity. For him, an ethnic
group is "a type of cultural collectivity; one that emphasizes the role of

myth of descent and historical memories, and that is recognized by one or more cultural differences like religion, customs or language" (Smith, 1991:120). Smith correctly distinguishes between two forms of ethnic group: ethnic categories and ethnic communities (or ethnies). An ethnic category is a group with marginal self-awareness but considered by non-group members, or outsiders, to constitute an objectively distinct cultural-historical grouping. An ethnie, on the other hand, is a group distinguishable both objectively and subjectively. Hutchinson and Smith (1996:6) define ethnie as "a named human population with myths of common ancestry, shared historical memories, one or more elements of common culture, a link with a homeland and a sense of solidarity among at least some of its members". The subjective dimension of ethnie is particularly important because it makes the group conscious of its distinctiveness. Equally important, this self-awareness serves as a base for the ethnie's demands for recognition as an equal from other such groups (Smith, 1991:21). Often, however, an ethnie makes demands beyond equality of treatment. When an ethnie demands corporate recognition of the group and self-government, and is successful in attaining these objectives within an existing or new state, then it becomes a nationality (Davies, 1996:84).

The salience of contemporary issues related to identity has led to new reconceptualizations of culture and identity which emphasize "social constructedness as opposed to primordialism, optionality as opposed to determinism, fragmentation and diversification as opposed to integration and homogenization, and multidimensionality and dynamism as opposed to static unidimensionality (Lapid, 1996:7). This line of theorizing also opens up new possibilities for reconceptualizing the state. For example, it provides insights for understanding the state as a social actor "embedded in social rules and conventions that constitute its identity and the reasons for the interests that motivate actors" (Katzenstein, 1996:23). The focus on culture and identity to analyze the state also shows that although nation-states remain as central pillars of global as well as territorial constructions of collective identities, they are not homogeneous bodies but "collectivities full of people with multiple identities and loyalties" (Krause and Renwick, 1996:xii). Perhaps most importantly, it suggests that even at sub-nation-state levels "identities are constructed and can, therefore, be deconstructed and reconstructed anew" (Krause and Renwick, 1996:xii-xiii). This is particularly relevant in Africa given the complexities of post-colonial state formation and the construction and reconstruction of identities within an overall climate of instability and frequent violence. Within this context, modern nation-building projects seek to create a sense of solidarity and belonging within heterogeneous entities where populations are faced with the realities of competing loyalties between the new and artificial formations and older cultural identities. When conflicts arise between these competing loyalties due to disaffection with the construction of post-colonial national identities, ethnic or "tribal" bonds provide ready-made alternatives especially in times of real or perceived insecurity for individuals or groups. In times of major transformations, as most post-colonial African states have experienced, newly created identities – including states – are often called into question as their constituting groups seek secessionist or irredentist alternatives. With one exception – the successful secession of Eritrea from Ethiopia – post-colonial African states have resisted pressures to redraw colonial borders for fear of opening the proverbial Pandora's Box. As Davies (1996:90) notes, "the potential for catastrophe has been largely acknowledged and few elites are prepared to take such risks". But fear of the potential chaos rightly expected to result from an exercise in redrawing colonial borders does not address the fact that "ethnicity retains its potency as a focus of identification in the absence of strong legitimate alternative identities" (Davies, 1996:90).

The Westphalian system in Africa produced problematic results in the sense that many African states continue struggling for domestic survival and international relevance. This condition was not entirely unpredictable especially given the role of ethnic identity in pre-colonial society. Pre-colonial Africa included hundreds of societies ranging from small bands of hunters and gatherers to large, agricultural-based communities with highly sophisticated and centralized political structures dominated by chiefs and kings. Most of these societies were held together by a strong sense of kinship and common territory.

As Thompson (1989:64–5) notes, despite their diverse forms of social, political, and economic organization, pre-colonial African societies had several features in common. These included the fact that "each society identified with a 'homeland', a specific territory defined not in the legalistic sense of a modern state boundary, but in the equally forceful sense of a 'common land' occupied since the beginning of the 'people' themselves". Even more important, as far as the issue of ethnic identity is concerned, Africans attached to each place "an emotional and cultural significance that could only be regarded as sacred" (Thompson, 1989:65). By choosing to ignore this realm – where the subjective domain of emotion, culture, and spirituality is anchored in a specific place – the departing colonial powers bequeathed upon the leaders of "independent" Africa a virtual ethnic time bomb. The boundaries of the new African states reflect colonial, not cultural or national, identities. The hastily arranged decolonization process, coupled with the personal ambitions of the would-be leaders of the newly independent states, did not allow for a more sober assessment of the costs and benefits of undertaking the post-colonial state building project guided by an essentially unaltered colonial map. Thus, predictably, independence did not usher in a new era of freedom, peace, and prosperity among Africa's peoples. Instead, several interstate and intrastate conflicts – many caused by difficulties of reconciling would-be pre-colonial nations and post-colonial states – have been fought with unsurprising frequency. Ironically, in some of the post-colonial wars – in Nigeria, Sudan, Liberia, Sierra Leone, Ivory Coast – nationalism has taken on a new meaning: it is no longer anti-colonial but anti-state. Its instrument of choice is no longer the liberation war but intercommunal strife. Could this have been prevented? The answer is, unfortunately, no. The inherited boundaries are artificial lines on a map, not communal boundaries. From this perspective, the post-colonial states are in many respects viewed as being just as artificial and illegitimate as the colonial entities they replaced. In this situation, it is inevitable that political parties will develop along ethnic lines and 'liberation armies' will be formed to subverte/reconfigure the new states. The reason for these conflicts does not simply reside in the existence of numerous, often unfriendly, ethnic communities, tribes or nations cohabiting within post-colonial states. Conflicts in Africa also reflect many post-colonial states' inability to develop an inclusive political system that takes into account their citizens' multiple allegiances. In some cases, African citizens' primary allegiances are not always to the post-colonial states. Often, that allegiance is given to the ethnic community because the citizens' sense of self is intrinsically attached to such factors as kinship ties, language, locality, religion, and tradition.

Many African states' lack of administrative and ideological capacity to govern make them even more unable to manage, let alone reconcile, national identity differences. Thus, a perennial source of conflict is related to the perceptions and realities of governance in Africa as a zero-sum proposition. More than a few post-colonial states have come under the control of one ethnic group, usually numerically dominant, which then uses the state's political and economic resources for its own benefit and to the detriment of others. This causes resentment, particularly when other groups perceive themselves as holders of certain tangible attributes and skills that could be translated into political or economic power. In such cases, when access to political power is denied, instability – even civil wars – often results. This should not come as a surprise especially in Africa where control of the state has become a vital political goal for ethnic groups, both dominant and subordinate, because it provides unobstructed access to power and wealth. For dominant groups, control of the state ensures political supremacy and economic dominance. Subordinate groups seek control of the state to ensure that their social, cultural, and economic interests are protected and their aspirations fulfilled. When the political arena does not accommodate ethnic communities as interest groups they become conflict groups with aspirations to insert the group's grievances, claims and anxieties into the national agenda/debate by all means necessary, including violence. Under such conditions, ethnic communities will produce political leaders like Savimbi in Angola who, expressing communal will or pursuing their personal ambitions, attempt to insert their group's grievances into the political agenda by politicizing ethnicity.

For Rothschild (1981:6), the politicization of ethnicity involves four elements, including:

1. to render people cognitively aware of the relevance of politics to the health of their ethnic cultural values and vice versa,

2. to stimulate their concern about this nexus,

3. to mobilize them into self-conscious ethnic groups, and

4. to direct their behaviour toward activity in the political arena on the basis of this awareness, concern, and group consciousness.

As numerous contemporary examples in Angola as elsewhere in Africa illustrate, ethnicity, once politicized, becomes a powerful political force that may ultimately "enhance, retard, or nullify the political integration of states, may legitimate or delegitimate their political systems, and stabilize or undermine their regimes and governments" (Rothschild, 1981:6). For post-conflict Angola, the challenge resides not so much in attempting to put the ethnic genie back in the bottle – or even in attempting to ignore it – but in channeling the power of ethnicity toward more positive ends like creating an open, inclusive, vibrant and multiethnic post-colonial state where differences are not simply respected but celebrated. This challenge arises mainly from the tremendous ethnic diversity in the country and the opportunities for politicizing these differences that remain even after the end of the civil war.

Diversity and the challenges of post-colonial governance

Inability to manage ethnic diversity was a major contributing cause of Angola's civil war. This diversity and accompanying political expressions pre-date colonialism. In Angola, as in many other parts of Africa, the pre-colonial process of state formation was carried out mainly along ethnic lines. When Portuguese explorer Diogo Cão first arrived in the Kingdom of Kongo in the early fifteenth century he found a complex process of state formation underway. Specifically, what Cão found in what later became Angola was not one homogenous state but a large number of distinct ethnolinguitic groups varying considerably in size, economic development, and political organization. Some were small "tribes" while others constituted larger "nations". The colonial presence halted whatever political processes – state-building or otherwise – were underway within those distinct groups and spaces. Moreover, by forcibly including within their colonial possession different ethnolinguistic groups with different histories and aspirations, Portuguese colonialism set the stage for very complicated processes of state building in Angola after independence. Not incidentally, the main combatants in Angola's civil war derived much of their popular support from the major ethno-linguistic groups in the country – Ovimbundu (UNITA), Mbundu (MPLA), and Bacongo (FNLA) – that once constituted distinct kingdoms. The Ovimbundu are, by far, the largest ethno-linguistic group. They represent thirty-five to forty per cent of Angola's population and dominate the areas with the highest population density in the country – the central plateau provinces of Huambo and Bié as well as the coastal province of Benguela. Their cultural, linguistic and economic domination in the central part of Angola is such that at least one writer describes them as "a nation rather than an assembly of tribes" (Van Der Waals, 1993:16). The Mbundu, representing about twenty-five per cent of the population, occupy the areas around the capital city, Luanda, and east as far as the Cassange area of Malanje province. A distinct ethnic subgroup has developed within the larger Mbundu region. The impact of the colonial presence on the western part of the Mbundu domain, more specifically around Luanda, brought to the region individuals from all Angolan ethnic groups. Over time, they constituted a unique group – heavily influenced by Portuguese language and customs – called Luandas (Redinha, 1965:7) or Caluandas. The Bacongo represent about fifteen per cent of Angola's population and reside mainly in the northern provinces of Cabinda, Zaire, and Uige.

This diversity has dominated politics and society in Angola since the first contact with Europeans. For example, the fractured nature of resistance against Portuguese encroachment and dominance facilitated the imposition of colonial rule. Although sporadic anti-colonial resistance took place during Portugal's presence in Angola, the various kingdoms and chiefdoms threatened by colonial domination were unable to create a united front. From this perspective, the disunity that characterized the anti-colonial movement after WWII and the inability to establish an inclusive political system after independence have long historical antecedents.

Unlike other colonial powers, Portugal did not participate in the European drive to de-colonize Africa after WWII. Thus, an anti-colonial war – led by MPLA, FNLA, and UNITA – was fought from 1961 until the collapse of the colonial regime in 1974. However, contrary to the experience of other former Portuguese colonies, the liberation movements in Angola never succeeded in creating a united front because, among other factors, they were never able to overcome their ethnic differences. As discussed above, MPLA was founded in 1956 to lead the struggle against colonialism. But its popular base of support remained circumscribed to the predominantly Kimbundu region that produced much of the MPLA leadership. MPLA had minor enclaves of support throughout the country especially among *assimilados*, mulattos, and even some members of the settler community. FNLA was created through the merger of several groups whose main objective was the restoration of the ancient Kongo kingdom in northern Angola. Thus, FNLA's main constituency remained almost exclusively restricted to the Bakongo ethnic group. Attempts to expand this constituency to include elements from other ethnic groups consistently failed. Similarly, there was an important ethnic rationale for creating UNITA. Many Ovimbundu believed that, as the major ethnic group in Angola, it was critical that they had their own "liberation movement" to counterbalance the role and power of the movements representing the other two major ethnic groups. Thus, in important respects, the political project of some of these movements was primarily sub-national. Beyond the rhetoric, FNLA and UNITA, in particular, were primarily concerned with the aspirations of particular ethnic groups – respectively, the Bacongo and Ovimbundu – not with the creation of an ethnically inclusive post-colonial state. For these liberation movements, the colonial state was an artificial and oppressive construct in need of dismantling as a pre-requisite for the reconstruction or reinvention of their respective "nations".

The ethnic factor became critical in the period leading up to independence and in subsequent years. As previously mentioned, the bulk of MPLA's leadership was drawn from the Kimbundu. Consequently, more than the other two major groups, the Kimbundu were the group perceived to be the main beneficiary of the post-colonial political economy. Both UNITA and FNLA resented, and were threatened by, this perceived unfair advantaged enjoyed by the Kimbundu who, predictably, used it to sustain MPLA's long stay in power. Overcoming these divisions, both real and perceived, represents a major challenge for post-conflict governance.

The challenges of governance in a divided society

Good governance involves political and bureaucratic accountability, freedom of association and participation, freedom of information and expression, and a sound autonomous judicial system. The preoccupation with good governance in Africa is not new. More than two decades ago, the International Financial Institutions (IFIs) diagnosed Africa's affliction as a "crisis of governance" reflected in the extensive personalization of power, the denial of fundamental rights and freedoms, widespread corruption, and the prevalence of non-elected and unaccountable governments (World Bank, 1989:60). Since then, the IFIs as well as Africanist intellectuals and development practitioners have sought the appropriate remedies to help Africa overcome this crisis.

The recommended prescription emphasized "political renewal" premised in "a systematic effort to build a pluralistic institutional structure, a determination to respect the rule of law, and a vigourous protection of the freedom of the press and human rights" (World Bank, 1989:60–61). At the time, even critics of adjustment policies in Africa accepted this position. For example, in its "African Alternative Framework", the United Nations Economic Commission for Africa suggested that governance was the key to fundamental change in Africa. For ECA (1989:60–61), governance involved the "democratization of the decision-making process at national, local and grassroots levels so as to generate the necessary consensus and people's support". In this sense, governance was seen as serving two important purposes. First, it pushed African rulers to become more accountable to the populations over which they claim authority. Second, it could "facilitate a relationship of bargaining through which the interests of the state and those in society can be adjusted to each other so that the exercise of state power might be regarded as legitimate by those subject to it" (Apter and Rosberg, 1994:91). This, for Hyden (1992:10), results in a situation "where politics is a positive-sum game; where reciprocal behaviour and legitimate relations of power between governors and governed prevail; and where everybody is a winner not only in the short run but also in the long run".

From a practical perspective the effectiveness of a system of governance depends largely on how it is perceived. Governments that acquire authority or legitimate power to govern through a credible electoral process have a better chance of becoming real agents of change. Similarly, good governance requires arrangements to make bureaucrats more accountable through regular performance monitoring of public agencies and officials. This is essential to achieve transparency in bureaucracies, particularly in terms of rigorous financial management.

Good governance has been especially problematic in Angola where, due to civil war and kleptocratic mismanagement, a decaying state has been unable to carry out vital functions associated with governance since independence. The inability to establish a regime of good governance in Angola can be understood by analyzing the ways the new state was organized, particularly in terms of how power was exercised. Although Angola achieved independence in extremely difficult conditions, MPLA succeeded in gaining control of the government and was able to extend and consolidate its administration throughout most of the country. Angolans expected, in retrospect unrealistically, that the winning side would introduce a system of good governance and impose measures to establish a viable political order as a foundation for promoting national unity, ethnic harmony and economic development. Instead, for a decade and a half after independence, the new regime erected an intolerant, inflexible political order based on Marxism-Leninism. The one-party regime attempted to either co-opt or destroy most elements of civil society. Political participation could only take place when mobilized and organized by the state – through "mass organizations" representing women, workers, youth, and children – to serve its own specific purposes.

Simultaneously, the governing party mandated revolutionary hostility to all forms of traditional authority and the aspirant petty bourgeoisie for alleged collaboration with the colonial regime. Lost in the initial Marxist-Leninist ideological fervour was the basic contractual relationship between state and citizen. Beyond the rhetoric, the new state regarded the citizens primarily as instruments for serving the regime's interests and not the other way around. This contributed to ethnic favouritism and divisions, corruption and injustices, as well as the economic decline that combined to add fuel to an already devastating civil war. With most avenues for political participation closed by the state – and in the presence of highly centralized, yet dysfunctional and decaying political and economic structures – the citizens became consumed almost exclusively by concerns affecting their immediate survival: the search for food, shelter, and security. Meanwhile, powerful and rapacious state elites – incubated in and protected by the regime's structures – emerged and, by usurping political power and economic benefits, further contributed to a widening gap between state and citizens. This gulf between the state and citizens manifested itself in various domestic conflicts involving class, race and ethnicity within an overall context of problematic governance. Ironically, in the war against colonialism and during its first years in power, MPLA considered itself a "movement of the masses". This populist rhetoric gradually disappeared after independence as a relatively small group of individuals used their party connections to dominate the post-colonial state and economy. In other words, instead of strengthening the ties with workers and peasants that began to develop during the anti-colonial war, the governing elites grew increasingly detached from the common citizen and used the repressive means of the state to preserve their privileged status.

Given their pivotal position, members of the Angolan ruling elite have enormous resources of patronage. These resources have been used to create extensive and intricate patron/client networks mainly along ethnic, class and racial lines. It is within these networks that most political deals are made and significant economic transactions take place. Such networks are an indispensable base to hold political office or even to seek public employment. Accordingly, the ruling elites have used these networks for political control and financial aggrandizement. In the process, however, they engendered high levels of corruption and seriously contributed to the erosion of public trust in government. From the ordinary citizen's point of view, the elite's grip on state power has assumed hegemonic proportions and represents a throwback to colonial times when power, prestige, and privilege were closely associated with class and race.

Regrettably, Angolan citizens cannot count on the main opposition to provide alternative forms of governance. UNITA demonstrated throughout its years of insurgency that it is no better equipped to facilitate the development of a healthy civil society than MPLA. In many respects political participation in the areas controlled by UNITA was even more restricted than in government-held zones. Several reasons account for this situation. Although UNITA portrayed itself as a democratic organization it was clearly anti-democratic both in political orientation and practice. As a result it created very centralized structures both at the political and military levels. For example, military structures dominated the organization in the sense that no civilians were allowed to hold leadership positions. During the civil war, all members of UNITA's Politburo and its Political Commission (the decision-making body) had a military rank. The merging of military and political positions and functions gave UNITA a particularly rigid and oppressive character. In other words, both the government and UNITA had put in place decidedly dysfunctional and oppressive systems of governance that favoured only a small percentage of the population with the right political, ethnic, or racial connections.

The war's end has added a new impetus for improving state-society relations. But this process is revealing important paradoxes. During the civil war, the MPLA regime had created both dissent and dependency. The dissent, which lay mostly dormant throughout the repressive years, is now serving as the catalyst for the mushrooming of all types of organizations. Paradoxically, however, many of these organizations continue to depend on the state or international organizations for resources. Thus, political parties, churches, cultural groups, women's organizations and other would-be civil society organizations are spreading not so much as a counterweight to the state but mainly to benefit from it in terms of financial assistance and all the other benefits traditionally allotted to the state elites.

As mentioned before, during the single party regime, the MPLA relied on "mass organizations" it created for workers, youth, women, and children to ensure participation of officially sanctioned groups while making the formation of autonomous organizations illegal. Mass organizations were expected to provide unconditional support for the MPLA's political, economic, and social programmes. However, since the introduction of economic reforms in the late 1980s and political liberalization initiatives in the early 1990s, allowing the emergence of autonomous organized groups, MPLA has tried to influence key groups in society by either direct cooptation or by binding them into organizations that have become dependent on patronage. Thus, the regime could both continue to influence society by extending its organization, coordination, and supervision over as much of the population as possible as well as stave off mass opposition.

In terms of the regime's survival strategies, the practice of allowing organized groups commonly associated with civil society to emerge while keeping them dependent on the state has been successful in the sense that this political liberalization provided the ruling party with sufficient democratic credentials to remain in power. But the structures being created in this more liberal era will not necessarily strengthen civil society because they are a product of state corporatism. Their continued existence, not to mention degree of influence and well-being, depend on the whims of the state, particularly the party controlling it. By polluting the space of civil society, MPLA has thus far succeeded in preventing alternatives from emerging with important implications for the deepening of the democratization process. Furthermore, this ensures that both the governing party and the state can avoid real popular accountability. Actually, the international community – not domestic civil society – has taken the leading role in demanding governmental accountability and transparency.

The end of the civil war provides the Angolan state with an opportunity to place good governance at the top of its priority list. Good governance for Angola will greatly depend on the extent to which the state can be perceived as legitimate in the eyes of the common citizen. In other words, from the citizens' perspective, the nature of the state must change radically – from its current form as an artificial colonial construct with a propensity for falling prey to predatory elites – to an entity whose primary function is to facilitate the materialization of all the citizens' aspirations as they seek the good life, however this is individually defined. This involves a drastic design change in the current overly centralized post-colonial state with the objective of creating an institutional framework that makes the state both more accountable and more responsive to the citizens. This can only occur through a radical devolution of power to sub-state levels where people tend to find innovative and – with the necessary judicial safeguards – peaceful ways to govern themselves in accountable, transparent, and responsible governance.

Post-war governance

The end of Angola's civil war and the approaching of the post-dos Santos era provide opportunities to rethink the idea of the post-colonial state with a view to undertaking fundamental transformations aimed at changing its rigid, sometimes authoritarian, highly centralized character into a modern, pluralistic, and decentralized entity. Given the make-up of the post-colonial state, especially in light of the fact that it agglomerates many peoples with distinct languages and cultures and political aspirations, successful post-civil war governance can only be achieved if it rests on a system whereby these peoples – living in distinct regions, provinces, municipalities, etc. – have greater power and responsibility in the management of those political, economic, and other matters pertaining to their existence.

In other words, sustainable peace in Angola requires devolution of power and responsibilities away from centre. Reducing the power divide between centre and periphery is the necessary first step to addressing longstanding sources of tension in Angola – some of which, as in the festering conflict in Cabinda, remain unresolved – that could acquire important centrifugal dynamics. Therefore, new notions of the post-colonial state must be founded on the notion that decentralization – including greater regional and/or provincial autonomy – could strengthen the state by empowering its constituting parts.

As discussed above, Angola, like many other African states, must cope with serious and deep regional differences and work toward reconciling the various ethnic groups that make up society. In this context, it is ultimately counterproductive to stubbornly hold on to modern and Western ideas of nation-state and ignore the strength of other conceptualizations especially when, in some areas, citizens identify themselves more readily with the group, province or region than with the nation-state. From the perspective of the post-colonial Angolan state, there is only *one nation* whose centre is the capital city Luanda. However, this notion is not shared by all those who inhabit the periphery. For many, there is *one state* with a government in Luanda. However, this state includes several nations – real or imagined – with distinct cultures and languages. These long-standing tensions between centre and periphery can be repressed with varying degrees of success for considerable periods. However, as multiple examples from Africa and elsewhere indicate, they are rarely extinguished. This suggests that, in places like Angola, the unitary state is often structurally inadequate to deal with the multiple pressures arising from the diversity of its constituting parts. A more decentralized structure better equipped to deal with the many peculiarities and artificialities of the post-colonial state to ensure its long-term viability, even survival, must therefore be sought. Decentralization – including devolution of power – must not be confused with self-determination. It may not even have to amount to autonomy. Indeed, the state must retain the constitutional framework that guarantees its integrity and indissolubility. Conversely, given the wider pressures of globalization, it is unlikely that sub-state units would be able to manage the turbulences of global relations individually. Decentralization simply enhances the viability of the state while correcting some of the most negative effects of colonialism by devolving to the constituting units within the post-colonial state their own space to express and celebrate their distinct forms of ethnic, political, economic, cultural, linguistic and other identities on their own terms.

Specifically, the post-war state in Angola must transform itself in ways whereby the current administrative division of the country evolves into a structure that better captures the political realities of the country. In other words, provinces – which currently are administrative units whose main function is to carry out the decisions of the central government through appointed officials – must be allowed to develop their own political structures and people's representatives elected by universal suffrage. These political structures and elected officials can then exercise those executive, legislative and judicial powers devolved by the centre. Thus, while the centre would retain under its exclusive jurisdiction such areas as international affairs, defence, justice, and finance, important areas like cultural affairs, public works, housing, town planning, tourism, and social welfare are most suitable under the jurisdiction of sub-state regions. Both levels of government can share jurisdiction in areas like education, health, and environmental protection that clearly require coordination among various levels of government. While the central government is ultimately responsible for financial matters the provinces and/or autonomous regions must have the financial wherewithal to carry out their functions in an authoritative manner. Therefore, these sub-state structures must be guaranteed a portion of the state funds as well as be allowed to collect local taxes and borrow funds in accordance with the overall policy frameworks set by the state as the entity ultimately responsible for the overall well-being of all its citizens. Critically, for a resource-rich state like Angola, the provinces must be granted the ability to negotiate the modalities for the exploration of natural resources and the formulas for sharing the accrued funds with the central government. This may go a long way to help address the simmering intra-state resource war in Cabinda while preventing others, especially in the diamond-rich and independent-minded Lunda Norte and Luanda Sul provinces, from breaking out.

To impact the lives of citizens in positive ways, the devolution of power away from the centre must be accompanied by a profound reorganization and democratization of local administration. This involves creating the legal and institutional frameworks that not only clearly define the nature of local, municipal, and provincial institutions but also establish guidelines for sharing power and responsibilities among the various levels of government. Although such change in the idea of the post-colonial state requires substantial constitutional revisions this does not constitute sufficient reason to prevent forward movement because, in any event, the Angolan constitution can at best be regarded as a work in progress. More fundamentally, it is fair to question the practical value of this document in a country where the vast majority of the population cannot read it. In Angola, then, as in many other African countries, the constitution is a document whose value is more readily recognized by political elites who, therefore, often change it to suit their transient political calculations, not the fundamental aspirations of the citizens upon whom national sovereignty really resides.

A more useful approach is to strengthen both the institutions and practices of governance. Specifically, greater power must be given to the people's representatives – both at the national and local levels – by revising current electoral practices. Admittedly, Angola's multi-party electoral system – tried only once since the introduction of multi-party politics – represents an important change from the previous single-party system. However, it is not designed to divide power either horizontally or vertically. It is mainly designed to elect a president and the unicameral parliament. Consequently, there is an unhealthy concentration of power in the presidency and parliament. A healthier division of power entails additional executive and legislative structures elected directly by the people. Thus, for example, Angola can benefit from a clearer separation of powers between the head of state and head of government – both of whom would govern with mandates renewable in periodic but not simultaneous elections. Likewise, the executive at all sub-state levels of government must be elected by the people, not appointed by the central government. Equally critical given the diversity of the national units that constitute the Angolan state, constitutional provisions are urgently needed to allow for the creation of sub-state political formations whose purpose is competition for local, municipal, provincial and, in future, autonomous regional governments. In addition, the parliament also needs to be reformed by at least transforming it into a bicameral body. An upper chamber representing the interests of the post-colonial state's diverse regions and peoples will go a long way in removing some regions' sense of political isolation and, consequently, allay some potentially centrifugal tendencies. Equally important, if designed as co-equals, the interactions between both chambers of parliament will require pluripartisan approaches to manage major issues facing the state. This could develop into a strong foundation for an inclusive political system.

In sum, then, successful post-civil war governance in Angola depends on the extent to which society is able to accept political models that do not necessarily privilege the state and give more importance and power to its constituting units within a more decentralized structure. This entails, first and foremost, recognizing, promoting, and protecting group identity rights, particularly those of ethnic and linguistic minorities, as a first step toward ultimately establishing a culture of peace and tolerance where the state's many conflicts can be peacefully managed.

Angola, like all other former colonies, cannot return to pre-colonial forms of governance. It must, therefore, adapt according to the requirements of the modern state. However, this does not necessarily entail a rejection of diversity, including ethnic identity, as a key pillar in the modern state edifice. Being an Angolan and a member of an ethnic group must not be mutually exclusive. But this goal will only be realized when all ethnic groups perceive the state to be an expression of their aspirations and sense of self-worth. In concrete terms, this is translated into equality of opportunities for access to power and wealth. In the absence of an equitable division of power and wealth within a democratic system, Angola's future will remain grim.

CHAPTER 8

Toward a Citizen-Friendly State

A radical reformulation of the nature of the post-colonial, post-civil war state in Angola is critical to build sustainable peace. But it is unrealistic to expect that such reformulation will originate from those – specifically the ruling elites – that have thus far most benefited from the peculiarities of the post-colonial state. Likewise, it is unlikely that Angola's other traditional political formations – FNLA and UNITA – will be able to provide alternative models of governance because they face several important existential challenges. Their most immediate challenges continue to revolve around undertaking their own internal transformations as a first step toward changing their public image and thus recuperating some of the political space they have lost to MPLA since independence. UNITA, for example, must resolve its current internal debate about the party's ideological orientation, i.e. whether to maintain a "right of centre" or "left of centre" posture. The ultimate resolution of this low-intensity debate – however shortsighted given the political realities on the ground, particularly the hegemonic position achieved by the governing MPLA – and the way UNITA is able to effectively advocate for the social reintegration of its former fighters and civilian cadres will determine in important ways the former rebels' long-term survivability as the main opposition force. Another important challenge for UNITA is related to its ability to stave off MPLA's aggressive co-opting strategies – involving, for example, offering posts in government, army, and civil service, as was done with FNLA in the 1980s and 1990s – that could eventually render the former rebels inoffensive, if not inoperative. In other words, left alone, the traditional political formations in Angola are unlikely to assume a role as catalysts for the type of fundamental changes Angola desperately needs.

Since the liberation movements, once driven by revolutionary ideals, have become conservative forces that are increasingly unable to respond to society's urgent needs for change, alternative forms of governance in Angola must be sought elsewhere. Angola's civil society, now with potentially greater space and voice in the aftermath of the civil war, has a unique opportunity to reconstitute itself and become useful again as a source for the creation, aggregation, and articulation of local/indigenous demands that can act to improve prospects for both political and economic development. These useful demands must be incorporated into public policies by competent and politically committed leaders working to restore the effectiveness and legitimacy of the state and break the cycle of structural violence. But since the interests of state and society are often at odds, the state may continue to hamper civil society from playing its crucial role in the political arena, particularly in terms of achieving accountable governance through the articulation of popular demands and their incorporation into public policies.

The restructuring of state-society relations is particularly important in post-conflict societies like Angola where diverse groups must find new ways to articulate their interests and have their voices count as new reconstruction strategies are elaborated and priorities set for their implementation. This interaction is crucial for the central authorities to be aware of society's real needs and aspirations as well as its sense of priorities for allocating scarce resources. Equally important, this state-society interaction can constitute a critical foundation for building a democratic system which ensures that all citizens are represented and have a voice in setting the national agenda. In this sense, civil society also provides a healthy counterbalance to the power of the state. Given its many levels of diversity, the role of civil society – especially in terms of achieving a mutually reinforcing and beneficial relationship with the state – will determine the sustainability of the current peace. But in Angola the role of civil society is, in itself, very problematic. One of the consequences of Angola's long civil war is that most elements of civil society have been captured by either the party-state or eliminated by the rebels. Thus, one of the main tasks ahead for Angola is to reconstitute its civil society and imbue it with the vibrancy necessary to become a site where peaceful alternatives to conflict are developed. Equally crucial, an unfettered and strong civil society can play a crucial role in developing and nurturing a tolerant, democratic culture. This is essential if Angola is to turn a new page, decisively away from its long post-colonial flirtation with state collapse and toward establishing a citizen-friendly state.

The pact between MPLA and UNITA elites that constituted the main political framework to end the civil war is a necessary but ultimately shaky foundation for sustainable peace especially if it does not go beyond its current role as a mechanism to co-opt former enemies into a corrupt and decaying system. A stronger foundation for a peaceful citizen-friendly state must involve the active participation of civil society as a critical source for the creation, aggregation, and articulation of both demands and opinions that can improve overall governance and, ultimately, prospects for political and economic development. These useful demands must be incorporated into public policies by competent and politically committed leaders working to restore the effectiveness and legitimacy of the state. To realize the positive-sum possibilities of this interaction in Angola it is critical for the state not to regard civil society as a threat, i.e. it must abstain from earlier attempts to subjugate civil society as a way of protecting a fragile regime. Thus, even as the opposition weakens and flirts with irrelevance by accepting cooptation and incorporation into national MPLA-dominated structures, civil society can play a decisive role as a check on renewed corporatism and authoritarianism. Just as important, in the absence of an effective political opposition, only civil society can counterbalance the power of central authorities and ensure that the post-conflict state focuses on "reviving livelihoods and civil institutions previously suppressed, eroded or rendered powerless by war, with the aim of strengthening local capacities to participate in the reconstruction process" (Green and Ahmed, 1999:195). This chapter discusses the character of Angola's post-colonial civil society and assesses its roles as possible guarantors of sustainable peace.

The notion of civil society

Post-conflict societal rebuilding with a view to achieving sustainable peace depends greatly on the role of civil society. Civil society refers to diverse spheres of activity within a country that exist outside the direct control of the state. It includes "that set of diverse non-governmental institutions which is strong enough to counterbalance the state and, while not preventing the state from fulfilling its role of keeper of the peace and arbitrator between major interests, can nevertheless prevent it from dominating and atomizing the rest of society" (Gellner, 1994:5). Civil society encompasses the space outside the state's realm where voluntary interests organize themselves and operate.

In current usage, civil society has become "an all-encompassing term that refers to social phenomena putatively beyond formal state structures – but not necessarily free of all contact with the state" (Woods, 1992:77). It is part of a complex triangular relationship that, in most contemporary societies has the state and the market as the other two interlinked poles. Therefore, an understanding of the character of national politics – comprising the arena represented by this triangular relationship – can hardly be achieved without reference to the nature and role of civil society. Unsurprisingly, therefore, the notion of civil society has been central to the general study of politics since the emergence of the modern industrial nation-state.

Many early theorists used the term "civil society" interchangeably with political society and the state (Karlson, 1993:76). Aristotle, for example, equated civil society with the "civilized" city-states in Greece which stood in contrast to the "barbaric" states in other areas. Others saw civil society as an urban society governed by civil laws (Karlson, 1993:76). In all such uses of this concept, civil society is contrasted with an "uncivilized" condition that characterizes other portions of humanity. This "uncivilized" condition has been generally depicted as the imaginary state of nature. Thus, the classical conception of civil society defines a point in societal development where a society can be characterized as "civilized" – a condition expressed, for example, in the social order of citizenship found in the Athenian polis or the Roman republic "where men (rarely women) regulate their relationships and settle their disputes according to a system of laws; where 'civility' reigns, and citizens take an active part in public life" (Karlson, 1993:377).

The modern idea of civil society – as the middle realm between the family and the state – originated in the writings of social contract theorists. Thomas Hobbes, for example, saw civil society emerging from people's rejection of the state of nature where life is "solitary, poore, nasty, brutish and short" (Hobbes, 1914:65). For Hobbes, the idea of civil society is founded in the readiness of each individual to forgo his or her individual quest for self-preservation in favour of a collective effort to provide security for all. The Hobbesian notion of the civil society is implicit in the social pact entered upon by individuals escaping the state of nature which involves the transfer of some powers from the citizen to the sovereign to protect civil society from its earlier destructive impulses. John Locke expanded upon Hobbes' formulation of civil society and viewed it as a more benign, higher level of human organization in which people agree upon basic principles for the mutual preservation of their lives and property (Locke , 1953:179).

From the rather narrow framework provided by Hobbes and Locke, the modern idea of civil society developed more fully in the eighteenth and nineteenth centuries, influenced by several major currents of thought. Natural rights theorists like Thomas Paine argued that most governments have a marked tendency to threaten the individual freedoms and "natural sociability" in civil society. In this context, the state can only be seen as a necessary evil while civil society is regarded as "a largely self-regulating sphere where the good life may be reached" (Karlson, 1993:77). The notion of civil society was also influenced by the work of Alexis de Tocqueville, particularly through his descriptive analysis of democratic life in America. Describing this new state and its innovative institutions, de Tocqueville argued that:

> All the citizens are independent and feeble; they can do hardly nothing by themselves.... They all, therefore, become powerless if they do not learn voluntarily to help one another. If men living in democratic countries had no right and no inclination to associate for political purposes, their independence would be in great jeopardy.... If they never acquired the habit of forming associations in ordinary life, civilization itself would be endangered (De Tocqueville, 1959:147).

Thus constituted, these associations also served to prevent the arbitrary and intrusive tendencies of the state. For de Tocqueville, civil associations such as scientific and literary circles, academic institutions, publishing houses, religious organizations, and so on, constituted powerful barriers against both political despotism and social injustice and inequality.

Current conceptions of civil society also draw from the work of Frederick Hegel who inverted the earlier liberal formulations and regarded civil society (*Gesellschaft*) as being identical with "the private and particularistic, and characterized by the self-seeking, conflicting and avaricious strivings of individuals and classes for largely materialistic ends" (Karlson, 1993:77). By contrast, he saw the state as the embodiment of universal values and rational civilization. Karl Marx later resolved this theoretical "conflict" between civil society and the state by arguing that, in future, civil society would somehow merge with the political sphere, resulting in a classless society. But for Marx, civil society was not necessarily dialectically superior to previous forms; it was "the site of crass materialism, of modern property relations, of the struggle of each against all, of egotism" (Bottomore, 1983:73). In important respects, Marx added to the understanding of civil society particularly as it relates to the state. He perceived the two to be symbiotically joined as "structure" and "superstructure".

Antonio Gramsci provided a more complete Marxian assessment of civil society. Like Hegel and Marx before him, Gramsci also addressed the relationship between civil society and the state. While defining civil society as the ensemble of "institutions, ideologies, practices, and agents ... that comprise the dominant culture of values" (Carnoy, 1984:70), Gramsci used the notion of "hegemony" to define the state-society relationship and interpret their interdependence. He suggests that the state uses "hegemony" to resolve its conflicts with the wider society. Gramsci depicts the state-civil society relationship as a formula whereby "State = political society + civil society, in other words, hegemony protected by the armour of coercion" (Texter, 1979:64). This suggests that there are two major hegemonic super-structural entities, i.e., the political society which rules directly through the coercive and judicial instruments available to the state and the civil society which promotes ethical values in the broader society through the exercise of ideological and cultural hegemony (Bratton, 1994:54). Thus the state and the dominant class within it are able to "postpone its demise" by both coercion and co-optation of "subordinate social formations". While Gramsci focused on how the state uses its power to secure the consent of the dominated classes through hegemony, post-Gramscian analyses view civil society in economic, political, and cultural terms both as the "ensemble of organisms" commonly called private and as "the political and cultural hegemony of a social group on the whole of society, as ethical content of the State" (Bobbio, 1979:31). In this context, civil society is a dynamic and innovative part of the superstructure that "represents the active and positive moment of historical development" (Bobbio, 1979:31). In sum, civil society can best be viewed as a product of both state and society, striving to limit the powers of the former while seeking to civilize the latter (Saich, 1994:261).

The post-colonial state and African civil society

Admittedly, the development of civil society in post-colonial Africa is at an embryonic stage. This may explain the reluctance by some Africanists to use this concept as a useful analytical tool to gain deeper understandings about how Africa works. Chabal and Daloz (1999:18), for example, dismiss "the current assumption about the emergence of such a recognizable civil society in Africa" as "eminently misleading" and suggest that the use of the concept "derives more from wishful thinking or ideological bias than from a careful analysis of present conditions". Most other Africanists, however, recognize the complex and dynamic relationship between state and civil society in Africa. Fatton (1992:141), for example, argues that the "state and civil society ... form two ensembles of an organic totality". However, this is a conflictual relationship in as much as civil society seeks to "breach and counteract" the simultaneous "totalisation" unleashed by the state (Bayart, 1986:111). In other words, civil society is "the private sphere of material, cultural, and political activities resisting the incursion of the state" (Fatton, 1992:4–5). It can be best understood as an aggregate of networks and institutions that evolve outside the contours of the state. These networks and institutions operate independently of the state and often develop and present alternative views. Thus, civil society occupies those increasingly important spaces or sites where "social actors mobilize their resources to exercise political power or to protect themselves from the predatory reaches of existing regimes" (Fatton, 1992:2). Civil society is, then, neither a discrete entity completely external to an equally discrete source of power nor a mere expression of dominated social groups. It encompasses "not only popular modes of political action but also the claims of those socially dominant groups (merchants, businessmen, clergy) which are no less excluded from direct participation in political power" (Bayart, 1986:112).

The reinvigoration of civil society on the continent occurred in the aftermath of the end of the Cold War and the East-West ideological rivalry that often turned Africa into a battleground. With the collapse of the Soviet Union and the triumph of Western orthodoxies, African states undertook a series of externally-prescribed or internally driven processes of democratization that involved abandoning single party systems and embracing multi-party politics. Civil society – hitherto of marginal relevance in many African countries – played critical roles in African transitions to democracy, especially in terms of legitimizing those transformations.

The marginalization of civil society in Africa until the late 1980s and early 1990s can be attributed primarily to the dominance of single-party politics and the unwillingness on the part of the dominant parties to appreciate its significance. But there was an even more basic reason. Paradoxically, post-colonial African leaders often retained the former colonial administrators' determination to control society's public and private spheres, albeit for different reasons – i.e. oppression to facilitate exploitation versus oppression to promote national unity as a prerequisite to build viable states on brittle foundations. Consequently, post-colonial African leaders regarded members of society who organized themselves outside the reach of the state as forces that exacerbated societal cleavages and retarded the process of political integration and state legitimization. Such leaders invariably regarded their societies as structurally "plural rather than pluralistic" (Apter and Rosberg, 1994:92). Thus, from this perspective, civil society – as an organized source of demands – constituted a threat to the establishment of a stable political order (Apter and Rosberg, 1994:92). Events in the 1990s showed that this view was too simplistic. Throughout the continent civil society has played important roles as African peoples have attempted to reclaim their central place in post-colonial political systems by reject-ing many autocratic, repressive regimes in favour of more citizen-friendly governments. For example, in the early 1990s, pressures arising from the grassroots contributed to forcing African governments to accept an innova-tive process for undertaking political reforms – i.e., national conferences – that have subsequently been sustained by several internationally moni-tored multi-party elections. Although in some parts of Africa the state has reasserted its dominant position by co-opting or, in extreme cases by bat-tering, civil society, it is unlikely that most African states will be able to monopolize political space as occurred for much of the first decades of post-colonial rule. This reassertion of civil society has generated some opti-mism about African futures because it has been viewed as "a hitherto miss-ing key to sustained political reform, legitimate states and governments, improved governance, viable state-society and state-economy relationships, and prevention of the kind of political decay that undermined new African governments a generation ago" (Harbeson, 1994:1–2).

As mentioned before, the idea of civil society has been dominant in Western political philosophy particularly since the advent of the modern nation-state. Its present uses in the context of African development occur at a time when the capabilities of some African states to even minimally sat-isfy the basic needs of their populations, let alone the political aspirations of nationalities and ethnic communities, are being seriously questioned and eroded. If the classical political thinkers saw civil society as a theoretical or analytical concept to further understandings of the relationships between society and state, in the present context civil society can be the "key to understanding and addressing the political and socio-economic crises in Africa and elsewhere, both on the ground and in contemporary theory" (Harbeson, 1994:2). This newer articulation of the notion of civil society addresses an important gap in the social sciences regarding the problems of political and socio-economic development in Africa – a theoretical short-coming has been highlighted by the unsuccessful post-colonial policies of most African governments. Civil society provides this "missing dimension" in social science theory and development policy by describing how, "in process terms, working understandings concerning the basic rules of the political game or structure of the state emerge from within society and the economy at large. In substantive terms, civil society typically refers to the points of agreement on what those working rules *should* be" (Harbeson, 1994:2). The usefulness of civil society as an element of theory rests on the possibilities this notion offers for a better understanding of state-society relations. The idea of civil society can serve to shift the focus from the question of power balances and/or conflicts between the state and society to the more important questions concerning their interdependence; in other words, while the state is the main political actor, civil society is the means by which the state and society at large are harmonized.

In Africa, as Bayart argues, the interests of the state and society are hardly harmonized because the former emerged as an "excrescence" developing in and upon society. It developed with a natural tendency to multiply its specialist apparatuses, subjecting populations, and finally subjecting the activities of society to its control (Bayart, 1986:112). This stands in stark contrast with modern liberal democracies where the state and civil society relate to each other in a situation of "balanced opposition". In such societies, "the state is not a separate and superior entity ruling over the underlying society, but it is conditioned by society and thus subordinated to it" (Bobbio, 1979:24). Civil society not only delineates the boundaries of the state by resisting its "predatory reach", it also has the potential to challenge the most repressive aspects of the state and force it to comply with the public will. In this sense, civil society often becomes both the foundation and the driving force for reform.

In post-colonial Africa, however, the relationship between the state and civil society is more problematic. There, for much of the post-colonial period:

> ... a heterogeneous state, either imposed by colonial rule or created by revolutionary will (often modeled on other states), has been deliberately set up *against* civil society rather than evolved in continual conflict with it (Bayart, 1986:112).

From this perspective, the ideologies adopted by many ruling parties in post-colonial Africa were used as a convenient cover to camouflage the "hegemonic imperative" of the state and its ruling classes in their attempts to control and shape society. The post-colonial African state sought to control and shape society by, among other things, defining the basis and criteria for access to sources of power and wealth. This often took the form of preventing subordinate groups from transforming themselves into autonomous and pluralistic organizations. This process was facilitated by the institutionalization of single-party regimes in Africa. In other words, during its critical formative post-independence period, Africa experienced the post-colonial hegemony of the African socialist project, with devastating consequences for good politics and good economics.

Problematically, structural adjustment further debilitated civil society in the sense that some of its constituting parts were transformed into receptors and reproducers of "reactionary forms of knowledge and codes of conduct that confine subaltern classes either to old, unchanging behaviour, or to ineffective, disorganized patterns of collective resistance" (Fatton, 1992:6). In some African countries like Angola, the dominant class has shrewdly used the newly "liberalized" market and the new types of relationships it imposes on social relations to further entrench its power and privilege. A post-colonial state besieged by war and eroded by corruption was unable to carry out important aspects associated with governance and, consequently, the forms of domination, the nature of surplus extraction, and the patterns of resource allocation not only increasingly escaped public accountability, they began to be formulated in the private spheres, albeit connected with the ruling party. The dictatorship of the proletariat had given way to an equally oppressive dictatorship of the market. In this new dictatorship, although the elites no longer overtly dominate power and wealth through their positions as the "vanguard" of the proletariat, their influence in society has increased. By effectively controlling the market through the ownership of former state owned enterprises as well as new companies that have been created since the introduction of liberal economic policies, the elites have the power to determine who gets what, when, and at what price. It is not surprising, therefore, that in Angola neither the withdrawal of the state from many of the functions it had performed with varying degrees of success since independence nor the move away from authoritarianism has led to the emergence of a more resourceful civil society. The exigencies of an authoritarian state have been replaced by the discipline of the market – both formal and informal – as well as the devising of more subtle ways for the state to maintain its hegemonic position. In this context, Angola's embryonic and vulnerable civil society is made up mainly of actors and structures developed around established institutions. The difficulties related to adapting to new conditions have led other potential elements of civil society to disengage from it, a phenomenon described by Hirschman (1970) as "exit".

For societies seeking to overcome post-colonial turmoil – especially in cases like Angola where such turmoil was of the military variety – exit can only compound the problems as it leaves the state once again as the only major player. A more appropriate course of action entails strengthening civil society, especially at the structural and normative levels. Only thus strengthened can civil society fulfil Bobbio's vision of it as:

... the place where, especially in periods of institutional crisis, *de facto* powers are formed that aim at obtaining their own legitimacy even at the expense of legitimate power; where, in other words, the processes of delegitimation and relegitimation take place. This forms the basis of the frequent assertion that the solution of a grave crisis threatening the survival of a political system must be sought first and foremost in civil society where it is possible to find new sources of legitimation and therefore new sources of consensus (Bobbio, 1979:26).

It cannot be taken for granted that post-colonial African countries – especially those with particularly problematic histories like Angola – will uncomplicatedly realize this idealized view of civil society in the short or medium term. Admittedly, civil society in many such countries exhibits important divisions and contradictions. In fact, civil society in post-colonial Africa is often as pathological as the state. Although this is an exaggeration, the idea of African civil society as an agent of political change – capable of achieving public accountability and sustaining participatory government – may be just as misleading. Contrary to East Europe, Latin America, or East Asia where the collapse of authoritarian regimes enabled civil societies to re-invigorate and re-assert themselves, African experiences have varied. In many African countries, basic issues of state legitimacy and authority, national identity and social cohesion still have to be resolved. Many of these factors are a direct result of the colonial experience. Others are related to the types of regimes and systems of governance that prevailed throughout most of Africa in the post-colonial period. Both prevented individuals and groups from fully developing their private interests due to the arbitrariness and highly parasitic behaviour of African states and their leaders. Thus, it can be argued that the present decline of predatory states and autocratic rule has only now opened up opportunities for the *formation* of civil society (Lewis, 1992:32). In other words, the emergence of civil society in many African countries is still at an embryonic stage and its development is problematic. The pertinent question in this context is whether this embryonic civil society – with its ethnic, regional, religious, class, or welfare orientation – will reinforce or transcend existing cleavages in African societies. That is to say that the maturation of civil society in Africa – a pre-requisite for fulfilling Bobbio's idea – will involve a lengthy and complicated process.

Much of what is referred to as civil society in Africa maintains a dependent relationship with state elites. There are few civil society organizations in Angola, for example, that can survive without handouts and favours from the state and its many tentacles. In many cases associations are led by intellectuals and members of the middle class. This is a social stratum that owes much of its relative social well-being to the state. Furthermore, their goals and objectives are often not very clear. For example, do civil society organizations exist primarily to help their members, or the population at large, attain higher levels of welfare or to help reshape the state along more democratic and institutionally accountable lines? Since such basic issues remain unresolved, Angolan civil society's impact in terms of aggregating, representing and defending the public realm has thus far been negligible.

Civil society and the post-colonial state in Angola

Many of the problems besetting Angola today – including perennially poor governance and related corruption – can be attributed to civil society's problematic relationship with the post-colonial state, a consequence of the MPLA regime's early ideological hostility toward civil society coupled with widespread societal frustration regarding the regime's slowness to solve the major political, military and economic crises that have faced the country since independence. As civil society succeeds in reinvigorating itself to occupy a more relevant space within post-civil war Angola, state-society relations can only be expected to improve, with positive effects for governance toward the creation of a citizen-friendly state.

The reinvigoration of civil society in Angola is a recent, albeit not entirely unanticipated, development. For much of the colonial and post-colonial eras, Angola's civil society was constrained by the nature of those regimes' state-society relations. Thus, given the totalitarian nature of the colonial regime, indigenous Angolan civil society organizations were relegated to the fringes of a system. Yet, as a testament to their resilience, small religious schools and recreation clubs constituted a strong enough base for organized anti-colonial protest. Post-World War II political protest first took the form of small leaflets criticizing the colonial regime. The brutality of that regime's response, however, forced the political leaders of that era to opt for a more violent form of political protest. Thus, from 1961 to 1974, the most important form of political participation involved membership of one of the three liberation movements that ultimately helped to bring down the colonial regime. But since, to a considerable degree, this participation took place along ethnic lines, it possessed within it the seeds of conflicts that have challenged post-colonial Angolan society.

Unable to form a common front either during the anti-colonial war or during the negotiation process with the departing Portuguese authorities, the three liberation movements failed to make the critical transition from armed guerrilla groups to political parties before independence. Instead, FNLA, MPLA, and UNITA kept their guerrilla armies intact – and sought to expand and strengthen them as the country slid into civil war – thus helping to militarize post-colonial society. Consequently, the overthrow of the colonial regime did not result in the expansion of the space and importance of civil society.

Although Angola gained independence in extremely difficult conditions, the MPLA government was able to extend and consolidate its administration throughout the country. It was expected, therefore, that the winning side would introduce measures to establish a viable political order which, in turn, could promote unity and harmony, social and regional equality, and economic development. Regrettably, as discussed earlier, MPLA succeeded only in winning the first important battle of a very long post-colonial conflict. Its regime would be continuously threatened militarily by a combination of national, regional, and international forces. Given this situation, it was unrealistic to expect the civil society to flourish during Angola's first quarter century as an independent state. In addition to the militarization of society, the early ideological orientation of the regime also contributed to the tightening of the space occupied by civil society.

Initially, MPLA created an intolerant and inflexible political order based on a dogmatic implementation of Marxism-Leninism. Lost in the early post-independence ideological fog was the basic contractual relationship between the state and citizen. Instead, the latter became a manipulable political commodity to further the goals of the one-party regime and the authoritarian post-colonial state. This resulted in ethnic favouritism and divisions, corruption and economic decline which, in combination, further complicated the dynamics of the civil war and hindered the development of civil society. With most avenues for political participation closed by the state and in the presence of a highly centralized and dysfunctional economy, Angolan citizens became almost exclusively consumed by concerns affecting their immediate survival, i.e., the search for human security. In other words, the atrophy of Angola's civil society after independence can be attributed both to the civil war and the political choices of the post-colonial one-party regime.

In hindsight, the Soviet-style model adopted by the MPLA to organize the post-colonial state in Angola could not have been expected to allow for the development of civil society. In fact, it discouraged even the most simple and innocuous initiatives from independent-minded individuals and groups. Thus, important segments of the population that had not been co-opted or incorporated into the regime – especially traditional leaders and religious groups but also a few intellectuals – were not only excluded from the political arena but also prevented from constituting an independent social sphere outside the realm of the state. Such atrophy of civil society is not unique to Angola. It was felt acutely in most societies where the state adopted Marxism as a guiding ideology. Such states centralized all aspects of life and developed a single political, economic, and ideological hierarchy which tolerated no alternative views. Consequently, outside the restricted confines of the spaces created or sanctioned by the governing party, society approximated an "atomized condition" where dissent became a mark of heresy and any dissenter could be labeled an "enemy of the people" (Gellner, 1994:1). In Angola this was tantamount to being exposed to severe state sanctions, ranging from ostracism to death. What accounted for this perverted state view of society?

Generally, states like Angola that were attempting to develop along Marxist lines regarded civil society as a fraud, a diversion, or even a threat. For such states, the idea of plurality of institutions that could both oppose and balance the state while, in turn, being protected by the state merely concealed a façade of political, economic, and social domination by elites. According to Gellner, Marxism claims to unmask both partners in this deception – the state which protects civil society, and civil society which provides a counterweight to the state – and rebukes both as redundant and fraudulent (Gellner, 1994:1–2). The formerly Marxist leaders in Angola, as elsewhere in other former Soviet client-states, internalized the Marxist dogma of the withering away of the state. Since the future socialist structure was meant to bring with it a harmonious order free of exploitation and oppression, civil society and other such institutions envisaged to counterbalance the state were deemed both "spurious and unnecessary" (Gellner, 1994:2). This served as justification – both ideological and practical – for attempts to destroy civil society. As Gray (1975:146) points out:

> The single most important feature of totalitarian orders is their suppression (partial or complete) of the institutions of civil society – the autonomous institutions of private property and contractual freedom under the rule of law, which allow people of different values and world-views to live in peaceful co-existence. Because they politicize economic life and repress voluntary associations, and because they are *Weltanschauung* states – that is to say, states which seek to impose a single world-view on all – totalitarian regimes have at their very core the project of destroying the key institutions of civil society. ... What-

ever its degree of success or completeness, totalitarianism is to be defined by its opposition to civil society, not by contrast with liberal democracy.

In the particular case of Angola, as the state became even more authoritarian as a consequence of both the military threat and economic decay, individuals were allowed only enough space for their daily struggle for survival. In those circumstances, very few sectors of civil society were able to muster enough strength to prevent complete subjugation by the state. The Catholic Church, in particular, made exceptional contributions in this regard through various pastoral letters highlighting the plight of the Angolan people and the decay of moral values in society and a more general overt posture against the excesses of the state, including its restrictions of the private sphere. During the first decade of independence as the ruling party attempted to build socialism, these restrictions on the private sphere were such that the governing MPLA required that popular participation in politics was carried out solely through officially sanctioned "mass organizations" that were expected to provide unconditional support for the party's broad political, economic, and social programmes. In reality, citizens became subordinate to the party and the state – and were manipulated to furthering the goals of the party and the totalitarian state it was erecting. This grotesque subversion of the state-citizen relationship – not just the civil war – created the peculiar conditions that intensified the structural violence inherited from the colonial state.

The unshackling of civil society in Angola started with the political and economic liberalization policies that began in the late 1980s. The period of greatest promise for civil society's flourishing occurred between the signing of the Bicesse Peace Accords in 1991 and the resumption of the civil war after the elections of September 1992 when a vast array of civil society organizations emerged and attempted to play a role in building what was expected to be post-electoral peace. Tragically, those hopes were dashed by the resumption of the war after the elections. However, that short period of bustling civil society activity revealed important paradoxes in state-society relations. As mentioned before, the would-be totalitarian regime had created both dissent and dependency. In important respects, then, in Angola as elsewhere in Africa where one-party structures had once flourished, the emergence of organized groups commonly associated with civil society and their dependent relationship with the state constitutes a politically astute regime survival political strategy. These groups' continued existence, not to mention degree of influence and well-being, depend on the whims of the state, particularly the party controlling it. By restricting the space of civil society MPLA is thus hindering important processes, including the emergence of alternatives – political and otherwise – with negative consequences for the pace and depth of democratization. Furthermore, with the entrenchment of this type of state corporatism, the governing party and the state – ruling over hybrid economic structures combined with centralized power – can afford to maintain its normative frameworks of opaque governance characterized by the use of public positions for private gain. Unfortunately for Angola and its process of transition to a new order, even some NGOs – important features of contemporary civil society – have become re-attached to the state apparatus. Others, equally problematically, operate as junior partners of their northern counterparts. This external component, especially in terms of their ability to secure financial resources from external donors, provided the means for some local NGOs to carry out several important social, humanitarian, and development projects thus enhancing their national clout at a time when – both due to overall inefficiency and the retreat of the state from the provision of services to many vulnerable groups – the work of NGOs often meant the difference between survival and death.

Since much of society was engaged in a desperate struggle for survival, it is not surprising that many would see the establishment of NGOs as avenues for their personal survival, not as potential instruments to enhance the public good. Most of these new associations were motivated primarily by economic considerations. In other words, they were created by individuals who wanted to take advantage of the real or perceived economic and financial advantages associated with having an NGO. This unprecedented sprouting of NGOs was further stimulated by the perception that financial help would be forthcoming from the government and, possibly, from international partners as well. Not surprisingly, the initial rush to create civil society organizations often also involved an aggressive search for financial support from state and external sources. Thus, although there is a rich and heterogeneous associational life thriving in spite of – and often as a response to – a severe crisis of governance, the activities of these organizations can be best interpreted as coping mechanisms, not as organized attempts to limit state power or provide alternative development frameworks.

Even more problematic is the fact that some organizations that could have developed to strengthen Angola's civil society have been co-opted by the state – instead of acting to change it, or at least to operate in "balanced opposition" to it – which has produced counterproductive effects in the sense that potentially key segments of civil society were thus unable to effectively influence the state to change its normative framework. In other words, by accepting co-optation or incorporation, civil society served as a legitimizing element for the state and its uses and abuses of power. For example, on the key issue of corruption and other forms of structural violence, co-opted members of civil society could not credibly confront the state on the issue because they also benefited from the system. The state, then, was the great beneficiary from civil society's dependence upon it and had obvious reasons for continuing to accommodate, even nurture, such a relationship. For as long as the continued existence, not to mention degree of influence and well-being, of important elements of civil society depend on the whims of the state, particularly the governing party, civil society is at risk of being rendered irrelevant again.

During the last decade of the civil war, MPLA successfully ensured that the state-society relations that emerged in the aftermath of the democratization process worked indefinitely to its benefit by continuously using Savimbi as the national boogeyman. Ironically, Savimbi's death now robs MPLA of a favourite instrument with which to frighten civil society into compliance, even co-optation. With Savimbi's death and UNITA's military implosion the civil war quickly came to an end. This has provided civil society with the second opportunity since independence to begin playing a more independent and meaningful role as a counterweight to the state. The Catholic Church is again leading the way by going as far as creating an independent radio station – Radio Eclesia – to broadcast credible information to the people untainted by regime propaganda. Equally important has been the role of the independent media. A significant number of independent newspapers and magazines – both print and electronic – have been created in the last decade. However, given the very high rates of illiteracy, this critical element of civil society has not reached much beyond key urban centres where the literate elites reside. Yet, they have already played an important role in reclaiming freedom of expression in Angolan society.

However critical their roles may be, the church and the media do not represent all elements of civil society. Besides, the various and concurrent challenges confronting post-civil war Angola require the participation of all segments of society. Specifically, these challenges can only be successfully met if a broad stratum of entrepreneurs, intellectuals, and activists in diverse fields emerge with the vision and skills to create independent institutions capable of mediating the interests of the citizen and the state. These institutions must then succeed in radically differentiating themselves from the state and the political class in the ways they operate. In other words, the overriding goals and objectives of such an organization must be centred on the creation of the good society for Angola. These social actors and institutions must have an existence of their own, which is not a result of the state's activities, and must justify their continuing existence through their ability to resist the state particularly by repudiating the state's propensity to seek a commanding position in the public sphere and by challenging the state's definition of the public good, whether in terms of economic growth or in terms of social consensus. Indeed, civil society can play an important role in post-civil war development by refusing to accept the state's claim to have the chief responsibility for providing the blueprints for this development while, on the other hand, asserting its own capacity and responsibility to provide alternatives to solve the problems of growth, social integration, and even national identity. Hence, civil society in Angola must work toward fundamental institutional changes in the political system that would shift the balance between the state and society in favour of the latter, in other words, to make the state subordinate to the citizens.

Such profound changes necessitate a rejection of usual politics as typified by both the "liberation movements" that have dominated post-colonial politics and their would-be opponents – the numerous political parties that have mushroomed since the end of single-party era but have generally failed to gain much public support partly because of their inability to provide credible alternatives for changing the post-colonial normative framework in fundamental ways. The end of the civil war provides Angola with a unique opportunity to embrace good politics – a citizen-centred system that focuses on creating and enhancing opportunities for human enrichment – as the norm. It is unlikely that the current political actors have the will to change a system that has been, or has the potential to be, beneficial to them singly or as individuals organized in political parties. The alternatives must, therefore, of necessity emerge from civil society.

CHAPTER 9

External Dimensions of Positive Peace

For much of the post-independence period – and mainly as a result of the civil war that raged until 2002 – Angola's external outlook reflected a constant preoccupation with the regime's internal preoccupation with its long-term survival. Therefore, the regime's policies to engage the world were initially driven by the overriding objective of securing a friendly regional environment conducive to the security of the internationally recognized borders of the post-colonial state. In important respects, then, Angola's principal foreign policy goals reflected the governing party's understanding of how its domestic security was directly linked to neighbouring countries' choices regarding what side to support in the devastating civil war that started in the months leading up to Angola's independence. Thus, an active regional engagement – first, through substantial support to the nationalist wars against settler rule in Zimbabwe, Namibia, and South Africa and, more recently, through direct military intervention in the Democratic Republic of Congo and in Congo-Brazzaville – found justification in terms of the domestic security dividends it was expected to produce. In other words, majority rule in the former settler colonies in Southern Africa and the removal of unfriendly governments in the two Congos was expected to fundamentally change Angola's domestic security predicaments by denying Angolan insurgents their life-lines. By seeking, first and foremost, to create a favourable regional environment as a first step to solving its domestic challenges, MPLA was able to create the conditions that would eventually enable it to defeat UNITA.

This chapter first addresses some of the key factors that have conditioned Angola's foreign policy during the civil war before touching on post-conflict challenges and opportunities for engaging the world. The chapter suggests that Angola's foreign policy has thus far reflected the unique circumstances under which the country emerged as an independent state and the strategic choices the governing MPLA made upon gaining independence. Although these choices ultimately ensured regime survival, the country still faces colossal domestic challenges while, internationally, its relevance within the global political economy derives almost solely from its position as sub-Saharan Africa's second major oil exporter and an important diamond producer. Yet, Angola's position within the global political economy provides it with important post-conflict opportunities on the world stage to continue using foreign policy as an important instrument to solve its domestic problems – now more developmental than military. Undoubtedly, Angola will require sustained international engagement as it overcomes the devastating effects of civil war. But within a crisis-prone international system, Angola's ability to place its own problems near the top of the international agenda will continue to be seriously challenged. The failure thus far to convince the world's major players to convene a "donors' conference" to help the Angola government raise post-war reconstruction funds, is evidence that Angola is no longer a main international preoccupation. Such failures, however, will not deter Angola's aggressive pursuit of external partners to assist in post-conflict reconstruction because this process, if successful, is critical to achieve both broad national reconciliation and sustainable peace.

The domestic rationale for external engagement

Angola's current domestic condition and international position – a resource-rich poor country just emerging from a devastating civil war – is particularly regrettable since the country was expected to achieve a measure of international relevance when it achieved independence in 1975. That expectation was neither unfounded nor unrealistic given Angola's considerable natural resource endowment, including important deposits of oil and diamonds. Unfortunately, such optimism was shattered in the process of decolonization. As mentioned earlier, decolonization in Angola and elsewhere in the Portuguese empire was precipitated by the military coup in Lisbon on 25 April 1974 which deposed the regime of Marcelo Caetano. The coup leaders – mostly mid-level military officers who opposed the old regime's colonial policies – sought to quickly end costly colonial wars. Thus, Portugal placed its colonies on the fast track to political independence. Sadly, Angola's decolonization process quickly degenerated into civil war as each of the three liberation movements attempted to grab power with the help of foreign allies: Zairian troops invaded Angola from the north in support of FNLA, South African troops invaded from the south in support of UNITA while MPLA succeeded in seizing and maintaining control of the capital and installing itself in power with the help of Cuban troops. Given the Cold War context of the time and since the outcome of the Angolan conflict was expected to have significant geo-strategic implications for Southern Africa, Angola also quickly became an important Cold War battleground. Unsurprisingly, both the United States and the former Soviet Union intervened directly or indirectly in Angola's civil war.

Although MPLA could count on direct Soviet and Cuban military support to stay in power, the US was not willing to allow the new Marxist regime in Angola to consolidate its rule. Nor was it willing to intervene directly. Fortunately for MPLA, in the aftermath of the Vietnam debacle the United States had developed an aversion to major foreign military interventions. This, however, did not prevent the US from pursuing destabilization strategies – through its UNITA surrogates – aimed at toppling the young Marxist-Leninist regime. Thus, focusing solely on the regime's ideological orientation provides incomplete explanations for post-colonial Angola's propensity for aggressive, even military, regional engagements. A fuller picture emerges when more pragmatic regime survival strategies are also taken into account. In other words, while the regime's ideological background predisposed it to participate in the liberation wars against settler minority rule in Southern Africa, these struggles were also regarded as being directly connected to the regime's long-term survival. For the MPLA government, support for the liberation of Zimbabwe, Namibia, and South Africa constituted an overt attempt to influence Angola's regional environment by supporting revolutionary change in neighbouring states – all at the time governed by settler regimes – that exhibited hostile intentions and/or provided support and sanctuary for UNITA and FNLA. There was also the additional pragmatic expectation that, once liberated, these neighbouring countries would provide the necessary military, economic, and diplomatic assistance to enable MPLA to solve its domestic problems – both military and developmental.

Angola's first president, Agostinho Neto, can be credited with giving Angola's foreign policy its original pragmatism. He believed that the consolidation of the MPLA regime in Angola could not be achieved without ensuring the new state's territorial security through the establishment of good relations with its neighbouring countries. Some of these, notably South Africa and Zaire, still exhibited hostile intentions and provided support and sanctuary for UNITA and FNLA. But Neto's pragmatism was not generally endorsed within MPLA. Angola's arduous birth as a sovereign state had a profound and traumatic effect on the wider MPLA leadership – with its various factions subscribing to different interpretations of the tragic events surrounding independence – that helped to cement their views of the world as essentially inhospitable for would-be revolutionary states. For some MPLA leaders, events in Angola – leading up to independence and beyond – could best be interpreted from a Cold War perspective. Thus, they perceived the actions of Zaire and South Africa in the context of a much wider and sinister Western "imperialist" conspiracy to establish a form of neo-colonial domination in Angola. Consequently, those who held this view argued for the establishment of very close relations with socialist countries, especially the former USSR and Cuba, to counter Angola's neighbours' alignment with the "imperialist" West. Neto had a more complex interpretation of the world and, therefore, did not fully endorse the ideological views propounded by some of his comrades. For him, the preservation of the nascent state's territorial integrity ultimately depended on its ability to establish good relations with neighbouring states like Zaire and South Africa, not necessarily change their regimes. Cold War dynamics, important as they were at the time, could be properly managed through membership of global organizations like the UN, regional organizations like the Organization of African Unity (OAU) and especially groupings like the Non-Aligned Movement (NAM).

Unlike some more doctrinaire members of the MPLA leadership, Neto wanted to limit the extent of Angola's cooperation with the USSR once the internal threat posed by UNITA and FNLA was brought under control through a combination of military efforts and political compromise. It is notable in this context that the first post-colonial Constitution included a clause prohibiting the establishment of foreign bases on Angolan soil. Additionally, as a show of non-alignment but also as a pragmatic response to Angola's economic realities, the new post-colonial government maintained a friendly posture toward Western oil companies operating in the country. Unfortunately for Angola, much of this early pragmatism died with Neto in 1979. Subsequently, attempts to make peace with Zaire and South Africa were unsuccessful and these neighbouring countries continued to interfere in Angola's domestic affairs on the side of UNITA, with devastating effects, until well into the 1990s.

Neto's successor, José Eduardo dos Santos, quickly abandoned non-alignment in favour of closer ties with the USSR and Cuba in an effort to find the means to handle a quickly deteriorating domestic situation. Unlike his predecessor, dos Santos was prepared to give greater latitude to the Soviets in determining the main guidelines of the new state's domestic and foreign policy. Previously frustrated with Neto's flirtation with non-alignment, the USSR welcomed this new foreign policy orientation because Angola provided an important base in Southern Africa from which to affect change during a period of great instability caused by both regional and Cold War dynamics. The former USSR was particularly interested in influencing events in South Africa, the richest and most developed state in the subcontinent, and thus fulfilling its self-proclaimed role as the vanguard of third world liberation movements.

Cuba – despite its own serious domestic and international problems – also agreed to provide additional support to Angola partly to further its own foreign policy objectives including, importantly, enhancing its claims to leadership within NAM (MacFarlane, 1992:87). However, given their own problems and limitations, neither the USSR nor Cuba could solve the MPLA's domestic problems. In particular, they could not help solve Angola's economic problems nor prevent UNITA from becoming a growing threat with Zairian, South African and American assistance. In fact, UNITA acted as a South African proxy army. Only the major global and regional changes that took place in the late 1980s and early 1990s – the end of the Cold War and the collapse of the minority regime in South Africa – relegated UNITA to irrelevance at the international and regional levels, thus contributing to its eventual demise. MPLA could rightfully claim to have played a part in accelerating the collapse of the settler regimes in Southern Africa. However, by abandoning Neto's pragmatic foreign policy, Angola exposed itself to the devastating military wrath of both Zaire and South Africa as well as, indirectly, that of the United States.

The regional environment

At independence, the new MPLA government could count on a single regional ally: the People's Republic of Congo, a relatively small and weak state. On the other hand, it was literally surrounded by enemies. Important regional actors – particularly South Africa and Zaire – overtly supported MPLA's main internal adversaries. The new Angolan regime understood that its ability to establish a viable state depended, to a considerable degree, on its ability to help establish friendly regimes in both neighbouring states. Thus, for the next two decades the MPLA regime sought to achieve this objective by actively helping domestic opponents of unfriendly neighbours. In the end, Angola achieved its foreign policy objectives, albeit at a devastating cost.

The wrath of apartheid

Angola's foreign policy toward apartheid South Africa involved open and unconditional military and diplomatic support for both African National Congress (ANC) and the South West Africa Peoples' Organization (SWAPO). South Africa's response to this aggressive foreign policy by the new Angolan state came in the form of the so-called "total strategy", a set of policies aimed at ensuring the survival of the apartheid system through a combination of repression at home and aggression abroad. For the main proponents of the "total strategy", aggression against South Africa's neighbours was justified because they – not the apartheid regime's failed policies – were seen as the main source of instability and conflict both inside South Africa and in the region. In a desperate attempt to save itself, the apartheid regime used a variety of strategies to persuade neighbouring states to refrain from actively supporting the armed liberation struggles in South Africa and Namibia. Apartheid South Africa also sought to ensure that no "communist power" gained a political or military foothold in the region. Given Angola's support for liberation struggles against settler regimes in the region and due to its condition as a key Soviet client, the MPLA regime was regarded by the apartheid regime as a major and direct threat to its survival. To counter this perceived external threat, South Africa further expanded its security and military apparatus to both suppress opposition at home and destabilize the region. As South Africa's principal enemy in the region – for being both SWAPO's main sanctuary and an important ANC base, for being uncompromisingly Marxist-Leninist in its ideological orientation, and for having significant economic potential – Angola suffered the brunt of the apartheid regime's total strategy.

South Africa used two main instruments to threaten Angola's territorial integrity. First, SADF carried out frequent and well-planned military invasions deep into Angolan territory. This strategy resulted in tremendous devastation both in human lives lost and infrastructures destroyed. Between 1975 and 1988, South Africa regularly mounted large-scale military invasions of Angola. These invasions, carried out under the pretext of responding to increased SWAPO attacks in northern Namibia from bases in southern Angola, usually involved several SADF infantry battalions, paratrooper units, tank battalions, long-range artillery groups, and military aircraft squadrons. The duration varied according to the real objective of the mission. Thus, for example, missions to destroy SWAPO bases did not take as much time as fighting alongside UNITA to prevent advances by Angolan government troops.

Second, South Africa transformed UNITA into a proxy army for its regional destabilization policies. Although virtually destroyed by MPLA and Cuban troops in 1975–6, UNITA was reorganized into a significant military force by 1979. As a result, by the end of the 1970s – while MPLA government and Cuban troops were preoccupied with building massive defensive systems to deter South African military aggression – UNITA's operations were moving northward from its bases in Angola's southeastern corner of Kuando-Kubango province into the country's central plateau. This was a significant movement for three reasons. First, this is a fertile, densely populated region inhabited by the Ovimbundo ethnic group – UNITA's traditional base of support. Second, military actions effectively rendered the vital Benguela Railway – one of the region's major transportation links to the Atlantic – inoperable. Third, UNITA could use its new bases in the central highlands to initiate military operations farther north with the objective of disrupting both oil and diamond exploration – the main pillars of Angola's economy.

In combination, apartheid South Africa's twin strategies toward Angola – regular military invasions and support for UNITA – convinced the Angolan government that a regional settlement with South Africa was in its best interest. Thus, belatedly reverting to Neto's pragmatism, the ruling MPLA accepted the Reagan Administration's policy of "linkage" tying the withdrawal of Cuban troops from Angola with Namibia's independence on the basis of UNSC Resolution 435 (1978) of 29 September 1978. This resolution had reaffirmed "the legal responsibility of the United Nations over Namibia" and approved a UN Secretary-General report containing a proposal for a settlement of the issue based on "the withdrawal of South Africa's illegal administration from Namibia and the transfer of power to the people of Namibia". The resolution also established a United Nations Transition Assistance Group (UNTAG) with a mandate to "ensure the early independence of Namibia through free elections under the supervision and control of the United Nations" (UNSC, 1978: paragraphs 1, 2, 3).

South Africa also had important domestic reasons for accepting a negotiated regional settlement. In the early 1980s important planks in South Africa's own regime-survival strategy plans – like the setting up of "Bantustans" aimed at resolving crippling political, economic and social problems – ran into successive dead-ends. Likewise, the idea of creating a "constellation of states" – the Bantustanization of the region – did not move much beyond the conceptual stage. Zimbabwe's independence in 1980 under the leadership of Robert Mugabe finally put an end to this idea.

In sum, their respective sets of internal and external pressures led both Angola and South Africa to accept American diplomatic involvement to help pave the way for a settlement of the interconnected regional conflicts. The New York Accord of 22 December 1988 was the culmination of this process. Signed by Angola, Cuba, and South Africa, it provided for the removal of Cuban troops from Angola in exchange for South African commitment to implement UNSC Resolution 435 (1978) regarding independence for Namibia. Angola saw this accord as a major foreign policy victory inasmuch as it was expected to bring MPLA closer to finally achieving a measure of domestic security. Specifically, the Angolan regime believed that full implementation of UNSC Resolution 435 (1978) would bring two important benefits. First, it would remove the South African threat from its southern border. Second, it would precipitate the collapse of UNITA as a military threat by eliminating its main supply routes via Namibia. This overly optimistic scenario partly explains MPLA's refusal to accept a broader regional peace deal that would also have included a settlement of Angola's civil war. The Angolan government believed that, without South African support, UNITA would accept the terms of President dos Santos' "harmonization policy" that promised jobs and houses to rebels who laid down their arms. However, this calculation was unacceptable to the rebels because surrender at a time when they were relatively strong militarily would not guarantee political survival for UNITA because, in the late 1980s, MPLA government still firmly adhered to the principles of one-party politics.

Consequently, the process leading to Namibia's independence produced only partial rewards for Angola. On the positive side, it marked the end of Angola's long suffering at the hands of South Africa. However, it did not fundamentally alter Angola's security predicament because UNITA still posed a major challenge even without South African support. The Angolan rebels could still count on their other major regional ally – Mobutu's Zaire – and were, therefore, able to continue their guerrilla war by shifting key logistical bases and areas of operation to the north, closer to the Zairian border.

Mobutu's Zaire

Like South Africa's, Zaire's support of UNITA was partly a response to Angola's aggressive regional foreign policy. Angola's foreign policy toward Zaire was driven by the ultimate desire to affect a change of regime in Zaire as a way to improve its own domestic security. Zaire's ill-fated invasion of Angola in support of FNLA's attempt to seize power during Angola's haphazard decolonization process convinced the MPLA leadership that their post-colonial state-building project would be threatened for as long as Mobutu remained in power. This calculation explains, to a large degree, two decades of hostile relations between the two neighbours. Even before consolidating its own regime in Angola, the new MPLA government nearly succeeded in helping to topple Mobutu by allowing Angola to be used as a staging area for two armed invasions of Zaire in 1977 and 1978. Both invasions were carried out by well-trained and well-equipped troops led by Moise Tschombe. These troops had fought and lost a secessionist war for Zaire's Katanga province (now Shaba) during that country's own civil war and they were then allowed into Angola by the Portuguese authorities who were keen to use them in their anti-insurgency war against Angolan nationalist groups, including MPLA. When the colonial regime finally ended in Angola, the Katangan gendarmes switched allegiance to MPLA which used them effectively in the defence of Luanda particularly against FNLA/Zairian forces. Now, MPLA – not keen on having a well-trained group it did not fully control within a new and weak state – was willing to send them back home and, in the process, attempt to affect a change of regime in Mobutu's Zaire.

These invasions provided Mobutu and his Western allies with an added rationale for continuing intervention in Angola. Mobutu's allies – including the US, France, Belgium and Morocco – promptly came to his rescue and quickly pushed the invading forces back to Angola. In retrospect, although the invasions of Zaire exposed Mobutu's vulnerability, they also significantly and negatively affected Angola for two decades. Within a Cold War context, Angola's actions – whether with or without Cuban and Soviet consent or help – were seen as an attempt to expand the "Soviet sphere of influence" into central Africa. Consequently and predictably, the United States and its allies responded with massive military support for Mobutu. Even more significant for Angola, Western intelligence services accelerated efforts to provide training and weapons to UNITA through Zaire. Thus in 1978, a large number of UNITA military officers were sent to Morocco for various types of military training while many more were trained in Zaire. Also, most of the equipment used during the Western operation to rescue Mobutu and in subsequent joint military maneuvers was handed over to UNITA. This Western-Zairian-UNITA connection seriously weakened the new Angolan state and constituted a major threat to its territorial security, exactly the reverse outcome of what MPLA had originally intended.

Angola's relations with Mobutu's Zaire remained severely strained through the 1980s and much of the 1990s. In the late 1990s, however, after the end of the Cold War, Mobutu's kleptocratic and undemocratic regime became an embarrassing liability to its main international backers, especially the United States. Without external support and with mounting internal problems, Mobutu was toppled in May 1997. Angola and several other states in the region, including Rwanda and Uganda, were instrumental in overthrowing Mobutu by providing direct military support to the forces led by Laurent Kabila. For Angola, the overthrow of Mobutu's regime had everything to do with domestic politics. Finally, for the first time since independence, Angola had a friendly government in Zaire, now renamed the Democratic Republic of Congo. Angola's tangible rewards would come in the form of the actions the new Kabila regime was expected to take in denying UNITA a vital route for the inflow of weapons and outflow of diamonds. Equally important, the new Kabila government was willing to allow the Angolan armed forces to conduct military operations within the DRC to destroy UNITA bases in Congolese territory and prevent fleeing UNITA rebels from seeking refuge in the neighbouring country. This denying of vital routes for UNITA contributed significantly to its demise as a military threat to MPLA. As far as Angola's domestic security was concerned, the last regional vestiges of the Cold War had disappeared. However, this did not lead to an immediate and substantial improvement in Angola's security situation. MPLA's best efforts could not prevent UNITA's final mutation during the civil war – into a criminal insurgency that used Angola's natural resources, namely diamonds, to finance its war for another five years.

The limits of Angola's aggressive regional foreign policy

South Africa's withdrawal from Angola in the late 1980s represented a hollow victory for the MPLA regime in the sense that it did not significantly alter the stalemate with UNITA on the ground. As mentioned above, it also came at a time of major international changes that included the disengagement by the former Soviet Union from international commitments due to its own internal crisis. In addition, this internal crisis in the former Soviet Union and its eventual disintegration affected Cuba, another major backer of the Angolan government.

These profound changes at the international level forced Angola to redouble diplomatic efforts towards solving pressing domestic problems within continental frameworks. To this end, President dos Santos invited several African heads of state – from Congo-Brazzaville, Gabon, Mozambique, São Tomé e Príncipe, Zaire, Zambia, and Zimbabwe – to Luanda on 16 May 1989 to discuss ways to end Angola's civil war. At the end of this summit the MPLA government accepted for the first time the notion that "national reconciliation" based on dialogue between the warring parties should be the basis for peace. As a direct result of this summit, dos Santos and Savimbi met for the first time on 22 June 1989 in Gbadolite, Zaire at a special summit of African heads of state convened by former Zairian president Mobutu to help the warring sides initiate the much-need dialogue to end the civil war. Both dos Santos and Savimbi used the occasion to publicly declare their mutual desire to end the conflict and begin the critical dialogue that would eventually lead to national reconciliation.

The Gbadolite summit's apparent peace breakthrough, however, did not last. Its participants – including the African heads of state – had different interpretations of what they had agreed upon. The summit's final communiqué stated that all the parties had reached agreement on three points, including a mutual desire to end the war and effect national reconciliation, proclamation of a cease-fire effective from 24 June 1989, and the establishment of a mixed UNITA-MPLA commission under the mediation of President Mobutu to negotiate the political future of Angola (RNA, 23 June 1989). However, this directly contradicted former president Mousa Traore's version of events. Traore, then acting OAU president, claimed that the leaders gathered at Gbadolite had discussed and agreed on six points, namely, an end to armed opposition, security for Savimbi and his followers, voluntary and temporary withdrawal of Savimbi, granting of a post to Savimbi, integration of UNITA elements, and conditions for their integration (RTM, 23 June 1989). UNITA categorically rejected the latter interpretation. The rebels' version of events was closer to the more general statements expressed in the final communiqué and was corroborated by the summit's host, President Mobutu, who asserted that the agreement included "nothing about exile" for Savimbi (*The Washington Post*, 25 June 1989, p.A21). Amid diverging interpretations of what was pledged at Gbadolite, dos Santos returned to Luanda to plot his next diplomatic move. The Gbadolite fiasco had shown the limits of aggressive Angolan diplomacy to end its civil war. In response to this diplomatic failure, the MPLA launched a major military offensive against one of UNITA's most important bases at Mavinga on 18 August 1989. Again, this offensive ended in failure partly due to prompt and effective American military assistance to the Angolan rebels.

Against the background of military conflict and public acrimony, and in an attempt to salvage some of the spirit of reconciliation displayed at Gbadolite, a follow-up summit of African leaders took place in Harare on 22 August 1989. Savimbi was not invited to participate partly because President Mugabe, given his close relationship with the dos Santos government, was not as willing as Mobutu to give the Angolan rebel leader the benefit of the doubt and an important regional diplomatic stage. The Harare summit's final communiqué revisited Gbadolite and asserted that three additional principles, previously undisclosed, had been agreed upon at the earlier summit: first, respect for the Constitution and laws of the People's Republic of Angola; second, integration of UNITA into existing MPLA institutions; and, third, acceptance of Jonas Savimbi's temporary and voluntary exile. As expected, Savimbi rejected this outcome just as emphatically as he had rejected Gbadolite. Again, Angola's best diplomatic efforts had failed to find a way to end the conflict.

The failures at Gbadolite and Harare constituted more than just diplomatic set-backs for the Angolan regime. They also showed how difficult it was for African leaders to find solutions for African problems. By embracing MPLA's approach to conflict resolution, African leaders could only focus on one facet of a complex situation. Thus, they failed to grasp the crux of the matter, i.e., that Savimbi was not likely to abandon his lifelong quest for personal power and a dominant position for his party in Angolan politics. Any framework for peace that included the disintegration of UNITA and exile for Savimbi always had little chance of success. In fact, as later events would show – and as discussed above within the context of the failure of the Bicesse peace process – not even direct superpower involvement succeeded in persuading Savimbi to change his position.

In the aftermath of the 1992 electoral fiasco, the MPLA regime was again forced to redouble its diplomatic efforts to withstand not only the post-electoral crisis but also a militarily reinvigorated UNITA ready to accomplish with bullets what it had been unable to achieve with ballots. As a direct result of intense diplomacy by the Angolan government, the international community remained diplomatically engaged in the complex Angolan situation even after UNITA reignited the civil war. This continuing engagement, not just the changing military situation on the ground, eventually persuaded UNITA to return to the negotiating table in 1993. Exploratory talks were held in Addis Ababa before peace talks resumed in

Lusaka under UN mediation. After more than a year of negotiations both parties signed yet another power-sharing agreement, the Lusaka Protocol, whose main achievement was a power-sharing agreement whereby UNITA was awarded four ministerial portfolios, seven junior ministerial positions, six ambassadorships, three provincial governorships, five deputy-governorships, thirty district administrator positions, and thirty-five deputy district administrator positions.

But having painfully learned on previous occasions that diplomacy alone was insufficient to achieve peace, government troops removed UNITA from most of the areas it had captured in 1992 including the rebels' headquarters at Huambo shortly before the signing of the Lusaka Protocol.

Predictably, like all other previous attempts to bring peace to Angola, the Lusaka Protocol failed to deliver peace. Despite Savimbi's public embrace of dos Santos in Lusaka on 6 May 1995 and his promise to "cooperate in the consolidation of peace", he would never again return to Luanda – not even to participate in a government of national reconciliation as stipulated by the Lusaka agreement. Instead, UNITA continued to prevent the Angolan government from extending state authority into rebel controlled areas. Exasperated by UNITA's intransigence, the Angolan government adopted a two-pronged strategy to destroy the rebels once and for all. At the political level, the government announced that it no longer recognized Savimbi as a legitimate interlocutor. Instead, the MPLA government attempted to implement the Lusaka Protocol in cooperation with a breakaway rebel faction, UNITA-Renovada, led by Eugenio Manuvakola, the former UNITA secretary-general who had signed the Lusaka Protocol on behalf of the rebels and then defected to Luanda in 1997. At the military level, the government successfully evicted UNITA from key strategic areas in the central plateau including, in October 1999, its military headquarters at Bailundo and Andulo.

Finally, after more than a quarter century of civil war, the MPLA government was on the verge of crushing its main domestic military threat. Having helped establish friendly regimes in the sub-region – Zimbabwe in 1980, Namibia in 1990, South Africa in 1994, Zaire (now DR Congo) in 1997, and Congo-Brazzaville in 1998 – the Angolan government could now dedicate all its efforts to eliminating its domestic military threat with the knowledge that the weakened rebels could find no sanctuary in neighbouring countries to lick their wounds and regain their strength to fight another day.

The international environment: From constraints to opportunities

Independence for Angola came at the height of the Cold War – a period when one of the United States' major foreign policy goals was to contain the spread of communism around the world. Angola, as a Soviet and Cuban client, could not avoid being targeted by the United States especially during the Reagan years when the United States adopted a more militant and militarist foreign policy stance – beyond containment – to "roll back" communism around the world. Angola would become a test case in this new American strategy that hinged on the creation and/or support of insurgent movements, like UNITA in Angola or the *Contras* in Nicaragua, to overthrow pro-Soviet regimes.

Initially, the new MPLA regime underestimated American commitment to "roll back" communism. Thus, Agostinho Neto attempted to navigate the Cold War turbulence by adopting a non-aligned foreign policy discourse – even if, in practice, MPLA could not realistically hope to abandon the Soviet embrace without threatening its very survival. Angola's non-alignment did not find much receptivity, let alone support, in the United States. Washington continued to actively support the overthrow of the MPLA government even as American oil companies achieved dominance in the exploration of Angola's vast offshore fields. Indeed, from independence until the end of the civil war, the MPLA government had to manage this peculiar American strategy toward Angola – the primacy of economic interests coupled with American desire for stronger energy security dictated continuing engagement in Angola's oil sector while ideological interests induced the American government into actively supporting the overthrow of the MPLA government.

Neto believed that, ultimately, American economic and energy security interests would prevail and lead to strong economic ties between the United States and Angola. This, coupled with MPLA's professed non-alignment was viewed by the Angolan leadership as being sufficient to eventually change Washington's posture toward Angola. Paradoxically, however, Angola's commitment to non-alignment depended on the United States' willingness to reduce the pressure – via UNITA – upon the regime. In the absence of a fundamental American policy shift in favour of normal relations with the MPLA government – including, at minimum, formal diplomatic recognition of the new Angolan state – the regime's survival could only be assured by stronger ties with Cuba and the former Soviet Union. This even closer relationship with its main international backers entered a new era with Neto's death in September 1979, less than four years after taking office. His successor, Eduardo dos Santos, a Soviet trained petroleum engineer, quickly abandoned any pretence of non-alignment in favour of even closer ties with the former USSR and Cuba due to a quickly deteriorating domestic situation.

Unlike his predecessor, dos Santos was prepared to give greater latitude to Angola's Soviet and Cuban allies in determining the main guidelines of the new state's domestic and foreign policy. Previously disappointed with Neto's flirtation with non-alignment, the Soviet leadership welcomed this new foreign policy orientation because Angola provided an important base in Southern Africa from which to affect change during a period of great instability caused by both regional and Cold War dynamics. The former USSR was particularly interested in influencing events in South Africa, the richest and most developed state in the subcontinent, as a way of fulfilling its self-proclaimed role as the vanguard of third world liberation movements and, more strategically, to help set up friendly regimes throughout this strategically important region. Dos Santos also strengthened his government's ties with Cuba which, as mentioned above, was all too willing to assist at various levels. However, as argued earlier, both the former USSR and Cuba were beset by their own set of domestic problems. Thus, they were not in a position to effectively help MPLA solve its domestic challenges. In particular, they could not help solve Angola's economic problems nor prevent UNITA from becoming a growing threat with Zairian, South African and American assistance. America, in particular, had not yet satiated its appetite for Angola.

Unlike the USSR, American interest and involvement in Southern Africa predated the collapse of the Portuguese colonial regime. The US, like other Western countries, had historically maintained a presence in Southern Africa to safeguard its access to the region's vast deposits of minerals. During the Cold War, the containment of the perceived Soviet expansionist threat in the region provided a new rationale for deeper involvement. However, the US's involvement in post-colonial Angola was bound to be problematic due to its intervention on the side of FNLA and UNITA during the chaotic transition to independence. This was followed by the withholding of diplomatic recognition of the MPLA regime and continued support for UNITA. Consequently, US-Angola relations during the civil war never moved past mutually beneficial commercial interests, notably with American companies' exploration of the vast Angolan oil fields. Although this commercial relationship, initiated during the colonial period, continued uninterrupted when the MPLA assumed power, the US preferred not to deal with the MPLA government at a political level – using diplomatic recognition as an enticing carrot – until democratic elections were held in Angola. Admittedly, the insistence on "free and fair" elections for Angola was not simply driven by American belief that their Jeffersonian institutions could be replicated in places like Angola. More instrumentally, it was assumed in Washington that elections would bring an American ally – UNITA – to power since this party's main base of support was among the majority Ovimbundu ethno-linguistic group.

Beginning in the early 1980s, partly as a result of its inability to force MPLA into holding elections, or at least enter into a power-sharing agreement with UNITA, the US under Ronald Reagan pursued a clear and unambiguous policy to overthrow the MPLA government. Angola would become an important target of the "Reagan Doctrine" – a global campaign aimed at confronting the former Soviet Union and undermining its allies by, among other things, providing overt American support for anticommunist guerrilla movements around the world. The Reagan Doctrine had an almost immediate impact on the Angolan civil war since UNITA became a major recipient of modern American weaponry, including sophisticated "Stinger" anti-aircraft missiles that, for a period of time, upset the air supremacy enjoyed by the MPLA government.

This doctrine also further emboldened the apartheid regime into intervening even more aggressively in Angola on the side of UNITA. Consequently, all major military offensives mounted by the MPLA forces to dislodge the Angolan rebels from their bases in southern Angola ended in failure. For example, massive American and SADF assistance was crucial in saving UNITA in 1988 from advancing MPLA and crack Cuban units during the battle for Cuito-Cuanavale, in what has been described as one of the fiercest conventional battles on African soil (Campbell, 1989:1).

The battle for Cuito-Cuanavale proved to Cuba and South Africa – both small, sub-imperial interventionist states – that protracted military engagements would result in unbearable loss of lives. Consequently, both countries accepted the inevitability of a negotiated framework for regional peace involving both the withdrawal of Cuban troops from Angola and the implementation of UNSCR 435/78 regarding Namibia's independence (Crocker, 1992:506–11). It can be argued, therefore, that the military stalemate on the ground hastened the cease-fire accord reached between the governments of Angola, Cuba and South Africa on 8 August 1988 and the historic agreement by these same governments on 22 December in New

York, providing for the phased withdrawal of 50,000 Cuban troops from Angola over a period of twenty-seven months in return for the implementation of the UN plan for Namibia's independence. Both accords marked the culmination of eight years of mediating efforts by the US and were heralded as a major diplomatic coup for the Reagan administration – proof that the "Reagan Doctrine" worked. The agreements eased Namibia's transition to independence but did little to speed up the resolution of the civil war in Angola itself, partly because they did not involve UNITA.

On the surface, the New York Accord was a major diplomatic coup for Angola inasmuch as it removed the South African military threat from its southern border, through Namibia. Moreover, independence for Namibia would deny UNITA vital supply routes in the south. In a wider regional context, this represented another important step in liberating Southern Africa from settler minority rule, a development that was expected to pay immediate domestic security dividends for Angola. But the accrual of these dividends would be delayed for more than a decade partly because of an important flaw in the New York Accord. By excluding UNITA, the New York Accord did not accelerate the resolution of the civil war in Angola because the perception of their marginalization forced the Angolan rebels to rethink their military and political strategies as a way to ensure continuing relevance, if only temporarily. Thus, at the military level UNITA moved a considerable portion of its operations away from its traditional bases in the southeast into the north and northeast. This placed UNITA both closer to the Zairian border and in control of important diamond producing areas. By moving north UNITA also hoped to achieve important political goals. For example, it could claim that its struggle against the regime was deeply implanted in most of the country's provinces.

The failure to include UNITA in the talks leading to the New York Accord was a result of the Angolan government's paradoxical insistence on removing its own domestic issues from the wider regional peace process. Oddly, this occurred while, given the interconnectedness between its domestic security predicament and the wider regional dynamics, Angola's foreign policy was geared to ensure the survival of the regime by changing its regional environment issues. In any event, the negotiations were conducted along two tracks. Track I involved negotiations regarding the removal of Cuban troops from Angola in return for South African withdrawal from Namibia, paving the way for its independence. Track II entailed consultations aimed at achieving national reconciliation between MPLA and UNITA. Both tracks were supposed to be pursued simultaneously.

However, since the parties to the negotiations had previously agreed that the question of national reconciliation for Angola was an internal matter, no pressure was put on either the MPLA government or UNITA to settle their differences within the framework of the negotiations. Therefore, Track II led to a dead-end because, at the time, the Angolan government was not prepared to end the war through political means as this would have required negotiating a comprehensive power-sharing framework with UNITA. For the MPLA government, negotiations with UNITA were still contrary to its guiding principles. As President dos Santos explained at the time, "the Angolan state is a one-party state and so the acceptance of such a political organization [UNITA] is out of the question" (Reuters, 1 October 1988). Instead, he suggested that his government would seek "national harmonization" – through a policy of clemency and reintegration of UNITA members into Angolan society – that would eventually lead to the end of the civil war. Dos Santos argued that "the idea is to bring all Angolans together under the same anthem and flag, under the same state" (Reuters, 1 October 1988). This position was based on the view that UNITA did not constitute a legitimate political force because it was armed and financed by outside forces.

Dos Santos and his government were planning to address the possibility of ending the civil war only after UNITA was sufficiently weakened through the disengagement of South Africa through the signing of a regional peace accord. Thus Angola's main diplomatic efforts after the signing of the New York Accord were directed toward ensuring that it was fully implemented. The MPLA government believed that even without direct military support from Cuba its armed forces could crush the rebels once South Africa withdrew from Namibia through a combination of political and military operations. This approach to internal conflict resolution seriously underestimated UNITA's military strengths and resourcefulness. Indeed, the MPLA government's efforts to isolate UNITA diplomatically while attempting to crush it militarily did not succeed within the optimistic timeframe it had envisaged mainly because South Africa's role as UNITA's main backer was simply taken over by the United States which used Mobutu's Zaire to channel help to the Angolan rebels.

Unable to settle the civil war militarily, and given the mounting international pressures associated with the collapse of communism and the end of the Cold War, eventually both MPLA and UNITA accepted an externally-imposed framework for peace. This greater inclination to accept international involvement occurred at a time when the US and the former

USSR were developing a warmer post-Cold War relationship that involved attempts to settle all major contentious issues that confronted them. For both global powers at the end of the Cold War, Angola provided a good opportunity to remove an important festering irritant in their bilateral relations. To this end, the superpowers signalled to both MPLA and UNITA that major diplomatic rewards would be forthcoming with the successful completion of a peace process in Angola. For example, the American government promised diplomatic recognition once free and democratic elections were held. Another positive external factor was Portugal's willingness to become involved again in helping its former colony settle the turmoil that followed independence.

On 25 April 1990, the Angolan government announced that it would enter into direct talks with UNITA. The two major powers, along with Portugal, actively participated in the peace negotiations and went as far as formulating the main documents for negotiations between the two rivals. These documents covered five basic political principles and technical-military issues: first, Angola would become a democratic and multi-party nation; second, the international community would guarantee a cease-fire; third, there would be free and fair elections in Angola, verified by the international community; fourth, the signing of a cease-fire would be preceded by an accord on the date for free and fair elections; and fifth, all military assistance from abroad would stop once a cease-fire accord was signed.

These principles formed the basis for the Bicesse Peace Accord signed in Portugal, on 31 May 1991 by Angolan President dos Santos and former UNITA leader Jonas Savimbi. In principle, this peace accord appeared solid. Yet, much like the ones before, the Bicesse Accord was doomed from the beginning because UNITA perceived it as another MPLA ploy to prolong its hold on power. In other words, at that time, there was little good will at the domestic political level to support a lasting settlement of the civil war. Although both the MPLA government and UNITA participated in the implementation of the Bicesse Accord, it amounted to no more than a tragic exercise in make-believe intended to satisfy the demands of the international community, particularly the United States. Predictably, once the internationally supervised process resulted in UNITA's defeat at the polls, Savimbi removed his generals from the embryonic unified army and sent them back to war. Tragically for Angola, the international community – especially the UN and the guarantors of the peace process (US, the former USSR, and Portugal) – could not prevent a renewal of the conflict.

In sum, the domestic, regional, and international environments severely restricted Angola's foreign policy options during the 1970s and 1980s. In the 1990s, however, important changes at the international and regional levels – brought about by the end of the Cold War and the dismantling of the apartheid regime in South Africa – were expected to improve Angola's foreign policy environment. Angola attempted to reap important dividends by taking advantage of new, more favourable, regional and international environments to redirect its foreign policy toward enhancing the regime's ability to achieve and sustain domestic peace and security. This objective, however, was delayed for a decade until the civil war ended after the death of rebel leader Jonas Savimbi.

Post-conflict diplomatic challenges

Having achieved its key objective – regime survival through the elimination of its main domestic threat partly by helping to create a favourable regional environment – the Angolan state must now reassess its priorities away from its single-minded focus on regime survival. With peace in Angola – except for the simmering conflict in the Cabinda enclave – a new, more inclusive foreign policy framework is urgently needed. This framework must be based on a redefinition of what constitutes the Angolan state's broader national interest. Thus far, the governing MPLA has cleverly defined party interest as national interest. In other words, what is good for the party is good for the nation. But such a framework is highly exclusive in the sense that it restricts foreign policy inputs to selected segments of society. Not incidentally, these are the groups at whose behest national foreign policy is conducted and who most benefit from state policies – both foreign and domestic.

A redefined national interest must go far beyond the governing party's traditional interest – regime security – toward broader human security. The focus on human security would force the Angolan government to deal with not only such issues pertaining to the adversities caused by the armed conflict – demilitarization of society, full reintegration of displaced persons, de-mining and so on – but also non-military issues that threaten the survival and dignity of citizens. This latter set of issues involves insecurities caused by poverty, infectious diseases, human rights violations, and all types of inequalities and vulnerabilities resulting from a grossly uneven distribution of wealth and power. Dealing with both sets of issues is crucial for achieving sustainable peace and development.

To successfully tackle these challenges as well as others yet unforeseen that will likely arise in the long and difficult struggle for national reconciliation and reconstruction, there is a pressing need for fundamental transformations at the state level – particularly in terms of democratic governance and transparent management of the country's revenues accrued especially from the sale of natural resources like oil and diamonds. In other words, a pseudo-democratic kleptocracy must undergo fundamental reform at the state level while, simultaneously, seeking to develop strong relationships with key global players – especially the US, but also the EU – to help sustain the peace and facilitate the commencement of a development process that has been delayed by almost three decades of civil war and mismanagement. In the final analysis, then, internal conditions in Angola will continue to have a major impact on how its engagements with the world are pursued. Now, strategic and governance issues – not ideology – will guide this engagement.

Angola: *The West's new best friend in Africa?*

The relationship with the US, in particular, cannot be expected to indefinitely hinge on oil alone. Admittedly, as mentioned before, oil has been a critical element in the complex relationship between the US and Angola. Currently, Angola accounts for five per cent of US global oil imports – a level greater than American oil imports from Kuwait and which is expected to double over the next ten years. Thus, Angola's relevance to the US is assured because it can make an important non-OPEC contribution to American energy security at a time when the US is actively diversifying its sources of energy supplies away from the volatile Middle East region. But the US is well aware that, as history has shown in Iran and more recently in the Gulf states, tying US foreign policy too closely to an illiberal regime holds obvious negative ramifications for American interests. Therefore, to avoid repeating the mistakes clearly evident in its Middle East foreign policy, the US can be expected to pursue a wider set of complementary policy goals – away from a singular focus on energy security – to foster the conditions that will ensure continued access to a 'friendly' source of oil. In other words, the nurturing of a stable, democratic, transparent, and accountable government as well as a healthy civil society will go hand-in-hand with greater investment in the oil sectors of countries like Angola.

The US is already making efforts – albeit low-key and overly cautious – to develop a comprehensive approach to Angola that would promote a post-conflict reconstruction based upon democratic values of good governance. This reflects a pragmatic understanding that a solid base for a successful US-Angolan partnership must move beyond a convergence of transnational petro-elite interests. It must also engage those sectors of Angolan civil society most interested in creating a flourishing democracy and market economy. In the absence of such engagement, the US will be justifiably regarded as a supporter of a corrupt regime and could run the risk of replicating the foreign policy failures that have regularly come back to haunt it in the Middle East.

Specifically, in the short run, American foreign policy toward Angola must involve a more active engagement in key critical issue areas of governance even if, as can be expected, this generates some discomfort among the governing elites. While continuing and strengthening its presence in Angola's growing oil sector, American foreign policy must recognise that this involvement – although critical for the long-term survival of those elites – alienates and embitters the majority of Angolans who, by and large, remain as peripheral participants in Angola's political economy and, consequently, do not have access to the country's oil wealth. However important Angolan oil may be for American security interests, a broader, longer-term perspective is critical lest the United States be regarded as a partner in corruption and, as such, an enemy of the Angolan people. As many examples around the world attest, highly corrupt regimes often engender populist movements. For the US, therefore, it would not be in its long-term national security interests to be identified with the Angolan regime's corruption. A more pragmatic American foreign policy toward Angola must, therefore, include a visible governance component. Through direct or indirect action, the United States must avoid the development of a generalized perception in the minds of average Angolans that it is simply interested in Angola's oil, regardless of the Angolan people's misery. In other words, the United States must develop a more overt political component to its foreign policy toward Angola to complement the well-established economic motive. This will ensure long-term sustainability for this important relationship.

Other Western countries – including France, Portugal, and the UK – also have important economic interests in Angola's oil sector. Thus, oil diplomacy will remain important in their interaction with Angola. But Western interaction with Angola will continue to encounter some very rough patches as some governments – especially in Europe – respond to their domestic civil society constituencies' demands to refrain from doing business as usual with a country like Angola that, according to Transparency International, is one of the most corrupt in the world. Prodded by important elements of their civil societies, some European governments are increasingly more willing to place human rights, transparency, and governance concerns at the centre of their relationships with third world countries – especially those resource-rich states like Angola that could better look after the needs of the populations they govern through improved management of resources. Thus, unsurprisingly, those governments have responded with a lessened sense of urgency to calls for post-conflict development aid – e.g. a "donors' conference" – coming from Angola because the ruling elite's looted wealth could fund a comprehensive reconstruction effort. The Angolan government can, therefore, expect continued pressure by Western governments to clean up its corruption now that the war is over and the regime is no longer distracted by urgent existential issues. Similar pressures can also be expected in Angola's interactions with the IFIs.

Angola and the IFIs: Prospects for effective engagement

Notwithstanding the efforts by important segments of Western civil society to force their governments to take a more forceful position vis-a-vis Angola with a view to ammeliorate its governance system, Western governments are more likely to succeed by exerting such pressure more indirectly via, for example, the IFIs. Unlike multinational oil companies, the power relationships between Angola and the IFIs are such that the latter cannot be easily bullied. To put it bluntly, Angola needs to make a concerted effort to develop a better relationship with both the IMF and the World Bank as it attempts to restructure its shattered economy to face the enormous tasks of post-conflict reconstruction. The relationship with the IMF is particularly important because it could enable Angola to secure long-term financing from the Fund instead of continuing to rely on expensive short-term loans for its financial needs. Angola's relations with these institutions – perhaps more so than any other set of foreign relations – are of critical importance as its undertakes to implement post-conflict reconstruction programmes. But the relationship between Angola and the IFIs will not be unproblematical because of these institutions' propensity for probing deeply into sensitive financial and governance issues and the rigidity of their prescriptions.

For the IFIs, a major challenge will revolve around finding ways to help the Angolan regime appreciate – and find the means to overcome – the corrosive effects of corruption on the economy and society as a whole. Specifically, this will involve finding the right mix of carrots and sticks to induce Angola to direct its considerable oil revenues strictly toward national development purposes and not use them for the personal enrichment of the governing elites. As mentioned earlier, oil is currently – and will be for several decades – the cornerstone of Angola's economy. In and of itself, this is a very problematic situation given the country's enormous potential in various other non-oil sectors. But even more alarming, however, is the fact that a considerable portion of oil revenues does not fund the country's development needs – it simply disappears into a "Bermuda triangle" comprising the state oil company SONANGOL, the president's office, and the central bank. In 2003, more than $900m disappeared in this triangle. According to the IMF, at least $4 billion had disappeared in the previous five years as the civil war was winding down.

No longer militarily at war with itself, Angola can now move ahead more firmly with the development tasks of reconstructing the economy, restoring financial stability, re-establishing market structures with the objective of reducing widespread poverty and, ultimately, create the enabling conditions to ensure that all citizens have the opportunity to achieve their individual socio-economic goals. This, however, will require both political will and technical expertise. No longer at risk, the regime may finally muster the political will to improve governance and trasparency. However, the lack of expertise that still plagues a country emerging from decades of civil war preceded by centuries of colonialism, will require sustained international engagement both for peace consolidation and economic development.

International engagement through the IFIs can help Angola implement key basic policies that would, over time, lead to greater transparency and accountability. For example, a truly autonomous central bank – free from political interference and with a clear mandate to design and implement policies to facilitate rapid economic growth – is an immediate necessity. Similarly, the national oil company must be both autonomous and transparent – shielded from political interference, regularly audited by reputable international firms, and legally compelled to publish all of its financial information – to ensure that it serves the broader national interest, not the interests of the governing party or the presidency. This is especially critical as oil production is expected to double and reach about 2 million barrels a day within 5 years. Without immediate efforts to fundamentally change the oil-power nexus – i.e. how oil wealth increases the power of the minority to the detriment of the majority – the doubling of oil production may lead to even greater corruption and structural violence.

The average Angolan citizen may, therefore, welcome this international involvement if it leads to better governance, especially as far as the management of public funds is concerned. But, as is apparent in other countries in Africa and around the world that experienced this type of international involvement, the implementation of the IFIs' prescriptions is not a guarantee of success in changing the structure and functioning of highly debilitated political and economic systems. Different patients have responded differently to the IFIs' medicine. In some cases, the implementation of structural adjustment programmes had profound negative effects on vulnerable segments of society like the urban underclasses, children, women, and the elderly. In other words, in attempting to get back in the IFIs' good graces by being a "good pupil", Angola may replicate the experiences of countries where structural adjustment programmes enhanced the economic disparities between the haves and the have-nots.

Recent bilateral discussions between Angola and the IFIs, perhaps the most significant both in terms of content as well as context since Angola joined the IMF and the World Bank in 1989, have focused on four key issues: first and foremost, they dealt with governance, transparency and accountability issues; second, short-term macroeconomic outlook and policies; third, poverty reduction strategy; and, fourth, structural reform (IMF 2003. See also World Bank 2003). Not unexpectedly, regarding the key issues of governance, transparency and accountability, the critical aspect of how best to manage Angola's oil revenues rose to the top of the agenda with the IFIs emphasizing the need to take appropriate measures to ensure that oil operations are managed in a transparent manner. In particular, tax payments by all the players involved in the oil sector – both domestic and international – must come under proper fiscal control. As far as the key domestic player in the oil sector is concerned, the IFIs would like to see SONANGOL adhere to international accounting standards. The ensuing regular reporting and auditing of its operations would go a long way to ensure transparency, reduce its exposure to the rapacity of the elites, and enable its revenues to become an important base for overall sound macroeconomic management of the economy. A related topic concerns the importance of a unified budget. In this regard, the government stressed that, for the first time, its 2003 budget would include the quasi-fiscal operations of SONANGOL as well as other government operations – particularly the provision of goods and services to the military – that thitherto had been conducted outside the regular budgetary norms. As far as transparency and accountability are concerned, this is a major improvement because these areas provided the greatest opportunities for non-transparent activities leading to the personal enrichment of many members of the governing elite. The "signature bonuses" given by multinational oil companies upon being granted oil exploration rights – often amounting to several hundred million dollars per year – were not, as a rule, included in the budget. Another favourite scheme for elite enrichment during the war involved opaque military procurement practices that included large kickbacks for groups of individuals responsible for purchasing weapons. A thorough cleansing of the budgetary process can, therefore, result in a considerable amount of funds being injected into the government coffers to be used for development efforts.

On the second issue – short-term macroeconomic outlook and policies – the picture is dominated by the government's sizeable fiscal deficit and very high inflation. In 2003, the fiscal deficit represented 8.9 per cent of GDP. In addition, the accumulation of external debt arrears represented 1 per cent of GDP. This situation forces the government to rely on costly commercial loans. Ammortization payments on those loans total $1.2 billion or 9.3 per cent of GDP (http://www.imf.org/external/pubs/cat/longres.cfm?sk=16871.0, p. 13). Inflation continues to be a major problem – perennially at the three-digit level – that continues to seriously threaten the prospects for economic recovery. The government hopes of bringing it down to just below the two-digit level, although commendable, may ultimately prove insufficient for the long-term health prospects of the economy. If the involvement of the IFIs elsewhere in the world is any indication, more drastic measures to fight inflation will be sought for Angola. But, for the government, this would be a risky course of action because tightening monetary policy could have adverse political consequences. For example, extra-budgetary activities – the critical lubricant of the system – would no longer be tolerable. More generally, it is not clear that a tight monetary policy would be appropriate for a country in need of almost entirely rebuilding itself after a devastating civil war. Indeed, most Angolans who are set to initiate the process of rebuilding their lives by becoming economic actors would understandably expect their government to make the necessary funds available cheaply and generously – especially given popular misperceptions about their country's wealth.

Poverty reduction is the third focus area for the IFIs in Angola where the vast majority of the population live in absolute poverty, i.e. survive on less than US$1 a day. But the more sensitive and equally problematic issue of relative poverty must also be addressed. As mentioned before, while the war led to the immiseration of most Angolans, it also provided opportunities for the ruling elite to accumulate fabulous wealth that is now flounted in many ways, including access to excessive food as well as luxurious housing and transportation at home in addition to education and health care abroad. Unchecked, this relative poverty gap will seriously undermine whatever base of legitimate governance the elites currently claim and lead to a new mutation of violence – back to more overt infliction of physical hurt upon individuals and property – as a way of redressing structural violence.

The reduction of both absolute and relative poverty can be best achieved through a wide-ranging structural reform of the economy, the fourth key area where the IFIs would like to see continuing improvements. The end of the civil war provides Angola with its first post-colonial opportunity to diversify its economy away from its current dependence on oil – even as the oil sector, by doubling its current production – continues to serve as the key economic base. However, this diversification must be designed to ensure the creation of opportunities for all citizens to participate in and benefit from revenue-generating economic activities. This, alas, is not as straightforward as it may seem given the elites' propensity to monopolize most wealth-producing activities. Unless this approach to state building undergoes a fundamental transformation, Angola will resemble other resource-rich African countries with a profoundly skewed wealth distribution system with all the adverse effects that such a situation produces.

The context within which Angola-IFI discussions have taken place highlights the unique opportunities and challenges facing Angola. For the first time since independence, regime survival is not an issue: the war's end removed all immediate and direct threats to the governing party. In a very real sense, Angola now has the opportunity to recapture the promise of building a good society in a post-colonial state – a realistic prospect given its wealth in human and natural resources. The war's end will also force the government to accept greater accountability because it removed the government's most convenient excuse for many of its setbacks. Dauntingly, however, the war's end exposed the magnitude of the challenges ahead as Angola attempts to overcome past ills and work toward creating a citizen-friendly state. No viable state can be built upon a base so seriously corroded by poverty and so viciously besieged by structural violence. The degree to which Angola can fully seize this window of opportunity will also determine future lending from the IFIs. But IFI lending can be counterproductive if it simply results in alleviating the government's multiple pressures while neglecting the more pressing needs of the wider society. In other words, unless IFI involvement at minimum results in creating the conditions for a transparent management of public resources, it will not significantly help the average citizen. Indeed, it may contribute to the perpetuation of structural violence that has already taken root in Angola.

Ultimately, the "one size fits all" approach to reform prescribed by the IMF and embraced by the MPLA regime will not result in a restructuring of economic activity in a way that improves the average citizen's opportunities for a better life. Indeed, they may lead to increasing structural violence. A more sustainable approach to economic development must involve a concerted effort to overcome one of the key aspects of the colonial economy – the heavy dependence on one or a handful of commodities like oil and diamonds. These commodities will produce a windfall for Angola only to the extent to which the revenues accrued from their exploration contribute to the development of human resources and the expansion of other economic sectors. Current approaches to development will only succeed in accelerating the expansion of the gap that separates the grotesquely rich and the impoverished masses. Given the potential for conflict associated with already existing societal fault lines – including ethnicity and race – popular perceptions concerning the elites' pauperization of the masses will continue to fuel instability and possibly conflict into the future.

Post-conflict opportunities

In September 2002, the government approved yet another typically ambitious economic programme for 2003-04. This new SAP aims to "consolidate the peace, achieve macroeconomic stability, improve service delivery, rehabilitate economic infrastructure, extend state administration across the nation, promote economic growth in the non-oil sectors, and create the conditions for new general elections" (http://www.worldbank.com/ao/reports/2003_Angola_tss.pdf, p.12). But the same report also gives a glimpse of Angola's many challenges. It says, bluntly, that:

> The macroeconomic situation in Angola continues to be extremely fragile and preliminary data indicate that the 2002 fiscal results were poor. Annual inflation, due to rapid increases in the monetary base and the velocity of money, largely fueled by fiscal laxity, was 106 per cent in December 2002. Oil revenues as reported by the government showed a decline as a share of GDP, but they may have been underestimated. Domestic payment arrears accumulated further, to about 2 per cent of GDP. The fiscal deficit for 2002 on an accrual basis exceeded 8 per cent of GDP, which was more than double the 2001 deficit and

also interrupted a trend-decline in overall fiscal deficits that started in 1999. In addition, financing of the deficit depleted Angola's offshore oil-bonus account, necessitated expensive international borrowing, and resulted in a large expansion of central bank credit to the government and a corresponding depletion of gross international reserves (these are now equivalent to one month of imports, the lowest level in a decade) (p.12).

In other words, colossal challenges lie ahead for Angola.

However daunting the current challenges may seem, Angola can still fulfil its enormous economic potential and provide its citizens with ample opportunities to achieve the good life – however they may define it. Its considerable oil and diamond resources can provide an important base for (re)launching the economy, especially in terms of reviving critical sectors like agriculture, industry, and fisheries. The fulfilment of this potential, however, will remain dependent on the country's ability to meet and overcome two key sets of challenges. The first set of challenges revolves around the critical – albeit more general – issues of transparency and accountability that will eventually determine the type of society Angola will become: open and vibrant or chronically debilitated by the corrosive effects of corruption. Thus, in the short run Angola will have to develop the institutional framework – grounded on a strong and independent judiciary – to improve its system of governance, particularly in terms of transparency. In addition, it must drastically improve overall productive efficiency by creating a system of social and economic rewards that promotes the development of good practices, ideas and, ultimately, innovation. Angola must also begin the more long-term process of creating a culture where all citizens – regardless of their position in society – are held accountable for their actions, particularly as far as the management of public resources is concerned.

The second set of challenges involves completing both the political and economic transitions that an open society requires. At the political level, the process of establishing a truly democratic regime is far from complete. Indeed, after winning the civil war, the governing MPLA is set to establish itself as a hegemonic political force willing to continue blurring the line between party and state. This dominant position will allow the governing party to use co-optation, if not coercion, to remain unchallenged for the foreseeable future – a quasi-one-party system where political opposition is tolerated simply for its usefulness in legitimizing the pseudo-democratic credentials of the party in power. A healthier political system would involve equally powerful opposing forces capable of governing from time to time.

Similarly, the economic transition from central planning to a free market economy remains to be completed. For example, key economic institutions like the central bank remain within the political grip of the governing party and its operations in the wider interests of society are often hampered by partisan political expediency. Political expediency has also thus far prevented the removal of the regulatory framework – i.e. red tape inherited from colonialism and the era of central planning – that severely constrains economic activities. The overall economic situation will also be greatly improved if the governing party is finally able to take advantage of the important contextual changes at the domestic level to design a sound macroeconomic management programme and find the political will to fully implement it.

At the economic level, Angola must finally take steps to use the dynamic and expanding oil sector to revive the moribund non-oil sectors. In particular, in a country richly endowed with an abundance of fertile lands, resuscitating the agricultural sector should be a top priority not only because of its employment generating potential but also to diminish the country's dependency on food imports. Reviving the agricultural sector is also of critical importance to reduce rural poverty. But to reduce rural poverty and revive Angola's agricultural sector the issue of land redistribution must rise toward the top of the country's post-conflict priorities.

How Angola chooses to prioritize its many post-conflict challenges will depend on the pressures, both internal and external, imposed upon the government. At the internal level, with the opposition still licking its wounds and civil society vulnerable to cooptation, the government can expect weak pressures. Also importantly, the government is likely to withstand external pressures to clean up its act partly due to its growing relationship with China.

The Chinese alternative

The Angola government has aggressively sought international assistance to rebuild its devastated country. However, Western governments and IFIs have not responded with the enthusiasm Angola originally expected. In fact, thus far, Angola has been unable to convince Western countries to hold a donors' conference where funds to finance post-conflict reconstruction could be sought. This has forced Angola to look elsewhere in search of external partners. China has emerged as Angola's best alternative to Western assistance. A growing global economic powerhouse, China is positioned to become Angola's largest trading partner. Angola is already China's second largest trade partner in Africa and, after Saudi Arabia, is China's second-largest supplier of oil. The trade volume between the two countries reached 4.9 billion US dollars in 2005 and is expected to grow at a rapid pace. China is particularly interested in having access to Angola's proven deposits of 10 billion barrels of oil to satisfy its own growing thirst for energy. There are, therefore, important complementarities to be exploited: China is in a position to supply Angola with much needed industrial goods and technical assistance while Angola can supply China with increasing quantities of oil.

Unlike Western interests which have scrambled for Angola's oil through production-sharing agreements, China is using soft loans to ensure access to this critical commodity. For example, in March 2004 China's Eximbank provided Angola with a $2 billion loan toward post-conflict reconstruction in return for 10,000 barrels of oil a day. The terms of the loan – 1.5 per cent over 17 years followed by an additional 5-year grace period – are particularly generous and suggest that China's goals are more long-term and strategic than short-term and commercial. For Angola, these loans enabled it to avoid dealing with the IFIs' demands for greater financial transparency and accountability as conditions for the provision of fresh loans. It also enables the country to urgently focus on the rebuilding of its devastated infrastructures – including power grids, water networks, roads, bridges and railways – without which the country's long-delayed development potential cannot be realized.

In many respects, China is making up for its initial miscalculations including the withholding of diplomatic recognition for eight years after Angola became independent. China's long hesitation partly reflected its early support for the two nationalist movements – FNLA and UNITA – that lost the pre-independence power struggle and subsequent civil war to the governing MPLA. It also indicated its disapproval of the MPLA regime's tight relationship with the former USSR – China's then communist rival. Now, for many members of the MPLA regime, China represents a model of pragmatism that must be emulated as Angola attempts to undertake its own colossal transformation from an impoverished war-debilitated country with enormous economic potential to a regional market-driven economic powerhouse.

Conclusion

Even by post-colonial African standards, Angola's recent history has been disappointing. This country was once justifiably expected to become an important regional political and economic player due to its rich endowment of natural resources. However, a combination of war and corruption have turned Angola into a problematic state where citizens must survive in miserable conditions while their leaders appropriate vast sums of public funds for their personal use. For most of its post-colonial history, Angola was a double-hostage caught between a criminal state that impoverished and battered the people in whose name it claimed to govern and a criminal insurgency with corresponding disregard for the people in whose name it claimed to fight. With the demise of the criminal insurgency, Angola has a unique opportunity to achieve peace. In important ways it represents an opportunity for the rebirth of a battered country, a chance for an entire generation to recapture its youthful optimism and attempt to realize postponed dreams. But these dreams – even basic aspirations like human security – are unlikely to come true any time soon due to the improbability that most Angolans will successfully extricate themselves from the second hostage condition Having won the war, the governing MPLA is set to remain in power for the foreseeable future while UNITA licks its wounds and the other opposition parties reinvent themselves. Given the lack of credible political alternatives, MPLA is unlikely to fundamentally disassemble the very structures that have kept it in power regardless of how corrupt and socially dysfunctional it may be. In other words, to achieve its potential and realize the aspirations of its citizens, Angola will require a new liberation – this time not from an external colonial power or domestic rebels but from an autochthonous system that excludes the many and empowers the few. This liberation will necessarily be long and arduous because the inherently structurally violent nature of the system will remain highly resistant to changes, especially of the cosmetic variety like leadership turnover and predetermined electoral exercises. Ultimately, liberation can only be achieved through citizen empowerment, i.e. by collective and sustained efforts to reestablish a more balanced relationship between state and society in which society's best interests guide the state's every action. Although organized elements of civil society can help, this process of liberation will necessarily be decided by the citizens themselves. In many respects, then, Angola must turn a new page in its political development and free itself from the grip of the "liberation movements" that, having led the anti-colonial struggle, subsequently brought despair to the very people they claimed to have liberated.

If anything, the post-independence period demonstrated the liberation movements' fundamental weaknesses in managing the complex processes involved in the transition from colony to independent statehood. In Angola's peculiar case, those weaknesses expressed themselves in various ways. For example, although MPLA and UNITA were the principal domestic participants in the war, they did not fully control all the elements involved in the conflict. For much of the conflict both sides acted as proxies of more powerful external forces and, as such, depended on and responded to external stimuli much more quickly than to domestic pressures. Thus, although both the government and the rebels were able to shut domestic civil society out of the formal political realm with varying degrees of success for much of the civil war period, external forces played a critical role in both the dynamics of war and the timing of the peace processes. But, ironically, the external dimension has been more decisive in conditions of war than peace: the United States and the former Soviet Union could force their respective proxies to the peace table but could not prevent a resumption of the war when one of them refused to play by the externally imposed rules of a game it was disinclined to play in the first place. Likewise, now admittedly in conditions of negative peace, the external powers are yet to deliver on the promises to help a devastated country achieve positive peace.

Rather than viewing the lack of eager external support as a handicap, Angola must seize it as a blessing and a unique opportunity to finally assume full responsibility to chart its future, away from the protracted flirtation with anarchy. This is the opportunity for the Angolan state to muster the resources necessary to establish credible, accountable, and functioning systems of governance as an essential base for development and sustainable positive peace. The political settlement ending the civil war, although necessary, is not enough to achieve such goals especially if it is seen by the people as simply a way to co-opt former enemies into a corrupt and decaying system. A viable state must allow civil society to reconstitute itself and again become useful as a source for the creation, aggregation, and articulation of local demands that can act to improve prospects for both political and economic development. These useful demands must be incorporated into public policies by competent and politically committed leaders working to restore the effectiveness and legitimacy of the state. This necessarily involves the critical process of institutional strengthening which is needed to break the cycle of institutionalized structural violence that, along with physical violence, has defined politics and society in post-colonial Angola. There is a connection, therefore, between the goal of achieving positive peace and a fundamental restructuring of state-society relations. The end of the civil war provides Angola with its best post-colonial opportunity to achieve the two critical goals of rehabilitating a profoundly traumatized society while simultaneously establishing new parameters for conducting politics and managing the economy to ensure sustainable peace.

As Barash and Webel (2002:485) argue, echoing Galtung, "peace implies a state of individual and collective tranquility, calm, and satisfaction". But, as they quickly point out, "it is very difficult to be tranquil or calm or satisfied when denied such basic needs as food, clothing, shelter, education, and medical care". This insight is particularly relevant for countries, like Angola, that are making the arduous trek upward from the abyss of war toward sustainable positive peace. In many respects, sustainable peace hinges on society's ability to successfully confront poverty and inequality. Specifically, Angola must reduce the gap between rich and poor to prevent the latter's further marginalization and dehumanization because this can ignite new cycles of physical violence as the poor and dehumanized masses attempt to redress their condition by mounting assaults on both the foundations and the beneficiaries of structural violence. Reducing the differences between the "haves" and "have-nots" is the price for sustainable peace. But reducing the gap between the few rich and many poor does not simply entail providing the many with the minimum means for subsistence. It requires a thorough structural dismantling in all its manifestations. At the economic level, all citizens must be exposed to real, equal, and open opportunities for self-fulfilment defined in terms of social betterment or their respective definitions of the "good life".

The political economy of inequality that currently prevails in Angola forces the citizens to endure traumas not too dissimilar to those associated with a state of war. Similar to the angst-filled powerlessness experienced by victims of war, poverty corrodes body, mind, and soul and produces "deep mental suffering: envy, shame, and either despair or anger" (Barash and Webel, 2002: 487). In Angola, where the highjacking of the public treasury by government and party officials has resulted in grotesque accumulations of personal wealth, large portions of the population are relegated to a life of poverty while exposed to the affluence of the powerful few. Urgent remedies are needed to address this situation.

Angola's record in the area of poverty alleviation and equitable income distribution has been horrendous, even if the distortions generated by the civil war are discounted. Alas, there is precious little evidence to suggest a concerted effort to reverse those trends. The consequences of persisting trends in inequitable income distribution mean that, for the general population, the road to positive peace will be long and arduous with little short-to-medium term improvement in their economic situation. Indeed, there is little evidence that Angola will escape the general continental trends in income distribution. In this regard, Nafzinger's admonition (1988:1) remains powerful:

> Maintaining past trends means degrading human dignity for the majority, with a rural population surviving on intolerable toil, disastrous land scarcity, and a worsening urban crisis, with more shanty towns, congested roads, unemployment, beggars, crime, and misery alongside the few unashamedly demonstrating greater conspicuous consumption, shopping at national department stores filled with luxury imports. The consequences of extreme wealth and poverty would be social tensions and continued financial crises threatening national sovereignty.

The implications for Angola are both profound and frightening. In other words, unless trends in income inequality are quickly reversed, the violence that has characterized post-colonial society will not effectively be confined to the past; it will simply mutate into different but equally devastating forms. These forms of violence will primarily involve, on one hand, the elites attempting to create innovative mechanisms to protect the wealth accrued due to the graft prevalent in the civil war years while also finding ways to enhance that wealth to acquire education and investment opportunities. On the other hand, the poverty-stricken masses will find equally creative means to destroy the elites' property because of the perception that it was illegitimately acquired. Ideally, the state should be able to mediate this potentially destabilizing violent conflict. However, the state's own standing is problematic because it is generally viewed as a tool of the powerful political and economic elites.

These extreme wealth discrepancies point to some of the key political challenges facing post-conflict Angola. The key political challenge for Angola does not reside so much in how power is divided among the political parties. Given the hegemonic position of the governing MPLA and the disarray within the other political parties – induced by both poor leadership and lack of funds – a quasi-one-party system will exist into the foreseeable future. In other words, the MPLA will govern unchallenged while the other parties will be allowed to survive simply to legitimize the "democratic" credentials of the ruling party. The key challenge, therefore, will revolve around how wealth is distributed among the citizenry. Continuing gross inequalities will seriously erode whatever legitimacy the state and its governing elites can currently claim. Unchecked, this widening wealth gap – and the disconnectedness it creates between those at the top and those at the bottom – may not necessarily lead to a new civil war but to an equally problematic situation of permanent violence.

More than three decades ago, Leys (1965:227) perceptively pointed out that ruling classes must be "induced to accept an altered perception of the nature of the public interest and so to redefine the purposes of the public offices and state institutions". In post-civil war Angola, sustainable peace will depend to a considerable degree on how quickly and how successfully such alterations and redefinitions take place. In practical terms, these alterations and redefinitions must result in more open and inclusive political systems as well as a more equitable and transparent system for distributing the country's wealth among its citizens. As Shleifer and Vishny (1993:610) correctly suggest, "countries with more political competition have stronger public pressure against corruption – through laws, democratic elections, and even the independent press – and so are more likely to use government organizations that contain rather than maximize corruption proceeds". Sustainable peace in Angola, then, also depends on the country's ability to create legitimate and effective post-civil war institutions that contain rather than maximize corruption.

List of Acronyms

AD-Coligaçâo — Aliança Democrática – Coligaçâo (Angola Democratic Alliance Coalition)

ALIAZO — Alianca dos Zombos (Aliance of Zombos)

ANANGOLA — Associacao dos Naturais de Angola (Association of Natives of Angola)

ANC — African National Congress

ANGOP — Angola Press (Angola News Agency)

ASSOMIZO — Associacao Mutua dos Zambos (Mutual Association of Zombos)

CNDA — Convençao Nacional Democática de Angola (Angolan National Democratic Convention)

CIA — Central Intelligence Agency

CCPM — Comissâo Conjunta Politico-Militar (Joint Political Military Commission).

FAA — Forcas Armadas de Angola (Angolan Armed Forces)

FDLA — Frente Democratica para a Libertaçâo de Angola (Democratic Front for the Liberation of Angola)

FISC — Federal Information Systems Corporation

FLEC — Frente de Libertaçâo do Enclave de Cabinda (Liberation Front of the Cabinda Enclave)

FNLA — Frente Nacional de Libertaçâo de Angola (National Front for the Liberation of Angola)

FNLC — Front National pour la Liberation du Congo (National Front for the Liberation of Congo)

FpD — Frente para Democracia (Front for Democracy)

GRAE — Governo Revolucionário de Angola no Exilio (Angolan Revolutionary Government in Exile)

LNA — Liga Nacional Africana (African National League)

MDIA — Mouvement de Defense des Interets de l'Angola (Movement for Defence of Angola's Interests

MDIPA — Movimento para Defesa dos Interesses do Povo de Angola (Movement for the Defence of the Angolan People's Interests)

MINA — Movimento de Independência Nacional de Angola (Movement for National Independence of Angola)

MNA — Movimento Nacional Angolano (National Movement of Angola)

MPLA — Movimento Popular de Libertaçâo de Angola (Popular Movement for the Liberation of Angola)

MUDAR — Movimento de Unidade Angolana para Reconstrucçâo (Movement of Angolan Unity for Reconstruction)

NGWIZAKO	NGWIZAKO-NGWIZANI a Kongo
PAL	Partido Angolano Liberal (Liberal Party of Angola)
PCA	Partido Comunista de Angola (Angola Communist Party)
PCP	Partido Comunista Português (Portuguese Communist Party)
PDA	Partido Democrático de Angola (Democratic Party of Angola)
PDLA	Partido Democrático Liberal de Angola (Liberal Democratic Party of Angola)
PDPA	Partido para a Paz e Democracia em Angola (Party for Peace and Democracy in Angola)
PDP-ANA	Partido Democrático para o Progresso-Aliança Nacional de Angola (Democratic Party for Progress – National Alliance of Angola)
PLUA	Partido da Luta Unida dos Africanos de Angola (Party of the United Struggle of Africans of Angola)
PNEA	Partido Nacional Ecológico de Angola (National Ecological Party of Angola)
PRD	Partido Renovador Democrático (Democratic Renewal Party)
PSDA	Partido Social Democrático de Angola (Social Democratic Party of Angola)
RENAMO	Resistencia Nacional Mocambicana (Mozambican National Resistance)
RNA	Radio Nacional de Angola (Angola National Radio)
RPI	Radiodifusão Portuguesa Internacional
RTM	Radiodiffusion-Television Malliene (Mali Radio-TV)
SADF	South Africa Defense Force
SWAPO	South West Africa People's Organization
UNITA	União Nacional para Independência Total de Angola (National Union for Total Independence of Angola)
UNTA	União Nacional dos Trabalhadores Angolanos (National Union of Angolan Workers)
UPA	União dos Povos de Angola (Union of the Peoples of Angola)
UPNA	União dos Povos do Norte de Angola (Union of the Peoples of Northern Angola)
VORGAN	Voz da Resistência do Galo Negro (Voice of the Resistance of the Black Cockerel) UNITA's radio station.

Bibliography

Abshire, David M., 1969, "From the Scramble for Africa to the 'New State'", in David M. Abshire and Michael A. Samuels (eds), *Portuguese Africa: A Handbook*. London: Pall Mall Press.

Adebajo, Adekeye, 2002, *Building Peace in West Africa: Liberia, Sierra Leone, and Guinea Bissau*. Boulder: Lynne Rienner.

Africa News, "Angola: UNITA Brings Offensive Close to Luanda", 30 July 1999.

Aguilar, Renato, 2003, "Angola's Private Sector: Rents Distribution and Oligarchy", Paper presented at the conference on Lusophone Africa: Intersections between the Social Sciences, Ithaca, Cornell University, 2–3 May 2003.

Akinosho, Toyin, 1999, "Producers Untangling Angola's Complex Deepwater Geology", *Offshore*, February 1999.

Ali, Taisier and Robert Matthews (eds), 2004, *Durable Peace: Challenges for Peacebuilding in Africa*. Toronto: University of Toronto Press.

Allison, Graham T., 1971, *The Essence of Decision: Explaining the Cuban Missile Crisis*. Boston: Little, Brown and Company.

Andreopoulos, George, 1994, "The Age of National Liberation Movements" in Michael Howard et al. (eds), *The Laws of War*. New Haven: Yale University Press.

Arato, Andrew, 1993, *From Neo-Marxism to Democratic Theory: Essays on the Critical Theory of Soviet-Type Societies*. Armonk. New York: M.E. Sharpe.

Arend, Anthony C. and Robert J. Beck, 1993, *International Law & the Use of Force*. New York: Routledge.

Aron, Raymond, 1966, *Peace and War: A Theory of International Relations*. New York: Doubleday.

Apter, David and Carl Rosberg, 1994, *Political Development and the New Realism in Sub-Saharan Africa*. Charlottesville: University of Virginia Press.

Ayittey, George, 2000, "Combating Corruption in Africa: Analysis and Context", in Kempe Hope and Bornwell Chikulo (eds), *Corruption and Development in Africa: Lessons from Case-Studies*. New York: St. Martin's.

Bhagavan, M.R., 1986, *Angola's Political Economy 1975–1985*. Uppsala: Scandinavian Institute of African Studies.

Bailey, Norman A., 1969, "Native and Labor Policy", in David M. Abshire and Michael A. Samuels (eds), *Portuguese Africa: A Handbook*. London: Pall Mall Press.

Barash, David P., 1991, *Introduction to Peace Studies*. Belmont, CA: Wadsworth.

Barash, David P. and Charles P. Webel, 2002, *Peace and Conflict Studies*. Thousand Oaks, CA: Sage.

Bardhan, Pranab, 1997, "Corruption and Development: A Review of Issues", *Journal of Economic Literature*, 35(3).

Barth, Fredrik, 1969, *Ethnic Groups and Boundaries*. London: Allen and Unwin.

Bayart, Jean-Francois, 1986, "Civil Society in Africa", in Patrick Chabal (ed.), *Political Domination in Africa*. Cambridge: Cambridge University Press.

Bayley, David H., 1966, "The Effects of Corruption in a Developing Nation", *The Western Political Quarterly,* 19(4), December.

BBC, 1981, "Angola reports new Zaire-based rebel organization", *BBC Summary of World Broadcasts,* 24 December.

—, 1989a, "Angolan agency comments on government peace plan, policy of reintegration and military measures against 'subversives'", *BBC Summary of World Broadcasts,* 13 March.

—, 1989b, "Angola Dos Santos on 'shortcomings' in diplomacy, prospects for economic development and co-operation in the region", *BBC Summary of World Broadcasts,* 8 May.

—, 1990, "Angolan President addresses traditional leaders on peace, economic prospects", *BBC Summary of World Broadcasts,* 24 September.

—, 1998, "MPLA Central Committee issues communique at end of meeting", *Summary of World Broadcasts,* 7 December, quoting Televisao Publica de Angola, Luanda, 3 December 1998.

—, 1999, "President Dos Santos says government, not UN, will restore peace", *BBC Summary of World Broadcasts,* 19 January.

—,1999a, "Army Source Says Capture of UNITA Bases at Andulo, Bailundo Imminent", *BBC Summary of World Broadcasts,* 21 July.

—, 1999b, "Officer Says Armed Forces Were Caught Off Guard in Catete", *BBC Summary of World Broadcasts,* 27 July.

—, 1999c, "Angola Asks SADC Summit for Human, Material Support Against UNITA", *BBC Worldwide Monitoring,* 18 August 1999, quoting SAPA news agency, 18 August 1999.

—, 1999d, "Angola: UNITA Leader's Letter to Ruling Party Calls For Dialogue", *BBC Worldwide Monitoring,* 31 August, quoting SAPA news agency web site, Johannesburg, 30 August 1999.

—, 1999e, "Angola: UNITA Reports Government Offensive on Four Fronts", *BBC Worldwide Monitoring,* 19 September, quoting KUP (UNITA) news agency web site 16 September 1999.

—, 1999f, "UNITA Communiqué Says 'Unprecedented Offensive' Under Way", *BBC Summary of World Broadcasts,* 20 September, quoting KUP (UNITA) news agency web site 18 September 1999.

—, 1999g, "Angola Announces Recapture of Bailundo, Andulo, Other Regions from UNITA", *BBC Summary of World Broadcasts,* 25 October, quoting Noticias de Angola web site 21 October 1999.

—, 2000a, "Angola to boycott OAU summit over Togo's backing for UNITA", *BBC Summary of World Broadcasts,* 18 May.

—, 2000b, "MPLA chief criticizes South African 'destabilizing' circles", *BBC Summary of World Broadcasts,* 14 January.

Beaudet, Pierre et al., 1993, "Angola in the New Regional Order", in Nancy Thede and Pierre Beaudet (eds), *A Post-Apartheid Southern Africa*. New York: St. Martin's Press.

Beer, Francis A., *Peace Against War: The Ecology of International Violence*. San Francisco: W.H. Freeman, 1981.

Bender, Gerald, 1989, "Peacemaking in Southern Africa: The Luanda-Pretoria Tug of War", *Third World Quarterly*, 11.

Bernhard, Michael, 1993, *The Origins of Democratization in Poland*. New York: Columbia University Press.

Bienen, Henry, 1980, "Perspectives on Soviet Intervention in Africa", *Political Science Quarterly*, 95(1) Spring.

Birmingham, David, 1966, *Trade and Conflict in Angola: The Mbundu and Their Neighbours Under the Influence of the Portuguese 1483–1790*. London: Clarendon Press.

—, 1975, "Central Africa from Cameroun to the Zambezi", in Roland Oliver (ed.), *The Cambridge History of Africa, Vol. 4 from c.1600 to c.1790*. Cambridge: Cambridge University Press.

—, 1976, "The Forest and the Savanna of Central Africa", in John Flint (ed.), *The Cambridge History of Africa, Vol.5 from c.1790 to c.1870*. Cambridge: Cambridge University Press.

—, 1977, "Central Africa from Cameroun to the Zambezi", in Roland Oliver (ed.), *The Cambridge History of Africa, Vol. 3 from c. 1050 to c. 1600*. Cambridge: Cambridge University Press.

—, 1982, "A Question of Coffee: Black Enterprise in Angola", *Canadian Journal of African Studies*, 16(2).

Bobbio, Norberto, 1979, "Gramsci and the Conception of Civil Society", in Chantal Mouffe (ed.), *Gramsci and Marxist Theory*. London: Routledge.

Bottomore, Tom (ed.), 1983, *A Dictionary of Marxist Thought*. London: Basil Blackwell.

Boulding, Kenneth E., 1978, *Stable Peace*. Austin: University of Texas Press.

Boutros-Ghali, Boutros, 1995, *An Agenda for Peace*. New York: United Nations.

Boxer, C.R., 1963, *Race relations in the Portuguese colonial empire*. Oxford: Clarendon Press.

Bradshaw, York and Stephen Ndegwa (eds), 2000, *The Uncertain Promise of Southern Africa*. Bloomington and Indianapolis: Indiana University Press.

Bragança, Aquino de, and Immanuel Wallerstein (eds), 1982, *The African Liberation Reader, Volume 1: The Anatomy of Colonialism*. London: Zed Press.

Bratton, Michael, 1994, "Civil Society and Political Transitions in Africa", in John W. Harberson et al. (eds), *Civil Society and the State in Africa*. Boulder: Lynne Rienner.

Bridgland, Fred, 1987, *Jonas Savimbi: A Key to Africa*. New York: Paragon.

—, 1990, *The War for Africa: Twelve Months That Transformed a Continent*. Gibraltar: Ashanti.

Brittain, Victoria, 1986, "Beleaguered Angola Looks to Kremlin", *The Guardian*, (London), 7 May.

—, 1996, "Eighteen years later ... speaking to Lucio Lara", *African Communist*, No.143, First Quarter.

Brooks, Robert C., 1909, "The Nature of Political Corruption", *Political Science Quarterly*, 24(1), March.

Brown, Chris, 1992, *International Relations Theory: New Normative Approaches*. New York: Columbia University Press.

Bull, Hedley, 1984, *Intervention in World Politics*. Oxford: Clarendon Press.

Buzan, Barry, 1991, *People, States and Fear: An Agenda for International Security Studies in the Post-Cold War Era*. Boulder: Lynne Rienner.

Cabral, Amilcar, 1982a, "The Facts about Portugal's African Colonies", in Aquino de Bragança and Immanuel Wallerstein (eds), *The African Liberation Reader, Volume 1: The Anatomy of Colonialism*. London: Zed Press.

—, 1982b, "A Situation of Permanent Violence", in Aquino de Bragança and Immanuel Wallerstein (eds), *The African Liberation Reader, Volume 2: The National Liberation Movements*. London: Zed Press.

Cadornega, Antonio de Oliveira, 1940, *Historia Geral das Guerras Angolanas*, Vol. III, part 3, Lisbon.

Cady, Duane L., 1989, *From Warism to Pacifism: A Moral Continuum*. Philadelphia: Temple University Press.

Campbell, Horace, 1989, "The Military Defeat of South Africans in Angola", *Monthly Review*, 40(11).

—, 2000, "Militarism, Warfare, and the Search for Peace in Angola", in York Bradshaw and Stephen Ndegwa (eds), *The Uncertain Promise of Southern Africa*. Bloomington and Indianapolis: Indiana University Press.

Carnoy, Martin, 1984, *The State and Political Theory*. Princeton: Princeton University Press.

Carter Center, 1990, *African Governance in the 1990s*. Atlanta: Carter Center.

Chabal, Patrick and Jean-Pascal Daloz, 1999, *Africa Works: Disorder as Political Instrument*. Oxford and Bloomington: James Currey and Indiana University Press.

Chatfield, Charles and Ruzanna Ilukhina (eds), 1994, *Peace/Mir: An Anthology of Historic Alternatives to War*. Syracuse: Syracuse University Press.

Chazan, Naomi et al., 1999, *Politics and Society in Contemporary Africa*, (3rd edition). Boulder: Lynne Rienner.

Chilcote, Ronald H., 1967, *Portuguese Africa*. Englewood Cliffs: Prentice Hall.

—, 1972, *Emerging Nationalism in Portuguese Africa: Documents*. Stanford: Stanford University Press.

Cockell, John G., 2002, "Conceptualising Peacebuilding: Human Security and Sustainable Peace", in Michael Pugh (ed.), *Regeneration of War-Torn Societies*. New York: St. Martin's Press.

Conchiglia, Augusta, 1990, *UNITA, Myth and Reality*. London: ECASAAMA/UK.

Coolidge, Jacqueline and Susan Rose-Ackerman, 2000, "Kleptocracy and Reform in African Regimes: Theory and Examples", in Kempe Hope and Bornwell Chikulo (eds), *Corruption and Development in Africa: Lessons from Case-Studies.* New York: St. Martin's.

Cousens, Elizabeth, 2001, "Introduction", in Elizabeth Cousens and Chetan Kumar (eds), *Peacebuilding as Politics: Cultivating Peace in Fragile Societies.* Boulder: Lynne Rienner.

Crocker, Chester, 1992, *High Noon in Southern Africa: Making Peace in a Rough Neighborhood.* New York: W.W. Norton.

Curtin, Philip D., 1969, *The Atlantic Slave Trade: A census.* Madison: University of Wisconsin Press.

Da Cruz, Viriato, 1972, "Problems of the Angolan Revolution", in Ronald H Chilcote, *Emerging Nationalism in Portuguese Africa: Documents.* Stanford: Stanford University Press.

—, 1982, "Two Groups of *Assimilados*", in Aquino de Bragança and Immanuel Wallerstein (eds), *The African Liberation Reader, Volume 1: The Anatomy of Colonialism.* London: Zed Press.

Daley, Suzanne, 1999, "Hunger Ravages Angolans in Renewed Civil War", *The New York Times*, 26 July 1999, p. A1.

Davies, Richard, 1996, "Ethnicity: Inside Out or Outside In?", in Jill Krause and Neil Renwick (eds), *Identities and International Relations.* New York: St. Martin's Press.

Davis, Nathaniel, 1978, "The Angola Decision of 1975: A Personal Memoir", *Foreign Affairs*, 57(1).

Davis, R. Hunt and Gwendolen M. Carter, 1989, "South Africa", in Peter J. Schraeder (ed.), *Intervention in the 1980s: U.S. Foreign Policy in the Third World.* Boulder: Lynne Rienner.

De Andrade, Mário, 1982, "Hierarchy of Privilege in Portuguese Colonial Society", in Aquino de Bragança and Immanuel Wallerstein (eds), *The African Liberation Reader, Volume 1: The Anatomy of Colonialism.* London: Zed Press.

De Carvalho, Henrique Dias, 1890, *Expedição Portugueza ao Muatiânvua.* Lisbon.

De Tocqueville, Alexis, [1835, 1840] 1959, *Democracy in America.* New York: Vintage Books.

Diamond, Larry, 1987, "Class Formation in the Swollen State", *The Journal of Modern African Studies,* 25(4).

Dietrich, Christian, 2000, "UNITA's Diamond Mining and Exporting Capacity", in Jakkie Cilliers and Christian Dietrich (eds), *Angola's War Economy: The Role of Oil and Diamonds.* Pretoria: Institute for Security Studies.

Dougherty, James E. and Robert L. Pfaltzgraff, 2001, *Contending Theories of International Relations: A Comprehensive Survey.* New York: Longman.

Duffy, James, 1959, *Portuguese Africa.* Cambridge: Harvard University Press.

—, 1962, *Portugal in Africa.* Cambridge: Harvard University Press.

Duner, Bertil, 1981, "Proxy Intervention in Civil Wars", *Journal of Peace Research*, 18(4).

ECA (United Nations Economic Commission for Africa), 1989, *African Alternative Framework to Structural Adjustment Programmes for Socio-Economic Recovery and Transformation*. Addis Ababa, ECA.

Elbl, Ivana, 1997, "The Volume of the Early Atlantic Slave Trade, 1450–1521", *The Journal of African History*, 38(1).

Facts on File, 1978, "Angola Requests U.S. Relations", *Facts on File World News Digest*, p. 562 F1, 28 July.

Falk, Richard, 1984, "Intervention in National Liberation", in Hedley Bull (ed.), *Intervention in World Politics*. Oxford: Clarendon Press.

Farrands, Chris, 1996, "Society, Modernity and Social Change: Approaches to Nationalism and Identity", in Jill Krause and Neil Renwick (eds), *Identities and International Relations*. New York: St. Martin's Press.

Fatton, Robert, 1992, *Predatory Rule: State and Civil Society in Africa*. Boulder: Lynne Rienner.

Fishman, Robert, 1990, "Rethinking State and Regime: Southern Europe in Transition to Democracy", *World Politics*, 42(3).

Frank, Thomas M., 1998, "A Holistic Approach to Building Peace", in Olara A. Otunn and Michael Doyle (eds), *Peacemaking and Peacebuilding for the New Century*. Lanham: Rowman & Littlefield.

Frankel, Glenn, 1985, "Angola Breaks Off Peace Talks with U.S.; Move Protests Congressional Vote Allowing Aid to Rebel Forces", *The Washington Post*, 14 July 1985.

Galtung, Johan, 1969, "Violence, Peace, and Peace Research", *Journal of Peace Research* 6(3):167–191.

—, 1976, *Peace, War, and Defence – Essays in Peace Research, Vol. 2*. Copenhagen: Christian Ejlers.

—, 1985, "Twenty-Five Years of Peace Research: Ten Challenges and Some Responses", *Journal of Peace Research*, 22(2):141–158.

Galtung, Johan and Tord Hoivik, 1971, "Structural and Direct Violence", *Journal of Peace Research*, 8(1):73–76.

Gellner, Ernest, 1994, *Conditions of Liberty: Civil Society and Its Rivals*. New York: Penguin Books.

Geertz, Clifford, 1963a, *Old Societies and New States: The Quest for Modernity in Asia and Africa*. New York: Free Press.

—, 1963b, "The Integrative Revolution", in C. Geertz (ed.), *Old Societies and New States*. New York: Free Press.

Global Witness, 1998, *A Rough Trade: The Role of Companies and Governments in the Angolan Conflict*. London: Global Witness.

—, 2000, *Conflict Diamonds: Possibilities for the Identification, Certification and Control of Diamonds*. London: Global Witness.

Gordon, April A. and Donald L. Gordon (eds), 1996, *Understanding Contemporary Africa*. Boulder: Lynne Rienner.

Gordon, Chris, 1999, "Eastern Europe Aid Bolsters UNITA", *Mail and Guardian* (Johannesburg), 15 January 1999.

GRAE, 1962, "Glimpses of the Angolan Nationalist Organizations", in Ronald H Chilcote, 1972, *Emerging Nationalism in Portuguese Africa: Documents*. Stanford: Stanford University Press.

Gray, Christine, 2000, *International Law and the Use of Force*. Oxford: Oxford University Press.

Gray, John, 1991 "Post-Totalitarianism, Civil Society, and the Limits of the Western Model", in Zbigniew Rau (ed.), *The Reemergence of Civil Society in Eastern Europe and the Soviet Union*. Boulder: Westview Press.

Gray, Richard, 1975, "Introduction", in Richard Gray (ed.), *The Cambridge History of Africa, Vol. 4 from c.1600 to c.1790*. Cambridge: Cambridge University Press.

Green, Reginald Herbold and Ismail I. Ahmed, 1999, "Rehabilitation, Sustainable Peace and Development: Towards reconceptualisation", *Third World Quarterly*, 20(1).

Guelke, Adrian, 1974, "Force, Intervention and Internal Conflict", in Northedge, F.S. (ed.), *The Use of Force in International Relations*. New York: The Free Press.

Gunn, Gillian, 1992, "The Legacy of Angola", in Thomas G. Weiss and James G. Blight (eds), *The Suffering Grass: Superpowers and Regional Conflict in Southern Africa and the Caribbean*. Boulder and London: Lynne Rienner.

Hallett, Robin, 1978, "The South African Intervention in Angola, 1975–76", *African Affairs*, 77(308).

Harbeson, John W., 1994, "Society and Political Renaissance in Africa", in Harbeson et al., *Civil Society and the State in Africa*. Boulder: Lynne Rienner.

Harsch, Ernest, 1993, "Accumulators and Democrats: Challenging State Corruption in Africa", *The Journal of Modern African Studies*, 31(1).

Helmore, Richard, 1984, "Diamond Mining in Angola", *Mining Magazine*, June.

Henderson, Lawrence H., 1979, *Angola: Five Centuries of Conflict*. Ithaca: Cornell University Press.

Henkin, Louis, 1991, "The Use of Force: Law and U.S. Policy", in Louis Henkin et al. *Right v. Might: International Law and the Use of Force*. New York: Council on Foreign Relations Press.

Herrick, A.B. et al., 1967, *Area Handbook for Angola*. Washington, DC: United States Government Printing Office.

Heywood, Linda M., 1987, "The Growth and Decline of African Agriculture in Central Angola, 1890–1950", *Journal of Southern African Studies*, 13(3).

Hinde, Robert A., 1990, "Human Aggression: Biological Propensities and Social Forces", in Paul Smoker, Ruth Davies and Barbara Munske (eds), *A Reader in Peace Studies*. Oxford: Pergamon Press.

Hirschman, Albert O., 1970, *Exit, Voice, and Loyalty* Cambridge: Harvard University Press.

Hobbes, Thomas, [1651] 1959, *Leviathan*. London: J.M. Dent.

Hoivik, Tord, 1997, "The Demography of Structural Violence", *Journal of Peace Research*, 14(1).

Holmes, Steven A., 1993, "Washington Recognizes Angola Government", *The New York Times*, 20 May 1993.

Hope, Kempe, 2000, "Corruption and Development in Africa", in Kempe Hope and Bornwell Chikulo (eds), *Corruption and Development in Africa: Lessons from Case-Studies*. New York: St. Martin's.

Hope, Kempe and Bornwell Chikulo, 2000, "Introduction", in Kempe Hope and Bornwell Chikulo (eds), *Corruption and Development in Africa: Lessons from Case-Studies*. New York: St. Martin's.

Hoper, Jim, 1989, "UNITA Guerrillas Attack with Impunity", *International Defense Review*, 22.

Howland, Nina D., 1989, "The United States and Angola, 1974–88: A Chronology", *Department of State Bulletin*, February 1989.

Hutchinson, John and Anthony D. Smith, 1996, "Introduction", in J. Hutchinson and A.D. Smith (eds), *Ethnicity*. Oxford: Oxford University Press.

Hydén, Göran, 1992, "Governance and the Study of Politics", in Göran Hyden and Michael Bratton (eds), *Governance and Politics in Africa*. Boulder: Westview.

IMF, 2003, "Angola: 2003 Article IV Consultation", (Country Report No. 03/291), in http://www.imf.org/external/pubs/cat/longres.cfm?sk=16871.0.

Johnston, Michael, 1986, "The Political Consequences of Corruption: A Reassessment", *Comparative Politics*, 18(4).

Karlson, Nils, 1993, *The State of the State: An Inquiry Concerning the Role of Invisible Hands in Politics and Civil Society*. Uppsala: Almqvist & Wiksell International.

Kabwegyere, Tarsis B., 1972, "The Dynamics of Colonial Violence: The Inductive System in Uganda", *Journal of Peace Research*, 9(4).

Kaiser, Robert G. and Don Oberdonfer, 1978, "Africa Turnabout: Concern over Soviets, Cubans Transforms U.S. Africa Policy", *The Washington Post*, 4 June 1978.

Kaplan, Robert, 1994, "The Coming Anarchy", *Atlantic Monthly*.

Karabell, Zachary, 1999, *Architects of Intervention: The United States, the Third World, and the Cold War, 1946–1962*. Baton Rouge: Louisiana State University Press.

Katsikas, Suzanne, 1982, *The Arc of Socialist Revolutions: Angola to Afghanistan*. Cambridge: Schenkman.

Katzenstein, Peter J., 1996, "Introduction: Perspectives on National Security", in Peter J. Katzenstein (ed.), *The Culture of National Security: Norms and Identity in World Politics*. New York: Columbia University Press.

Kellas, James, 1991, *The Politics of Nationalism and Ethnicity*. New York: St. Martin's Press.

Kempton, Daniel, 1989, *Soviet Strategy toward Southern Africa: The Liberation Movement Connection*. New York: Praeger.

—, 1990, "New Thinking and Soviet Policy towards South Africa", *The Journal of Modern African Studies*, 28(4).

Kirkpatrick, Jeane J. and Allan Gerson, 1991, "The Reagan Doctrine, Human Rights, and International Law", in Louis Henkin et al., *Right v. Might: International Law and the Use of Force*. New York: Council on Foreign Relations Press.

Kissinger, Henry, 1999, *Years of Renewal*. New York: Simon & Schuster.

Klare, Michael T., 1989, "The Development of Low-Intensity Conflict Doctrine", in Peter J. Schraeder (ed.), *Intervention in the 1980s: U.S. Foreign Policy in the Third World*. Boulder: Lynne Rienner.

Korten, David C., 1984, "People-Centered Development: Toward a Framework", in David Korten and Rudi Klauss (eds), *People Centered Development: Contributions toward Theory and Planning Frameworks*. West Hartford: Kumarian.

Krause, Jill and Neil Renwick, 1996, "Introduction", in Jill Krause and Neil Renwick (eds), *Identities and International Relations*. New York: St. Martin's Press.

Lapid, Yosef, 1996, "Culture's Ship: Returns and Departures in International Relations Theory", in Yosef Lapid and Friedrich Kratochwil (eds), *The Return of Culture and Identity in IR Theory*. Boulder: Lynne Rienner.

Lapid, Yosef and Friedrich Kratochwil, 1996, "Revisiting the 'National': Toward an Identity Agenda in Neorealism?", in Yosef Lapid and Friedrich Kratochwil (eds), *The Return of Culture and Identity in IR Theory*. Boulder: Lynne Rienner.

Le Billon, Philippe, 2001, "Angola's Political Economy of War: The Role of Oil and Diamonds 1975–2000", *African Affairs*, 100(398):55–80.

Lederach, J.P., 1995, *Preparing for Peace: Conflict Transformation across Cultures*. Syracuse: Syracuse University Press.

—, 1997, *Building Peace: Sustainable Reconciliation in Divided Societies*. Washington, DC: United States Institute of Peace.

Lemarchand, Rene, 1986, "Ethnic Violence in Tropical Africa", in John F. Stack (ed.), *The Primordial Challenge: Ethnicity in the Contemporary World*. New York: Greenwood Press.

Lentner, Howard H., 1974, *Foreign Policy Analysis: A Comparative and Conceptual Approach*. Columbus, Ohio: Charles E. Merril.

Lewis, Peter M., 1992, "Political Transition and the Dilemma of Civil Society in Africa", *Journal of International Affairs*, 46(1).

Leys, Colin, 1965, "What Is the Problem about Corruption?", *The Journal of Modern African Studies*, 3(2).

Locke, John, [1868] 1953, *Two Treatises on Government*. London: J.M. Dent.

Lodico, Yvonne, 1996, "A Peace That Fell Apart: The United Nations and the War in Angola", in William J. Durch (ed.), *UN Peacekeeping, American Politics and the Uncivil Wars of the 1990s*. New York: St. Martin's Press.

MacFarlane, S. Neil, 1983–84, "Intervention and Security in Africa", *International Affairs* (Royal Institute of International Affairs), 60(1).

—, 1992, "Soviet-Angolan Relations, 1975–90", in George W. Breslauer (ed.), *Soviet Policy in Africa*. Berkeley: University of California Press.

—, 2002, *Intervention in Contemporary World Politics*. New York: Oxford University Press.

MacKenzie, Ian, 1995, "S. African Visit Gives Boost to Angola's UNITA Chief", *Reuters World Service*, 18 May.

Macridis, Roy C., 1976, *Foreign Policy in World Politics*. Englewood Cliffs, NJ: Prentice Hall.

Malaquias, Assis, 1999, "Angola: The Foreign Policy of a Decaying State", in Stephen Wright (ed.), *African Foreign Policies*. Boulder: Westview Press.

Marcum, John, 1969, *The Angolan Revolution. Volume I: The Anatomy of an Explosion (1950–1962)*. Cambridge: The MIT Press.

—, 1976, "Lessons from Angola", *Foreign Affairs*, 54(3).

—, 1978, *The Angolan Revolution. Volume II: Exile Politics and Guerrilla Warfare (1962–1976)*. Cambridge: The MIT Press.

Martelli, George, 1962, "The Future in Angola", *African Affairs*, 61(245).

Matheson, Neil, 1982, *The 'Rules of the Game' of Superpower Military Intervention in the Third World 1975–1980*. Washington, DC: University Press of America.

Mbaku, John, 2000, "Controlling Corruption in Africa: A Public Choice Perspective", in Kempe Hope and Bornwell Chikulo (eds), *Corruption and Development in Africa: Lessons from Case-Studies*. New York: St. Martin's.

McFaul, Michael, 1989, "Rethinking the Reagan Doctrine in Angola", *International Security* 14, Winter.

McGreal, Chris, 1999, "Profits Fuel Angola's War", *Manchester Guardian Weekly*, 14 July.

McKinley, James C Jr., 1997, "Congo's Neighbors Played Crucial Role in Civil War", *The New York Times*, 22 May.

Mead, Margaret, 1940, "Warfare Is Only an Invention – Not a Biological Necessity", *Asia*, August 1940.

Minix, Dean A. and Sandra M. Hawley, 1998, *Global Politics*, Belmont. CA: West/Wadsworth.

Minter, William, 1988, *Operation Timber: Pages from the Savimbi Dossier*. Trenton: Africa World Press.

—, 1994, *Apartheid's Contras: An Inquiry into the Roots of War in Angola and Mozambique*. Johannesburg: Witwatersrand University Press.

Morgenthau, Hans J., 1973, *Politics among Nations: The Struggle for Power and Peace*. New York: Alfred A. Knopf.

Mosley, Paul, 1987, "Conditionality As a Bargaining Process: Structural-Adjustment Lending, 1980–86", *Essays in International Finance*, 168, Princeton University: International Finance Section, October.

MPLA, 1972, "Memorandum to the African Governments on the Formation of the So-Called Provisional Government of Angola (GRAE)", in Ronald H. Chilcote, *Emerging Nationalism in Portuguese Africa: Documents*. Stanford: Stanford University Press.

—, 1977, *Documents of the First Congress*. Luanda: MPLA.

—, 1980, *MPLA Extraordinary Party Congress Documents*. Luanda: MPLA.

—, 1982, "Cultural Racism", in Aquino de Bragança and Immanuel Wallerstein (eds), *The African Liberation Reader, Volume 1: The Anatomy of Colonialism*. London: Zed Press.

Munslow, Barry, 1999, "Angola: The Politics of Unsustainable Development", *Third World Quarterly*, 20(3).

Nafzinger, E. Wayne, 1988, *Inequality in Africa: Political elites, proletariat, peasants, and the poor*. Cambridge: Cambridge University Press.

Ndegwa, Stephen N., 1994, "Civil Society and Political Change in Africa: The Case of Non-Governmental Organizations in Kenya", *International Journal of Comparative Sociology*, (35):1–2.

Neto, Agostinho, 1972, "The FDLA and Unity", in Ronald H. Chilcote, *Emerging Nationalism in Portuguese Africa: Documents*. Stanford: Stanford University Press.

Newitt, Malyn, 1981, *Portugal in Africa: The Last Hundred Years*. London: C. Hurst & Co.

Northedge, F.S. (ed.), 1974, *The Use of Force in International Relations*. New York: The Free Press.

Nye, J.S., 1967, "Corruption and Political Development", *The American Political Science Review*, 61(2) June.

O'Brien, Tim, 1999, "The Worst Place on Earth to Live", *The Irish Times*, 18 September.

O'Meara, Dan, 1986, "Destabilization in Southern Africa: Total Strategy in Total Disarray", *Monthly Review*, 37, April.

Ogunbadejo, Oye, 1985, *The International Politics of Africa's Strategic Minerals*. Westport, Conn: Greenwood Press.

Oliver, Roland, 1977, "Introduction: Some interregional themes", in Roland Oliver (ed.), *The Cambridge History of Africa, Vol. 3 from c.1050 to c.1600*. Cambridge: Cambridge University Press.

Ottaway, David B., 1978a, "Lance Seeks Post at Area Bank Firm: Brzezinski's Strategists Confront Young's 'Africanists' in Policy Row", *The Washington Post*, 14 February.

—, 1978b, "Angolan Shakeup Signals Waning Soviet Influence", *The Washington Post*, 15 December.

Papp, Daniel S., 2002, *Contemporary International Relations: Frameworks for Understanding*. New York: Longman.

Paris, Roland, 1997, "Peacebuilding and the Limits of Liberal Internationalism", *International Security*, 22(2):54–89.

Perez-Diaz, Victor, 1993, *The Return of Civil Society: The Emergence of Democratic Spain*. Cambridge, Massachusetts: Harvard University Press.

Pincus, Walter and Robert G. Kaiser, 1978, "U.S. Envoy Dispatched to Angola", *The Washington Post*, 22 June.

Pitcher, M. Anne, 1991, "Sowing the Seeds of Failure: Early Portuguese Cotton Cultivation in Angola and Mozambique, 1820–1926", *Journal of Southern African Studies*, 17(1).

Potholm, Christian P., 1976, *The Theory and Practice of African Politics*. Englewood Cliffs: Prentice Hall.

Premoll, Camillo, 1992, "Angola Emerges As Exploration Target", *Engineering and Mining Journal*, July.

Price, Robert, 1978, *U.S. Foreign Policy in Sub-Saharan Africa: National Interest and Global Strategy*. Berkeley: Institute of International Studies, University of California.

Pugh, Michael, 1995, "Peacebuilding as Developmentalism: Concepts from Disaster Research", *Contemporary Security Policy*, 16(3).

Rapoport, Anatol, 1992, *Peace: An Idea Whose Time Has Come*. Ann Arbor: The University of Michigan Press.

Redinha, José, 1965, *Distribuição Étnica da Província de Angola*. Luanda: Centro de Informacao e Turismo de Angola.

Reno, William, 2000a, "Clandestine Economies, Violence and States in Africa", *Journal of International Affairs*, 53(2).

—, 2000b, "Shadow States and the Political Economy of Civil Wars", in Mats Berdal and David Malone (eds), *Greed and Grievance: Economic Agendas in Civil Wars*. Boulder: Lynne Rienner.

Riddler, Gordon, 1997, "Angola's Prospects", *The Mining Journal*, 31 January.

Rodman, Peter, 1994, *More Precious Than Peace: The Cold War and the Struggle for the Third World*. New York: Charles Scribner's Sons.

Rodney, Walter, 1981, *How Europe Underdeveloped Africa*. Washington, DC: Howard University Press.

Rosenau, James, 1998, "The Dynamism of a Turbulent World", in Michael Klare and Yogesh Chandrani, *World Security: Challenges for a New Century*. New York: St. Martin's.

Rothchild, Donald and Caroline Hartzell, 1995, "Interstate and Intrastate Negotiations in Angola", in I. William Zartman (ed.), *Elusive Peace: Negotiating an End to Civil Wars*. Washington, DC: The Brookings Institution.

Rothschild, Joseph, 1981, *Ethnopolitics: A Conceptual Framework*. New York: Columbia University Press.

Rourke, John, 2003, *International Politics on the World Stage*. Guilford: Dushkin.

Rubinstein, Alvin Z., 1984, "Soviet Intervention in the Third World", in John H. Maurer and Richard H. Porth (eds), *Military Intervention in the Third World: Threats, Constraints, and Options*. New York: Praeger.

Saich, Tony, 1994, "The Search for Civil Society and Democracy in China", *Current History*, (93):584.

Samuels, Michael A. and Norman A. Bailey, 1969, "African Peoples", in David M. Abshire and Michael A. Samuels (eds), *Portuguese Africa: A Handbook*. London: Pall Mall Press.

Sandberg, Eve (ed.), 1994, *The Changing Politics of Non-Governmental Organizations and African States*. Westport: Praeger.

Santos, Eduardo, 1965, *Maza: Elementos de Etno-Historia para a Interpretação do Terrorismo no Nordeste de Angola*. Lisboa: Ramos, Afonso e Moita.

Schechterman, Bernard and Martin Slann (eds), 1993, *The Ethnic Dimension of International Relations*. Westport: Praeger.

Schermerhorn, Richard, 1970, *Comparative Ethnic Relations*. New York: Random House.

Schraeder, Peter J., 1992, "Paramilitary Intervention", in Peter J. Schraeder (ed.), *Intervention into the 1990s: U.S. Foreign Policy in the Third World*. Boulder: Lynne Rienner.

Shleifer, Andrei and Robert W. Vishny, 1993, "Corruption", *The Quarterly Journal of Economics*, 108(3).

Small, Michael, 2001, "Peacebuilding in Postconflict Societies", in Rob McRae and Don Hubert (eds), *Human Security and the New Diplomacy: Protecting People, Promoting Peace*. Montreal and Kingston: McGill-Queen's University Press.

Smith, Anthony D., 1991, *National Identity*. Harmondsworth: Penguin.

Snow, Donald, 1998, *National Security: Defense Policy in a Changed International Order*. New York: St. Martin's Press.

Sparks, Samantha, 1988, "Angola: U.S. Sees Progress in Talks", *Inter Press Service*, 1 February.

Stevens, Christopher, 1976, "The Soviet Union and Angola", *African Affairs*, 75(299).

Strauss, Claudia and Naomi Quinn, 1997, *A Cognitive Theory of Cultural Meaning*. Cambridge: Cambridge University Press.

Tambiah, Stanley, 1996, "The Nation-State in Crisis and the Rise of Ethnonationalism", in Edwin N. Wilmsen and Patrick McAllister (eds), *The Politics of Difference: Ethnic Premises in a World of Power*. Chicago: University of Chicago Press.

Texter, Jacques, 1979, "Gramsci, Theoretician of Superstructures", in Chantal Mouffe (ed.), *Gramsci and Marxist Theory*. London: Routledge & Kegan Paul.

The Economist, 1982, "Angola: The detail that matters", 7 August 1982.

The Mining Journal, 1999, "Blessing or curse?", 15 October 1999.

—, 2000a, "The Diamond-Mining Scene", 16 June 2000.

—, 2000b, "De Beers Record", 23 June 2000.

—, 2000c, "New era for diamonds?", 30 June 2000.

Theobald, Robin, 1994, "Lancing the Swollen African State: Will It Alleviate the Problem of Corruption?", *The Journal of Modern African Studies*, 32(4)701–6.

—, 1999, "So What Really Is the Problem about Corruption?", *Third World Quarterly*, 20(3):491–502.

Thompson, Richard H., 1989, *Theories of Ethnicity: A Critical Appraisal*. Westport: Greenwood Press.

Timsar, Richard, 1981, "Marxist Angola Backs West's Namibia Blueprint", *The Christian Science Monitor*, 29 October.

Tickner, J. Ann, 1996, "Identity in International Relations Theory: Feminist Perspectives", in Yosef Lapid and Friedrich Kratochwil (eds), *The Return of Culture and Identity in IR Theory*. Boulder: Lynne Rienner.

UNITA, 1990, *The UNITA Leadership*. Jamba: UNITA.

USAID, 1993, "Economic Reform in Africa's New Era of Political Liberalization", *Proceedings of a USAID Workshop for SPA Donors*. Washington, DC: USAID.

UPA, 1982, "Portuguese Settlement in Angola", in Aquino de Bragança and Immanuel Wallerstein (eds), *The African Liberation Reader, Volume 1: The Anatomy of Colonialism*. London: Zed Press.

United Nations Security Council, 1978, Resolution 435.

—, 1993, Resolution 864.

—, 1997, Resolution 1127.

—, 1998, Resolution 1173.

—, 2000, *Report of the Panel of Experts on Violations of Security Council Sanctions against UNITA*. S/2000/203, 10 March 2000.

Van Der Waals, Willem, 1993, *Portugal's War in Angola 1961–1975*. Rivonia: Ashanti Publishing.

Vanneman, Peter, 1990, *Soviet Strategy in Southern Africa: Gorbachev's Pragmatic Approach*. Stanford: Hoover Institution Press.

Viotti, Paul R. and Mark V. Kauppi, 2001, *International Relations and World Politics: Security, Economy, Identity*. Upper Saddle River, NJ: Prentice Hall.

Weber, Max, 1947, *The Theory of Social and Economic Organization*. New York: Free Press.

Wehr, P. and J.P. Lederach, 1991, "Mediating Conflict in Central America", *Journal of Peace Research*, 28(1).

Weiss, Thomas G. and James G. Blight (eds), 1992, *The Suffering Grass: Superpowers and Regional Conflict in Southern Africa and the Caribbean*. Boulder and London: Lynne Rienner.

Weissman, Stephen R., 1979, "CIA Covert Action in Zaire and Angola: Patterns and Consequences", *Political Science Quarterly*, 94(2).

Wheeler, Douglas L., 1969, "The Portuguese Army in Angola", *Journal of Modern African Studies*, 7(3).

Williams, David and Tom Young, 1994, "Governance, the World Bank and Liberal Theory", *Political Studies*, 42(1).

Woods, Dwayne, 1992, "Civil Society in Europe and Africa: Limiting State Power through a Public Sphere", *African Studies Review*, (35)2.

World Bank, 1989, *Sub-Saharan Africa: From Crisis to Sustainable Growth*. Washington, DC: World Bank.

—, 1990, *Angola: An Introductory Economic Review*. Washington, DC: World Bank.

—, 2001, *World Development Report 2000/2001: Attacking Poverty*. Washington, DC: World Bank.

—, 2003, "Transitional Support Strategy for the Republic of Angola of March 2003", in http://www.worldbank,com/ao/reports/2003_Angola_tss.pdf.

Xinhua News Agency, 1983, "U.S. Vice-President Meets Angolan Interior Minister", 15 April 1983.

—, 1995, "UNITA Wishes to Benefit from Mandela's Experience: Savimbi", 14 October.

—, 1999, "Angolan Army to Launch Massive Attack against Rebels", 13 July.

Zartman, I. William, 1995, *Collapsed States: The Disintegration and Restoration of Legitimate Authority*. Boulder: Lynne Rienner.

Index